William Shakespeare's

As You Like It

MODERN CRITICAL INTERPRETATIONS

William Shakespeare's

As You Like It

Edited and with an Introduction by

Harold Bloom

Viva Books

New Delhi | Mumbai | Chennai | Kolkata | Bengaluru | Hyderabad | Kochi | Guwahati

First Indian Edition 2007
Reprinted 2011

VIVA BOOKS PRIVATE LIMITED

- 4737/23 Ansari Road, Daryaganj, New Delhi 110 002
  E-mail: vivadelhi@vivagroupindia.net, Tel. 42242200
- 76, Service Industries, Shirvane, Sector 1, Nerul, Navi Mumbai 400 706
  E-mail: vivamumbai@vivagroupindia.net, Tel. 27721273, 27721274
- Jamals Fazal Chambers, 26 Greams Road, Chennai 600 006
  E-mail: vivachennai@vivagroupindia.net, Tel. 28290304, 28294241
- B-103, Jindal Towers, 21/1A/3 Darga Road, Kolkata 700 017
  E-mail: vivakolkata@vivagroupindia.net, Tel. 22836381, 22816713
- 7, Sovereign Park Apartments, 56-58, K. R. Road, Basavanagudi, Bengaluru 560 004
  E-mail: vivabangalore@vivagroupindia.net, Tel. 26607409, 26607410
- 101-102 Mughal Marc Aptt., 3-4-637 to 641, Narayanguda, Hyderabad 500 029
  E-mail: vivahyderabad@vivagroupindia.net, Tel. 27564481, 27564482
- First Floor, Beevi Towers, SRM Road, Kaloor, Kochi 682 018, Kerala
  E-mail: vivakochi@vivagroupindia.net, Tel: 0484-2403055, 2403056
- 232, GNB Road, Beside UCO Bank, Silpukhuri, Guwahati 781 003
  E-mail: vivaguwahati@vivagroupindia.net, Tel: 0361-2666386

Published by arrangement with:

Facts on File, Inc.
132 West 31st Street
New York NY 10001
USA

ISBN : 978-81-309-1872-3

Published by Vinod Vasishtha for Viva Books Private Limited, 4737/23, Ansari Road, Daryaganj New Delhi - 110 002. Printed and bound by Anand Sons, Delhi - 110 092.

Contents

Editor's Note

My introduction meditates upon Rosalind's immense superiority to everyone else in her play. C.L. Barber begins the chronological sequence of criticism with his exegesis of Shakespeare's humorous recognition in *As You Like It* of the dramatic limits of representing "love's intensity as the release of a festive moment."

Existence in Arden is Ruth Nevo's subject, and informs her argument that Shakespeare attempted to replace Falstaff by the new combination of Rosalind and Touchstone.

Sexual politics, still one of our obsessive current concerns, is analyzed in its social aspects in the play by Peter Erickson.

Orlando's schooling by Rosalind is judged by Marjorie Garber to prefigure Prospero-as-educator, while René Girard fiercely pursues "mimetic rivalry" in the play, as is his wont.

The late Ted Hughes, poet laureate, relates *As You Like It* to "manipulative ritual," after which Andrew Barnaby gives us an account of the play's supposed "political consciousness."

Paul Alpers deepens our sense of pastoral context, while in my altogether archaic way I emphasize Rosalind's human qualities.

Memory theater is usefully invoked as a mode of visual location by Martha Ronk, after which Robert Leach sets *As You Like It* in the tradition of the Robin Hood May games and plays.

Nathaniel Strout concludes this volume by contrasting *As You Like It* to its prime "source," Thomas Lodge's *Rosalynde*.

HAROLD BLOOM

Introduction

As You Like It is Rosalind's play as *Hamlet* is Hamlet's. That so many critics have linked her to Hamlet's more benign aspects is the highest of compliments, as though they sensed that in wit, intellect, and vision of herself she truly is Hamlet's equal. Orlando is a pleasant young man, but audiences never quite can be persuaded that he merits Rosalind's love, and their resistance has its wisdom. Among Shakespearean representations of women, we can place Rosalind in the company only of the Portia of act 5 of *The Merchant of Venice*, while reserving the tragic Sublime for Cleopatra. All of us, men and women, like Rosalind best. She alone joins Hamlet and Falstaff as absolute in wit, and of the three she alone knows balance and proportion in living and is capable of achieving harmony.

That harmony extends even to her presence in *As You Like It*, since she is too strong for the play. Touchstone and Jaques are poor wits compared to her, and Touchstone truly is more rancid even than Jaques. Neither is capable of this wise splendor, typical of Rosalind's glory:

> ROSALIND: No, faith, die by attorney. The poor world is almost six thousand years old, and in all this time there was not any man died in his own person, *videlicet*, in a love-cause. Troilus had his brains dash'd out with a Grecian club, yet he did what he could to die before, and he is one of the patterns of love. Leander, he would have liv'd many a fair year though Hero had turn'd nun, if it had not been for a hot midsummer night; for, good youth, he went but forth to wash him in the

> Hellespont, and being taken with the cramp was drown'd; and the foolish chroniclers of that age found it was—Hero of Sestos. But these are all lies: men have died from time to time, and worms have eaten them, but not for love.

It seems a miracle that so much wit should be fused with such benignity. Rosalind's good humor extends even to this poor world, so aged, and to the amorous heroes she charmingly deromanticizes: the wretched Trolius who is deprived even of his honorable end at the point of the great Achilles's lance, and Marlowe's Leander, done in by a cramp on a hot midsummer night. Cressida and Hero are absolved: "men have died from time to time, and worms have eaten them, but not for love." Heroic passion is dismissed, not because Rosalind does not love romance, but because she knows it must be a sentimental rather than a naive mode. In the background to *As You Like It* is the uneasy presence of Christopher Marlowe, stabbed to death six years before in a supposed dispute over "a great reckoning in a little room," and oddly commemorated in a famous exchange between Touchstone and Audrey:

> TOUCHSTONE: When a man's verses cannot be understood, nor a man's good wit seconded with the forward child, understanding, it strikes a man more dead than a great reckoning in a little room. Truly, I would the gods had made thee poetical.
>
> AUDREY: I do not know what "poetical" is. Is it honest in deed and word? Is it a true thing?
>
> TOUCHSTONE: No, truly; for the truest poetry is the most feigning, and lovers are given to poetry; and what they swear in poetry may be said as lovers they do feign.

Touchstone is sardonic enough to fit into Marlowe's cosmos, even as Jaques at moments seems a parody of Ben Jonson's moralizings, yet Rosalind is surely the least Marlovian being in Elizabethan drama. That may be why Marlowe hovers in *As You Like It*, not only in the allusions to his death but in an actual quotation from *Hero and Leander*, when the deluded shepherdess Phebe declares her passion for the disguised Rosalind:

> Dead shepherd, now I find thy saw of might,
> Who ever lov'd that lov'd not at first sight?

Marlowe, the dead shepherd, defines *As You Like It* by negation. Rosalind's spirit cleanses us of false melancholies, rancid reductions, corrupting idealisms, and universalized resentments. An actress capable of the role of Rosalind will expose both Jaques and Touchstone as sensibilities inadequate to the play's vision. Jaques is an eloquent rhetorician, in Ben Jonson's scalding vein, but Arden is not Jonson's realm; while Touchstone must be the least likeable of Shakespeare's clowns. I suspect that the dramatic point of both Jaques and Touchstone is how unoriginal they are in contrast to Rosalind's verve and splendor, or simply her extraordinary originality. She is the preamble to Hamlet's newness, to the Shakespearean inauguration of an unprecedented kind of representation of personality.

Richard III, Iago, and Edmund win their dark if finally self-destructive triumphs because they have quicker minds and more power over language than anyone else in their worlds. Rosalind and Hamlet more audaciously manifest the power of mind over the universe of sense than anyone they could ever encounter, but their quickness of thought and language is dedicated to a different kind of contest, akin to Falstaff's grosser agon with time and the state. It is not her will but her joy and energy that Rosalind seeks to express, and Hamlet's tragedy is that he cannot seek the same. Richard III, Iago, and Edmund superbly deceive, but Rosalind and Hamlet expose pretensions and deceptions merely by being as and what they are, superior of windows, more numerous of doors. We could save Othello and Lear from catastrophe by envisioning Iago and Edmund trying to function if Rosalind or Hamlet were introduced into their plays. Shakespeare, for reasons I cannot fathom, chose not to give us such true clashes of mighty opposites. His most intelligent villains are never brought together on one stage with his most intelligent heroes and heroines. The possible exception is in the confrontation between Shylock and Portia in *The Merchant of Venice*, but the manipulated clash of Jew against Christian there gives Shylock no chance. Even Shakespeare's capacities would have been extended if he had tried to show Richard III attempting to gull Falstaff, Iago vainly practising upon Hamlet, or Edmund exercising his subtle rhetoric upon the formidably subtle Rosalind. Poor Jaques is hopeless against her; when he avers "why, 'tis good to be sad and say nothing," she replies: "why, then, 'tis good to be a post," and she sweeps away his boasts of melancholy experience. And what we remember best of Touchstone is Rosalind's judgment that, like a medlar, he will be rotten ere he is ripe.

Perhaps Rosalind's finest remark, amid so much splendor, is her reply when Celia chides her for interrupting. There are many ways to interpret:

"Do you not know I am a woman? When I think, I must speak. Sweet, say on." We can praise Rosalind for spontaneity, for sincerity, for wisdom, and those can be our interpretations; or we can be charmed by her slyness, which turns a male complaint against women into another sign of their superiority in expressionistic intensity. Rosalind is simply superior in everything whatsoever.

C.L. BARBER

The Alliance of Seriousness and Levity in As You Like It

In a true piece of Wit all things must be
  Yet all things there agree.
    —Cowley, quoted by T. S. Eliot in "Andrew Marvell"

Then is there mirth in heaven
When earthly things made even
  Atone together.
    —*As You Like It*

Shakespeare's next venture in comedy after *The Merchant of Venice* was probably in the Henry IV plays, which were probably written in 1597–98. Thus the Falstaff comedy comes right in the middle of the period, from about 1594 to 1600 or 1601, when Shakespeare produced festive comedy. *Much Ado About Nothing*, *As You Like It*, and *Twelfth Night* were written at the close of the period, *Twelfth Night* perhaps after *Hamlet*. *The Merry Wives of Windsor*, where Shakespeare's creative powers were less fully engaged, was produced sometime between 1598 and 1602, and it is not impossible that *All's Well That Ends Well* and even perhaps *Measure for Measure* were produced around the turn of the century, despite that difference in tone that has led to their being grouped with *Hamlet* and *Troilus and Cressida*.[1] I shall deal only with *As You Like It* and *Twelfth Night*; they are the two last festive plays, masterpieces that include and extend almost all the resources of the form whose development we have been following. What I would have to say about *Much Ado About Nothing* can largely be inferred from the discussion of the other festive plays. To consider the various other sorts of comedy which Shakespeare produced around the inception of the period when his main concern became tragedy would require another, different frame of reference.

As You Like It is very similar in the way it moves to *A Midsummer Night's Dream* and *Love's Labour's Lost*, despite the fact that its plot is taken over almost entirely from Lodge's *Rosalynde*. As I have suggested in the introductory chapter, the reality we feel about the experience of love in the play, reality which is not in the pleasant little prose romance, comes from presenting what was sentimental extremity as impulsive extravagance and so leaving judgment free to mock what the heart embraces.[2] The Forest of Arden, like the Wood outside Athens, is a region defined by an attitude of liberty from ordinary limitations, a festive place where the folly of romance can have its day. The first half of *As You Like It*, beginning with tyrant brother and tyrant Duke and moving out into the forest, is chiefly concerned with establishing this sense of freedom; the traditional contrast of court and country is developed in a way that is shaped by the contrast between everyday and holiday, as that antithesis has become part of Shakespeare's art and sensibility. Once we are securely in the golden world where the good Duke and "a many merry men ... fleet the time carelessly," the pastoral motif as such drops into the background; Rosalind finds Orlando's verses in the second scene of Act III, and the rest of the play deals with love. This second movement is like a musical theme with imitative variations, developing much more tightly the sort of construction which played off Costard's and Armado's amorous affairs against those of the nobles in Navarre, and which set Bottom's imagination in juxtaposition with other shaping fantasies. The love affairs of Silvius and Phebe, Touchstone and Audrey, Orlando and Rosalind succeed one another in the easy-going sequence of scenes, while the dramatist deftly plays each off against the others.

The Liberty of Arden

The thing that asks for explanation about the Forest of Arden is how this version of pastoral can feel so free when the Duke and his company are so high-minded. Partly the feeling of freedom comes from release from the tension established in the first act at the jealous court:

> Now go we in content
> To liberty, and not to banishment.
> (I.iii.139–140)

Several brief court scenes serve to keep this contrast alive. So does Orlando's entrance, sword in hand, to interrupt the Duke's gracious banquet by his threatening demand for food. Such behavior on his part is quite out of character (in Lodge he is most courteous); but his brandishing entrance gives Shakespeare occasion to resolve the attitude of struggle once again, this time by a lyric invocation of "what 'tis to pity and be pitied" (II.vii.117).

But the liberty we enjoy in Arden, though it includes relief from anxiety in brotherliness confirmed "at good men's feasts," is somehow easier than brotherliness usually is. The easiness comes from a witty redefinition of the human situation which makes conflict seem for the moment superfluous. Early in the play, when Celia and Rosalind are talking of ways of being merry by devising sports, Celia's proposal is "Let us sit and mock the good housewife Fortune from her wheel" (I.ii.34–35). The two go on with a "chase" of wit that goes "from Fortune's office to Nature's" (I.ii.43), whirling the two goddesses through many variations; distinctions between them were running in Shakespeare's mind. In Act II, the witty poetry which establishes the greenwood mood of freedom repeatedly mocks Fortune from her wheel by an act of mind which goes from Fortune to Nature:

> A fool, a fool! I met a fool i' th' forest, ...
> Who laid him down and bask'd him in the sun
> And rail'd on Lady Fortune in good terms, ...
> "Good morrow, fool," quoth I. "No, sir," quoth he,
> "Call me not fool till heaven hath sent me fortune."
> And then he drew a dial from his poke,
> And looking on itwith lack-lustre eye,
> Says very wisely, 'It is ten o'clock.
> Thus we may see.' quoth he, 'how the world wags.
> 'Tis but an hour ago since it was nine,
> And after one more hour 'twill be eleven;
> And so, from hour to hour, we ripe and ripe,
> And then, from hour to hour, we rot and rot;
> And thereby hangs a tale.'
>
> (II.vii.12–28)

Why does Jaques, in his stylish way, say that his lungs "began to crow like chanticleer" to hear the fool "thus moral on the time," when the moral concludes in "rot and rot"? Why do we, who are not "melancholy," feel such large and free delight? Because the fool "finds," with wonderfully bland wit, that nothing whatever happens under the aegis of Fortune. ("Fortune reigns in gifts of the world," said Rosalind at I.ii.44.) The almost tautological inevitability of nine, ten, eleven, says that all we do is ripe and ripe and rot and rot. And so there is no reason not to bask in the sun and "lose and neglect the creeping hours of time" (II.vii.112). As I observed in the introductory chapter, Touchstone's "deep contemplative" moral makes the same statement as the spring song towards the close of the play: "How that a life was but a flower." When they draw the moral, the lover and his lass are only thinking of the "spring time" as they take "the present time" when "love is crowned with the prime." (The refrain mocks them a little for their obliviousness, by its tinkling "the only pretty ring time.") But Touchstone's festive gesture is not oblivious.

The extraordinary thing about the poised liberty of the second act is that the reduction of life to the natural and seasonal and physical works all the more convincingly as a festive release by including a recognition that the physical can be unpleasant. The good Duke, in his opening speech, can "translate the stubbornness of fortune" into a benefit: he does it by the witty shift which makes the "icy fang / And churlish chiding of the winter wind" into "counsellors / That feelingly persuade me what I am" (II.i.6–11). The two songs make the same gesture of welcoming physical pain in place of moral pain:

Come hither, come hither, come hither!
  Here shall he see
  No enemy
But winter and rough weather.

(II.v.5–8)

They are patterned on holiday drinking songs, as we have seen already in considering the Christmas refrain, "Heigh-ho, sing heigh-ho, unto the green holly,"[3] and they convey the free solidarity of a group who, since they relax in physical pleasures together, need not fear the fact that "Most friendship is feigning, most loving mere folly."

Jaques speech on the seven ages of man, which comes at the end of Act II, just before "Blow, Blow, thou winter wind," is another version of the liberating talk about time; it expands Touchstone's "And thereby hangs a tale." The simplification, "All the world's a stage," has such imaginative reach that we are as much astonished as amused, as with Touchstone's summary ripe and rot. But simplification it is, nevertheless; quotations (and recitations) often represent it as though it were dramatist Shakespeare's "philosophy," his last word, or one of them, about what life really comes to. To take it this way is sentimental, puts a part in place of the whole. For it only is *one* aspect of the truth that the roles we play in life are settled by the cycle of growth and decline. To face this part of the truth, to insist on it, brings the kind of relief that goes with accepting folly—indeed this speech is praise of folly, superbly generalized, praise of the folly of living in time (or is it festive abuse? the poise is such that relish and mockery are indistinguishable). Sentimental readings ignore the wit that keeps reducing social roles to caricatures and suggesting that meanings really are only physical relations beyond the control of mind or spirit:

> Then a soldier, ...
> Seeking the bubble reputation
> Even in the cannon's mouth. And then the justice,
> In fair round belly with good capon lin'd ...
> (III.vii.149–154)

Looking back at time and society in this way, we have a detachment and sense of mastery similar to that established by Titania and Oberon's outside view of "the human mortals" and their weather.

Counterstatements

That Touchstone and Jaques should at moments turn and mock pastoral contentment is consistent with the way it is presented; their mockery makes explicit the partiality, the displacement of normal emphasis, which is implicit in the witty advocacy of it.

> If it do come to pass
> That any man turn ass,
> Leaving his wealth and ease
> A stubborn will to please ...
> (II.v.52–55)

The folly of going to Arden has something about it of Christian humility, brotherliness and unworldliness ("Consider the lilies of the field ..."), but one can also turn it upside down by "a Greek invocation to call fools into a circle" and find it stubbornness. Touchstone brings out another kind of latent irony about pastoral joys when he plays the role of a discontented exile from the court:

> *Corin*. And how like you this shepherd's life, Master Touchstone?
>
> *Touchstone*. Truly, shepherd, in respect of itself, it is a good life;

> but in respect that it is a shepherd's life, it is naught. In respect that it is solitary, I like it very well; but in respect that it is private, it is a very vile life. Now in respect it is in the fields, it pleaseth me well; but in respect it is not in the court, it is tedious. As it is a spare life, look you, it fits my humour well; but as there is no more plenty in it, it goes much against my stomach.
>
> (III.ii.12–22)

Under the apparent nonsense of his self-contradictions, Touchstone mocks the contradictory nature of the desires ideally resolved by pastoral life, to be at once at court and in the fields, to enjoy both the fat advantages of rank and the spare advantages of the mean and sure estate. The humor goes to the heart of the pastoral convention and shows how very clearly Shakespeare understood it.

The fact that he created both Jaques and Touchstone out of whole cloth, adding them to the story as it appears in Lodge's *Rosalynde*, is an index to what he did in dramatizing the prose romance. Lodge, though he has a light touch, treats the idyllic material at face value. He never makes fun of its assumptions, but stays safely within the convention, because he has no securely grounded attitude towards it, not being sure of its relation to reality. Shakespeare scarcely changes the story at all, but where in Lodge it is presented in the flat, he brings alive the dimension of its relation to life as a whole. The control of this dimension makes his version solid as well as delicate.

Although both Jaques and Touchstone are connected with the action well enough at the level of plot, their real position is generally mediate between the audience and something in the play, the same position Nashe assigns to the court fool, Will Summers, in *Summer's Last Will and Testament*.[4] Once Jaques stands almost outside the play, when he responds to Orlando's romantic greeting: "Good day and happiness, dear Rosalind!" with "Nay then, God b'wi'you, and you talk in blank verse!" (IV.i. 31). Jaques' factitious melancholy, which critics have made too much of as a "psychology," serves primarily to set him at odds both with society and with Arden and so motivate contemplative mockery. Touchstone is put outside by his special status as a fool. As a fool, incapable, at least for professional purposes, of doing anything right, he is beyond the pale of normal achievements. In anything he tries to do he is comically disabled, as, for example, in falling in love. All he achieves is a burlesque of love. So he has none of the illusions of those who try to be ideal, and is in a position to make a business of being dryly objective. "Call me not fool till heaven hath sent me fortune." Heaven sends him Audrey instead, "an ill-favour'd thing, sir, but mine own" (V.iv.60)—not a mistress to generate illusions. In *As You Like It* the court fool for the first time takes over the work of comic commentary and burlesque from the clown of the earlier plays; in Jaques' praise of Touchstone and the corrective virtues of fooling, Shakespeare can be heard crowing with delight at his discovery. The figure of the jester, with his recognized social role and rich traditional meaning, enabled the dramatist to embody in a character and his relations with other characters the comedy's purpose of maintaining objectivity.

The satirist presents life as it is and ridicules it because it is not ideal, as we would like it to be and as it should be. Shakespeare goes the other way about: he represents or evokes ideal life, and then makes fun of it because it does not square with life as it ordinarily is. If we look for social satire in *As You Like It*, all we find are a few set pieces about such stock figures as the traveller and the duelist. And these figures seem to be described rather to enjoy their extravagance than to rebuke their folly. Jaques, in response to a topical interest at the time when the play appeared, talks a good deal about satire, and proposes to "cleanse the foul body of th' infected world" (II.vii.60) with the fool's medicine of ridicule. But neither Jaques, the amateur fool, nor Touchstone, the professional, ever really gets around to doing the satirist's work of ridiculing life as it is, "deeds, and language, such as men do use."[5] After all, they are in Arden, not in Jonson's London: the infected body of the world is far away, out of range. What they make fun of instead is what they can find in Arden—pastoral innocence and romantic love, life as it might be, lived "in a holiday humour." Similar comic presentation of what is not ideal in man is characteristic of medieval fool humor, where the humorist, by his gift of long ears to the long-robed dignitaries, makes the point that, despite their pageant perfection, they are human too, that "stultorum numerus infinitus est." Such humor is very different from modern satire, for its basic affirmation is not man's possible perfection but his certain imperfection. It was a function of the pervasively formal and ideal cast of medieval culture, where what should be was more present to the mind than what is: the humorists' natural recourse was to burlesque the pageant of perfection, presenting it as a procession of fools, in crowns, mitres, caps, and gowns. Shakespeare's point of view was not medieval. But his clown and fool comedy is a response, a counter-movement, to artistic idealization, as medieval burlesque was a response to the ingrained idealism of the culture.

"all nature in love mortal in folly"

I have quoted already in the Introduction a riddling comment of Touchstone which moves from acknowledging mortality to accepting the folly of love:

> We that are true lovers run into strange capers; but as all is mortal in nature, so is all nature in love mortal in folly.
>
> (II.iv.53–56)

The lovers who in the second half of the play present "nature in love" each exhibit a kind of folly. In each there is a different version of the incongruity between reality and the illusions (in poetry, the hyperboles) which love generates and by which it is expressed. The comic variations are centered around the seriously-felt love of Rosalind and Orlando. The final effect is to enhance the reality of this love by making it independent of illusions, whose incongruity with life is recognized and laughed off. We can see this at closer range by examining each affair in turn.

All-suffering Silvius and his tyrannical little Phebe are a bit of Lodge's version taken over, outwardly intact, and set in a wholly new perspective. A "courting eglogue" between them, in the mode of Lodge, is exhibited almost as a formal spectacle, with Corin for presenter and Rosalind and Celia for audience. It is announced as

> a pageant truly play'd
> Between the pale complexion of true love
> And the red glow of scorn and proud disdain.
>
> (III.iv.55–57)

What we then watch is played "truly"—according to the best current convention: Silvius, employing a familiar gambit, asks for pity; Phebe refuses to believe in love's invisible wound, with exactly the literal-mindedness about hyperbole which the sonneteers imputed to their mistresses. In Lodge's version, the unqualified Petrarchan sentiments of the pair are presented as valid and admirable. Shakespeare lets us feel the charm of the form; but then he has Rosalind break up their pretty pageant. She reminds them that they are nature's creatures, and that love's purposes are contradicted by too absolute a cultivation of romantic liking or loathing: "I must tell you friendly in your ear, / Sell when you can! you are not for all markets" (III.v.59–60). Her exaggerated downrightness humorously underscores the exaggerations of conventional sentiment. And Shakespeare's treatment breaks down Phebe's stereotyped attitudes to a human reality: he lightly suggests an adolescent perversity underlying her resistance to love. The imagery she uses in disputing with Silvius is masterfully squeamish, at once preoccupied with touch and shrinking from it:

'Tis pretty, sure, and very probable
That eyes, which are the frail'st and softest things,
Who shut their coward gates on atomies,
Should be call'd tyrants, butchers, murtherers!
... lean but upon a rush,
The cicatrice and capable impressure
Thy palm some moment keeps; but now mine eyes,
Which I have darted at thee, hurt thee not, ...
(III.v.11–25)

Rosalind, before whom this resistance melts, appears in her boy's disguise "like a ripe sister," and the qualities Phebe picks out to praise are feminine. She has, in effect, a girlish crush on the femininity which shows through Rosalind's disguise; the aberrant affection is happily got over when Rosalind reveals her identity and makes it manifest that Phebe has been loving a woman. "Nature to her bias drew in that" is the comment in *Twelfth Night* when Olivia is fortunately extricated from a similar mistaken affection.

Touchstone's affair with Audrey complements the spectacle of exaggerated sentiment by showing love reduced to its lowest common denominator, without any sentiment at all. The fool is detached, objective and resigned when the true-blue lover should be

All made of passion, and all made of wishes,
All adoration, duty, and observance.
(V.ii.101–102)

He explains to Jaques his reluctant reasons for getting married:

Jaques. Will you be married, motley?
Touchstone. As the ox hath his bow, sir, the horse his curb, and the falcon her bells, so man hath his desires; and as pigeons bill, so wedlock would be nibbling.
(III.iii.79–83)

This reverses the relation between desire and its object, as experienced by the other lovers. They are first overwhelmed by the beauty of their mistresses, then impelled by that beauty to desire them. With Touchstone, matters go the other way about: he discovers that man has his troublesome desires, as the horse his curb; then he decides to cope with the situation by marrying Audrey:

Come, sweet Audrey.
We must be married, or we must live in bawdry.
(III.iii.98–99)

Like all the motives which Touchstone acknowledges, this priority of desire to attraction is degrading and humiliating. One of the hall-marks of chivalric and Petrarchan idealism is, of course, the high valuation of the lover's mistress, the assumption that his desire springs entirely from her beauty. This attitude of the poets has contributed to that progressively-increasing respect for women so fruitful in modern culture. But to assume that only one girl will do is, after all, an extreme, an ideal attitude: the other half of the truth, which lies in wait to mock sublimity, is instinct—the need of a woman, even if she be an Audrey, because "as pigeons bill, so wedlock would be nibbling." As Touchstone put it on another occasion:

If the cat will after kind,
So be sure will Rosalinde.
(III.ii.109–110)

The result of including in Touchstone a representative of what in love is unromantic is not, however, to undercut the play's romance: on the contrary, the fool's cynicism, or one-sided realism, forestalls the cynicism with which the audience might greet a play where his sort of realism had been ignored. We have a sympathy for his downright point of view, not only in connection with love but also in his acknowledgment of the vain and self-gratifying desires excluded by pastoral humility; he embodies the part of ourselves which resists the play's reigning idealism. But he does not do so in a fashion to set himself up in opposition to the play. Romantic commentators construed him as "Hamlet in motely," a devastating critic. They forgot, characteristically, that he is ridiculous: he makes his attitudes preposterous when he values rank and comfort above humility, or follows biology rather than beauty. In laughing at him, we reject the tendency in ourselves which he for the moment represents. The net effect of the fool's part is thus to consolidate the hold of the serious themes by exorcising opposition. The final Shakespearean touch is to make the fool aware that in humiliating himself he is performing a public service. He goes through his part with an irony founded on the fact (and it is a fact) that he is only making manifest the folly which others, including the audience, hide from themselves.

Romantic participation in love and humorous detachment from its follies, the two polar attitudes which are balanced against each other in the action as a whole, meet and are reconciled in Rosalind's personality. Because she remains always aware of love's illusions while she herself is swept along by its deepest currents, she possesses as an attribute of character the power of combining wholehearted feeling and undistorted judgment which gives the play its value. She plays the mocking reveller's role which Berowne played in *Love's Labour's Lost*, with the advantage of disguise. Shakespeare exploits her disguise to permit her to furnish the humorous commentary on her own ardent love affair, thus keeping comic and serious actions going at the same time. In her pretended role of saucy shepherd youth, she can mock at romance and burlesque its gestures while playing the game of putting Orlando through his paces as a suitor, to "cure" him of love. But for the audience, her disguise is transparent, and through it they see the very ardor which she mocks. When, for example, she stages a gayly overdone take-off of the conventional impatience of the lover, her own real impatience comes through the burlesque; yet the fact that she makes fun of exaggerations of the feeling conveys an awareness that it has limits, that there is a difference between romantic hyperbole and human nature:

> *Orlando*. For these two hours, Rosalind, I will leave thee.
> *Rosalind*. Alas, dear love, I cannot lack thee two hours!
> *Orlando*. I must attend the Duke at dinner. By two o'clock I will be with thee again.
> *Rosalind*. Ay, go your ways, go your ways! I knew what you would prove. My friends told me as much, and I thought no less. That flattering tongue of yours won me. 'Tis but one cast away, and so, come death! Two o'clock is your hour?
> (IV.i.181–190)

One effect of this indirect, humorous method of conveying feeling is that Rosalind is not committed to the conventional language and attitudes of love, loaded as these inevitably are with sentimentality. Silvius and Phebe are her foils in this: they take their conventional language and their conventional feelings perfectly seriously, with nothing in reserve. As a result they seem naïve and rather trivial. They are no more than what they say, until Rosalind comes forward to realize their personalities for the audience by suggesting what they humanly are beneath what they romantically think themselves. By contrast, the heroine in expressing her own love conveys by her humorous tone a valuation of her sentiments, and so realizes her own personality for herself, without being indebted to another for the favor. She uses the convention where Phebe, being unaware of its exaggerations, abuses it, and Silvius, equally naïve about hyperbole, lets it abuse him. This control of tone is one of the great contributions of Shakespeare's comedy to his dramatic art as a whole. The discipline of comedy in controlling the humorous potentialities of a remark enables the dramatist to express the relation of a speaker to his lines, including the relation of naïveté. The focus of attention is not on the outward action of saying something but on the shifting, uncrystallized life which motivates what is said.

The particular feeling of headlong delight in Rosalind's encounters with Orlando goes with the prose of these scenes, a medium which can put imaginative effects of a very high order to the service of humor and wit. The comic prose of this period is first developed to its full range in Falstaff's part, and steals the show for Benedict and Beatrice in *Much Ado About Nothing*. It combines the extravagant linguistic reach of the early clowns' prose with the sophisticated wit which in the earlier plays was usually cast, less flexibly, in verse. Highly patterned, it is built up of balanced and serial clauses, with everything linked together by alliteration and kicked along by puns. Yet it avoids a stilted, Euphuistic effect because regular patterns are set going only to be broken to underscore humor by asymmetry. The speaker can rock back and forth on antitheses, or climb "a pair of stairs" (V.ii.42) to a climax, then slow down meaningly, or stop dead, and so punctuate a pithy reduction, bizarre exaggeration or broad allusion. T. S. Eliot has observed that we often forget that it was Shakespeare who wrote the greatest prose in the language. Some of it is in *As You Like It*. His control permits him to convey the constant shifting of attitude and point of view which expresses Rosalind's excitement and her poise. Such writing, like the brushwork and line of great painters, is in one sense everything. But the whole design supports each stroke, as each stroke supports the whole design.

The expression of Rosalind's attitude towards being in love, in the great scene of disguised wooing, fulfills the whole movement of the play. The climax comes when Rosalind is able, in the midst of her golden moment, to look beyond it and mock its illusions, including the master illusion that love is an ultimate and final experience, a matter of life and death. Ideally, love should be final, and Orlando is romantically convinced that his is so, that he would die if Rosalind refused him. But Rosalind humorously corrects him, from behind her page's disguise:

> ... Am I not your Rosalind?
>
> *Orlando*. I take some joy to say you are, because I would be talking of her.
>
> *Rosalind*. Well, in her person, I say I will not have you.
>
> *Orlando*. Then, in mine own person, I die.
>
> *Rosalind*. No, faith, die by attorney. The poor world is almost six thousand years old, and in all this time there was not any man

died in his own person, videlicet, in a love cause. Troilus had his brains dash'd out with a Grecian club; yet he did what he could to die before, and he is one of the patterns of love. Leander, he would have liv'd many a fair year though Hero had turn'd nun, if it had not been for a hot midsummer night; for (good youth) he went but forth to wash him in the Hellespont, and being taken with the cramp, was drown'd; and the foolish chroniclers of that age found it was 'Hero of Sestos.' But these are all lies. Men have died from time to time, and worms have eaten them, but not for love.

Orlando. I would not have my right Rosalind of this mind, for I protest her frown might kill me.

Rosalind. By this hand, it will not kill a fly!

(IV.i.90–108)

A note almost of sadness comes through Rosalind's mockery towards the end. It is not sorrow that men die from time to time, but that they do not die for love, that love is not so final as romance would have it. For a moment we experience as pathos the tension between feeling and judgment which is behind all the laughter. The same pathos of objectivity is expressed by Chaucer in the sad smile of Pandarus as he contemplates the illusions of Troilus' love. But in *As You Like It* the mood is dominant only in the moment when the last resistance of feeling to judgment is being surmounted: the illusions thrown up by feeling are mastered by laughter and so love is reconciled with judgment. This resolution is complete by the close of the wooing scene. As Rosalind rides the crest of a wave of happy fulfillment (for Orlando's behavior to the pretended Rosalind has made it perfectly plain that he loves the real one) we find her describing with delight, almost in triumph, not the virtues of marriage, but its fallibility:

Say 'a day' without the 'ever.' No, no, Orlando! Men are April when they woo, December when they wed. Maids are May when they are maids, but the sky changes when they are wives.

(IV.i.146–150)

Ordinarily, these would be strange sentiments to proclaim with joy at such a time. But as Rosalind says them, they clinch the achievement of the humor's purpose. (The wry, retarding change from the expected cadence at "but the sky changes" is one of those brush strokes that fulfill the large design.) Love has been made independent of illusions without becoming any the less intense; it is therefore inoculated against life's unromantic contradictions. To emphasize by humor the limitations of the experience has become a way of asserting its reality. The scenes which follow move rapidly and deftly to complete the consummation of the love affairs on the level of plot. The treatment becomes more and more frankly artificial, to end with a masque. But the lack of realism in presentation does not matter, because a much more important realism in our attitude towards the substance of romance has been achieved already by the action of the comedy.

In writing of Marvell and the metaphysical poets, T. S. Eliot spoke of an "alliance of levity and seriousness (by which the seriousness is intensified)." What he has said about the contribution of wit to this poetry is strikingly applicable to the function of Shakespeare's comedy in *As You Like It*: that wit conveys "a recognition, implicit in the expression of every experience, of other kinds of experience which are possible."[6] The likeness does not consist simply in the fact that the wit of certain of Shakespeare's characters at times is like the wit of the metaphysicals. The crucial similarity is in the way the humor functions in the play as a whole to implement a wider awareness, maintaining proportion where less disciplined and coherent art falsifies by presenting a part as though it were the whole. The dramatic form is very different from the lyric: Shakespeare does not have or need the sustained, inclusive poise of metaphysical poetry when, at its rare best, it fulfills Cowley's ideal:

> In a true piece of Wit all things must be
> Yet all things there agree.

The dramatist tends to show us one thing at a time, and to realize that one thing, in its moment, to the full; his characters go to extremes, comical as well as serious; and no character, not even a Rosalind, is in a position to see all around the play and so be completely poised, for if this were so the play would cease to be dramatic. Shakespeare, moreover, has an Elizabethan delight in extremes for their own sake, beyond the requirements of his form and sometimes damaging to it, an expansiveness which was subordinated later by the seventeenth century's conscious need for coherence. But his extremes, where his art is at its best, are balanced in the whole work. He uses his broad-stroked, wide-swung comedy for the same end that the seventeenth-century poets achieved by their wire-drawn wit. In Silvius and Phebe he exhibits the ridiculous (and perverse) possibilities of that exaggerated romanticism which the metaphysicals so often mocked in their serious love poems. In Touchstone he includes a representative of just those aspects of love which are not romantic, hypostatizing as a character what in direct lyric expression would be an irony:

> Love's not so pure and abstract as they use
> To say who have no mistress but their muse.

By Rosalind's mockery a sense of love's limitations is kept alive at the very moments when we most feel its power:

> But at my back I always hear
> Time's winged chariot hurrying near.

The fundamental common characteristic is that the humor is not directed at "some outside sentimentality or stupidity," but is an agency for achieving proportion of judgment and feeling about a seriously felt experience.

As You Like It seems to me the most perfect expression Shakespeare or anyone else achieved of a poise which was possible because a traditional way of living connected different kinds of experience to each other. The play articulates fully the feeling for the rhythms of life which we have seen supporting Nashe's strong but imperfect art in his seasonal pageant. Talboys Dimoke and his friends had a similar sense of times and places when they let holiday lead them to making merry with the Earl of Lincoln; by contrast, the Puritan and/or time-serving partisans of Lincoln could not or would not recognize that holiday gave a license and also set a limit. An inclusive poise such as Shakespeare exhibits in Rosalind was not, doubtless, easy to achieve in any age; no culture was ever so "organic" that it would do men's living for them. What Yeats called Unity of Being became more and more difficult as the Renaissance progressed; indeed, the increasing difficulty of poise must have been a cause of the period's increasing power to express conflict and order it in art. We have seen this from our special standpoint in the fact that the everyday–holiday antithesis was most fully expressed in art when the keeping of holidays was declining.

The humorous recognition, in *As You Like It* and other products of this tradition, of the limits of nature's moment, reflects not only the growing consciousness necessary to enjoy holiday attitudes with poise, but also the fact that in English Christian culture saturnalia was never fully enfranchised. Saturnalian customs existed along with the courtly tradition of romantic love and an ambient disillusion about nature stemming from Christianity. In dramatizing love's intensity as the release of a festive moment, Shakespeare keeps that part of the romantic tradition which makes love an experience of the whole personality, even though he ridicules the wishful absolutes of doctrinaire romantic love. He does not found his comedy on the sort of saturnalian simplification which equates love with sensual gratification. He includes spokesmen for this sort of release in reduction; but they are never given an unqualified predominance, though they contribute to the atmosphere of liberty within which the aristocratic lovers find love. It is the latter who hold the balance near the center. And what gives the predominance to figures like Berowne, Benedict and Beatrice, or Rosalind, is that they enter nature's whirl consciously, with humor that recognizes it as only part of life and places their own extravagance by moving back and forth between holiday and everyday perspectives. Aristophanes provides a revealing contrast here. His comedies present experience entirely polarized by saturnalia; there is little *within* the play to qualify that perspective. Instead, an irony attaches to the whole performance which went with the accepted place of comedy in the Dionysia. Because no such clear-cut role for saturnalia or saturnalian comedy existed within Shakespeare's culture, the play itself had to place that pole of life in relation to life as a whole. Shakespeare had the art to make this necessity into an opportunity for a fuller expression, a more inclusive consciousness.

Notes

1. For the chronology, see E. K. Chambers, *William Shakespeare* (Oxford, 1930), I, 248–249 and 270–271.
2. I hope that a reader who is concerned only with *As You Like It* will nevertheless read the generalized account of festive comedy in Ch. 2, for that is assumed as a background for the discussion here.
3. See above, pp. 113–116.
4. See above, Ch. 4, pp. 61–67.
5. Ben Jonson, *Every Man in his Humour*, Prologue, I.21.
6. *Selected Essays, 1917–1932* (New York, 1932), pp. 255 and 262.

RUTH NEVO

Existence in Arden

The two great comedies composed during the last years of the sixteenth century share many features which place them in something of a class apart. One of these is the confident, even demonstrative nonchalance with which they relate to the Terentian tradition. It is as if Shakespeare reaches his majority in them, knows it, and would have us know it. It is almost as if we hear him indulging in a sly joke about the whole paternalistic New Comedy model when he has Rosalind, at some undramatized point, meet her father in the forest, where, as she later reports to Celia, she had much question with him: 'He ask'd me of what parentage I was. I told him of as good as he, so he laugh'd and let me go. But what talk we of fathers, when there is such a man as Orlando?' (III. iv. 36–9). With no parental obstacles, no separating misprisions or vows or oaths, with no reason (as has often been pointed out) for Rosalind's continuing disguise once she is safe in the forest and the writer of the execrable verses identified, *As You Like It* is the only comedy in which the two chief protagonists fall in love not as victims of blind Cupid, or of plots of one kind and another, or against their own conscious will, but freely, open-eyed, reciprocally and as if in godsent fulfilment of their own deepest desires.

Their meeting is finely, appropriately rendered. Orlando is hesitant, disconcerted, incredulous, speechless; Rosalind responds with the immediate

---

From *Comic Transformations in Shakespeare*. © 1980 by Ruth Nevo.

joyful, irrepressible spontaneity of her confession to Celia. Some of *her* speechlessness, she says, is 'for my child's father' (I. iii. 11). But this is a comic ending (or very near ending), rather than a comic beginning; and indeed the whole carriage of the play seems almost to set the comedy sequence on its head. The grave potential dangers are concentrated at the start, the tangle of mistaken identities occurs as late as the end of Act III.

'What', indeed, asks Barber, 'is the comedy in *As You Like It* about? What does Shakespeare ridicule? At times one gets the impression that it doesn't matter very much what the characters make fun of so long as they make fun.'[1] Sandwiched between *Much Ado* and *Twelfth Night*, Harold Jenkins notes:

> *As You Like It* is conspicuously lacking in comedy's more robust and boisterous elements—the pomps of Dogberry and the romps of Sir Toby ... [and] it has nothing which answers to those bits of crucial trickery ... which link events together by the logical intricacies of cause and effect. *As You Like It* takes Shakespearean comedy in one direction nearly as far as it could go before returning (in *Twelfth Night*) to a more orthodox scheme.[2]

The point is very well taken. The play exhibits not only a different direction but a markedly looser and more casual handling of the 'orthodox scheme', which I take to mean the Terentian formula; and it is this which makes inspired improvisation, the capacity to seize and make the most of one's opportunities, a key factor in the comic remedy itself. That which is therapeutic to the human condition is elicited here too by considerable anxiety and error, is winnowed clear of delusion and snatched by a hair's breadth from disaster. But what is prominently displayed, extruded, so to speak, as surface structure in *As You Like It* is the wisdom/folly dialectic of comedy itself, as antinomies are first exacerbated and then transcended. And what it embodies in its trickster heroine is comic pleasure itself, in practice and in action: a liberating playful fantasy, an expansive reconciliation of opposites of all kinds, enlivening and enchanting, to be enjoyed and rejoiced in; a heaven-sent euphoria. It is a play so self-assured as not to care whether we notice or not that it is talking about its own mode of being. It is a meta-comedy, in which the underlying principles of Shakespearean practice are drawn out for all to see and turned into the comic material itself.

The play polarizes harm and remedy in its initial catalogue of imperfections and deficiencies—the most dire we have yet encountered—and in the flight of its refugees. A youngest son seeks his proper place in the world. His elder brother keeps him rustically at home, like a peasant, breeds his horses better—they are not only fed but taught—allows him nothing but mere growth and, in short 'mines his gentility with his education'. For this servitude become unendurable. Orlando knows no wise remedy, and there begins his sadness. Elsewhere in the kingdom a duke is displaced by his younger brother and flees into exile, leaving his daughter mourning his absence. A thug is hired to dispatch the rebellious younger brother under cover of a court wrestling-match, and when the plan miscarries, the young man and his faithful retainer are unceremoniously turned out to make their way in the world as best they can. The usurping duke, unable to bear the accusing presence of his elder brother's daughter banishes her the court on pain of death. 'Thou art a fool', he says to his daughter, her friend, who entreats him to let her stay:

> She is too subtile for thee, and her smoothness,
> Her very silence, and her patience
> Speak to the people, and they pity her.
> Thou art a fool; she robs thee of thy name,
> And thou wilt show more bright and seem more virtuous
> When she is gone....
>
> (I. iii. 77–82)

His counterpart, Oliver, has a similar message concerning folly to deliver to his younger brother: 'What will you do, you fool', he says, in effect, 'when you have the meagre pittance your father left you? Beg when that is spent?'

This is the cold world of Edmund and Goneril in which there is no place for goodness and virtue, no room for undissimulated feeling; the tainted, radically corrupt world of court or city, of lust for gain and place, of craft and deceit. From wicked brother and wicked uncle there is no recourse for the oppressed but to take flight, which they do gladly. They go 'To liberty, and not to banishment' (I. iii. 138), to 'some settled low content' (II. iii. 68) as they say in their worldly folly, and arrive by a providential coincidence in the same wood, with nothing but their natural loyalty and generosity, their foolish good nature, and love, contracted at the wrestling-match. Back home, cunning and treachery—called worldly wisdom—grow ever more manifest under the impetus of their own accumulation. This is rendered with a splendid acid brevity in Act III, scene i, when Oliver declares his kinship to Duke Frederick in the matter of affection for his wayward brother Orlando:

> *Oliver* O that your Highness knew my heart in this! I never lov'd my brother in my life.

Duke Frederick More villain thou. Well, push him out of doors,
And let my officers of such a nature
Make an extent upon his house and lands.
(III. i. 13–17)

The exposition of *As You Like It* presents a whole society in need of cure, not a temporary emergency, or lunacy, to be providentially set right.

Since this is the case, however, a good deal of manoeuvering is required to keep the play within the orbit of comedy. The source story in Lodge is far fiercer—there are several deaths; but even Shakespeare's toning down of the violence, and a reduction of the casualties to Charles' broken ribs is not sufficient to make the initiating circumstances mere harmless aberrations, or, at worst, aberrations which only an accumulation of mishaps and ill-fortune will render disastrous. To transform the Lodge story into comedy, therefore, necessitated a shift of gear, and the production of what one might call a second order set of follies from the realm not of the reprehensible but of the ridiculous; a modulation from vice to error, and potentially liberating error at that. It is the flight into the forest during the long second act which effects this transformation.

The flight into the forest draws upon the tradition of that other time and other place of the nostalgic imagination—the *locus amoenus* where the return to nature from corrupt civilization allows the truth, simplicity and humility of innocence to replace the treachery, craft and arrogance of worldly sophistication. But the audience, following the courtiers in their flight from usurpation, cruelty, artifice and deceit discover in the forest the usurpation of Corin, the boorish rusticity of Audrey and William and the factitious elegancies of imitation courtly love masking sexual tyranny in the shepherd lovers; while, before the story is over, the forest's lionesses and snakes will have revealed in it possibilities no less inhospitable, not to say predatory, than those of the vicious court.

What we perceive is a plethora of disjunctive contraries. The whole of Act II bandies views of the good life about between defendants of court and country respectively, in a battery of claims and counter-claims which turns each into its opposite, revealing the absurdity of polarized and partial solutions. Shakespeare erects a burlesque dialectic during which, at every point, assumptions are refuted by realities and opinions fooled by facts.

Amiens sings to whoever

doth ambition shun,
And loves to live i' th' sun, (II. v. 38–9)

promising him no enemy but winter and rough weather. The disenchanted Jaques, whom there is no pleasing, caps Amiens' with another stanza (or stanzo—Jaques cares not for their names since they owe him nothing) pointing out that anyone who leaves his hearth and ease is an ass, and will find nothing but fools as gross as he in the greenwood. And Amiens' second song is less buoyant about winter and rough weather, not to mention friendship and loving, than the first.

Orlando, who has no illusions about 'the uncouth forest' swears to succour the fainting Adam: if there be anything living in the desert, he says, 'I will either be food for it, or bring it for food to thee'. It is as succinct a summary of nature red in tooth and claw as may be found, but oddly enough Orlando, who complained of the poverty of Nature, denied the benefits of Nurture, steeling himself for savagery, finds civility in the forest. 'Your gentleness shall force. / More than your force move us to gentleness', says the Duke, his rhetorical chiasmus figuring the contraries. More precisely: figuring the contraries resolved in a way that is characteristic, as we shall see, of the Duke.

According to the melancholy Jaques that 'poor dappled fool' the deer, who has his 'round haunches gored' in his own native 'city' is a standing reproach to all seekers of the good life in the forest. But Jaques' bleak account of human ageing in the seven ages speech (II. vii. 139ff.) is immediately refuted by Orlando's tender care for an old and venerable faithful servant. Jaques' various orations 'most invectively' pillory not only country, city and court, but 'this our life' in its entirety (II. i. 58). But Jaques' view that evil is universal and good an illusion is countered from yet another perspective by Touchstone's: that folly is universal and wisdom an illusion.

These two represent the play's opposing poles, but in asymmetrical opposition. They are a teasingly complex instance of Shakespeare's fools, referred to in Chapter I.

The meeting between them is reported exultantly by Jaques in Act II, scene vii, with much rejoicing, on the part of that arrogant nihilist, in the capacity for metaphysics of a mere fool. But the audience is quietly invited to perceive that there is an extraordinary similarity between Touchstone's oracular ripening and rotting and Jaques' own disenchanted rhetoric, and we are invited to wonder whether it is not after all the ironical fool who is mocking, by parody, the philosophical pretensions of the sentimental cynic. The scene plays handy dandy (like Lear) with the question most germane to comedy (as Lear's to tragedy): which is the Eiron, which the Alazon? Which is the mocker and which the mocked? Who is fooling and who is fooled?

What after all does Touchstone not mock? He dismantles,

systematically and with detached amusement, the entire structure of syllogistic reasoning with which his betters occupy their minds:

> Truly shepherd, in respect of itself, it is a good life; but in respect that it is a shepherd's life, it is naught. In respect that it is solitary, I like it very well; but in respect that it is private, it is a very wild life. Now in respect it is in the fields, it pleaseth me well; but in respect it is not in the court, it is tedious. As it is a spare life (look you) it fits my humor well; but as there is no more plenty in it, it goes much against my stomach. Hast any philosophy in thee, shepherd? (III. ii. 13–22)

A premise, to Touchstone is nothing but its own potential contrary, as he delights to demonstrate with his mock or anti-logic of all's one:

> That is another simple sin in you, to bring the ewes and the rams together, and to offer to get your living by the copulation of cattle; to be bawd to a bell-wether, and to betray a she-lamb of a twelve-month to a crooked-pated old cuckoldly ram, out of all reasonable match. (III. ii. 78–83)

Nevertheless, Touchstone is a fool. Audrey is there to remind us of that. And so what we come to see is that both monistic or polarized solutions—that evil is universal and good an illusion, and that folly is universal and wisdom an illusion are being mocked.

However, the play makes it clear which it prefers,[3] which it includes, finally. It finds a place—a key place, as we shall see—for the mother wit which Touchstone demonstratively parades, and parodies. It is Jaques, totally lacking in good humour, who is sent packing. First by the Duke, in terms which are significant, in view of comedy's concern with remedies for human ills. The Duke checks Jaques' enthusiasm about cleansing with satire the foul body of the infected world with the command, Physician, heal thyself:

> Most mischievous foul sin, in chiding sin:
> For thou thyself hast been a libertine,
> As sensual as the brutish sting itself;
> And all th' embossed sores, and headed evils,
> That thou with license of free foot hast caught,
> Would'st thou disgorge into the general world.
> (II. vii. 64–9)

And then by the lovers. 'I thank you for your company, but, good faith, I had as lief have been myself alone' is Jaques' opening ploy when he meets Orlando. He doesn't, it transpires, approve of Orlando's verse, of his love's name, of his 'pretty answers' (probably 'conn'd out of rings'), of his 'nimble wit' at which he learnedly sneers, of his being fool enough to be in love at all. What he would like to do, he says, is to sit down and 'rail against our mistress the world, and all our misery'. At the end of this dispiriting conversation Orlando sends him to seek the fool he was looking for in the brook (III. ii. 253–93 passim). And Rosalind, similarly tried by Jaques' disquisition on his own unique and inimitable brand of melancholy, would 'rather have a fool to make [her] merry than experience to make [her] sad—and travel for it too!' (IV. i. 28).

If (much virtue in 'if')—if we must choose between disjunctions, too cool a head is evidently preferable to too cold a heart. But must we choose? Certainly Act II (in particular) with its reiterated pastoral polemic, its multitude of syntactic, imagistic, situational figurations of either/or places us constantly in attitudes of indecision, or of quasi-dilemma. Nothing is happening, of course, so that these are not the impossible choices of tragic action; they are merely virtual. These constantly collapsing or exploding solutions of the greenwood constitute the comic disposition which the process of the play heightens and mocks. The characters all have answers to the question of the good life, but their answers keep being refuted; keep being invaded by aspects of reality they have not taken into account. Yet they continue tirelessly searching. Moreover, the comedy of this second act is an almost Chekovian dialogue of the deaf. Everybody is talking philosophically about life. Ah Life. But it is only themselves they really hear.[4] The Duke, who needs grist for his mill, loves, he tells us, to cope Jaques in his sullen fits, for 'then he's full of matter'. But Jaques, who has no patience with another's problems, has been trying all day to avoid him: 'He is too disputable for my company', says he, with sardonic derision. 'I think of as many matters as he, but I give heaven thanks, and make no boast of them' (II. v. 35–7).

If then disjunctive logic is the comic disposition in Arden (reflecting the disjunction of good and evil in the play's outer frame), any remedy will have to mediate or bridge the fissuring of human experience which is thus symbolized. It is the good Duke (meta-*senex* for a meta-comedy?) who points the way to such a resolution.

The Duke's stoicism is more than a brave show. His speech (II. i. 1–17) on the sweet uses of adversity and the preferability of biting winter winds to man's ingratitude and the ingratiation of court sycophancy is a profoundly dialectical *concordia discors*, transcending, with its paradoxes, diametrical contraries. He is, it is to be noted, as aware as Jaques of the universality of evil. It is he who first notices the anomaly of the deer hunt, though it is Jaques who rubs it in. He does not say that Arden is a rose garden. He only says that he recognizes the penalty of Adam.[5] Duke Senior does not deny the icy fangs of the winter wind, the ugly venom of the toad. On the contrary, he welcomes them because they 'feelingly persuade him what he is'. The contraries: painted pomp and icy fangs; chiding and flattery; feeling and persuasion (intuition and reason, we would say); books and brooks; sermons and stones, are all resolved in his remedial vision of the good life to be found in the hard discipline of nature, not in her soft bosom; in the riches of deprivation, not in the poverty of prodigality. 'Happy is your Grace', says Amiens, 'That can translate the stubbornness of fortune/Into so quiet and so sweet a style' (II. i. 18–20).

This Duke is indeed wise enough to be Rosalind's father but his wisdom of retreat, his embracing of penury, does not nurture a comic economy which requires bonus and liberating excess. He is the ideologue of resolutions, not their protagonist. Nor is the virtue that he makes of dispossession entirely victorious. They are doing their best, these exiles, to keep their spirits up, and there are moments of greenwood merriment, to be sure, but it doesn't take much to set off in them a yearning for better days. When the young man rushes on with his drawn sword shouting for food, and meets the Duke's courteous welcome, he also poignantly reminds him of the privations of a purely private virtue:

> what e'er you are
> That in this desert inaccessible,
> Under the shade of melancholy boughs,
> Lose and neglect the creeping hours of time;
> If ever you have look'd on better days,
> If ever been where bells have knoll'd to church,
> If ever sate at any good man's feast,
> If ever from your eyelids wip'd a tear,
> And know what 'tis to pity, and be pitied,
> (II. vii. 109–17)

The Duke echoes his sentiments with enthusiasm, and invites him to a meal served with as ducal a propriety as circumstances permit. The Duke can do much, but *As You Like It* requires, for its proper centre, his daughter. Which brings us to the lovers.

While the veteran refugees are thinking of many matters, these newcomers are thinking of one alone. Orlando, so far from finding settled low content in the forest, finds a compulsion to dream of fair women and to publish his poetasting upon every tree; and Rosalind, who had seized the opportunity, while she was about it, to satisfy a girl's tomboy fantasies:

> Were it not better,
> Because that I am more than common tall,
> That I did suit me all points like a man?
> A gallant curtle-axe upon my thigh,
> A boar-spear in my hand, and—in my heart
> Lie there what hidden woman's fear there will—
> We'll have a swashing and a martial outside,
> As many other mannish cowards have
> That do outface it with their semblances.
> (I. iii. 114–22)

now finds an echo to her own thoughts in the lovelorn Silvius. 'Alas, poor shepherd searching of [thy wound], / I have by hard adventure found my own' is her sympathetic response to Silvius' plaint (II. iv. 44–5ff.). The meeting precipitates the process of self-discovery which the comic device in Act II, the disguise whereby Rosalind both reveals and conceals her true identity, will infinitely advance.

'Arcadia', says Peter Marinelli (and the perceptive remark applies as well to Arden), 'is a middle country of the imagination ... a place of Becoming rather than Being, where an individual's potencies for the arts of life and love and poetry are explored and tested'.[6] Shakespeare's Arcadia offers a further turn: his comic heroine's own potencies for the arts of life and love and poetry are explored and tested by a variety of contingencies even while she is testing and exploring these same potencies in others.

Her initial absence of mind at the first encounter with Silvia is amusingly rendered by her failure to take in Touchstone's derisive parody of fancy shepherds:

> I remember when I was in love, I broke my sword upon a stone, and bid him take that for coming a-night to Jane Smile; and I remember the kissing of her batler and the cow's dugs that her pretty chopp'd hands had milk'd; and I remember the wooing of a peascod instead of her, from whom I took two cods, and giving her them again, said with weeping tears, 'Wear these for my sake'.
> (II. iv. 46–54)

All she hears, and that inattentively, is his epigrammatic ending: 'as all is mortal in nature, so is all nature in love mortal in folly'. Upon which she sagely replies, 'Thou speak'st wiser than thou art ware of', and misses again entirely the fool's ironic snub: 'Nay, I shall ne'er be ware of mine own wit till I break my shins against it' (II. iv. 58–9).

But this is the last time Rosalind is inattentive or absent-minded. Indeed it is her presence of mind which dominates and characterizes the middle acts.

From the moment when she finds herself trapped in her page role and exclaims in comic consternation, 'Alas the day, what shall I do with my doublet and hose?' to the moment of her unmasking, Ganymede releases in Rosalind her best powers of improvisation, intuition, and witty intelligence. Her quick wit transforms her page disguise into the play's grand comic device, and turns comic predicament to triumphant account. When she says to Celia: 'Good my complexion, doest thou think, though I am caparison'd like a man, I have a doublet and hose in my disposition? One inch of delay more is a South-sea of discovery.' (III. ii. 194–7), her gift for comic hyperbole as well as her ironic self-awareness are delightfully in evidence. But the master invention of the play lies in 'the inch of delay more' which she cannily, deliberately, takes upon herself (though with a handsome young fellow like Orlando wandering about the forest scratching 'Rosalind' on every tree there is nothing that would please her more than to be revealed) and in the 'South-sea of discovery' it allows her to make. For if Orlando discovers culture—sonnets and banquets—in the forest, Rosalind discovers nature, and rejoices in the occasion for the expression of her own ebullient, versatile and polymorph energies. It is a superbly audacious idea, this saucy lackey cure for love, if she can bring it off:

> At which time would I, being but a moonish youth, grieve, be effeminate, changeable, longing and liking, proud, fantastical, apish, shallow, inconstant, full of tears, full of smiles; for every passion something, and for no passion truly any thing, as boys and women are for the most part cattle of this color; would now like him, now loathe him; then entertain him, then forswear him; now weep for him, then spit at him; ... and this way will I take upon me to wash your liver as clean as a sound sheep's heart, that there shall not be one spot of love in't.
>
> (III. ii. 409–24)

And if she can bring it off, how can she lose? She is invisible. She is in control. She is master-mistress of the situation. She can discover not only what he is like, but what she is like; test his feelings, test her own; mock love and mask love and make love; provoke and bask in the attentions of the lover whose company she most desires, pretend to be the boy she always wanted, perhaps, to be, and permit herself extravagances everyday decorum would certainly preclude: 'Come, woo me, woo me; for now I am in a holiday humor, and like enough to consent. What would you say to me now, and I were your very very Rosalind?' (IV. i. 68–71).

It is no wonder the gaiety of this twinned character is infectious, the ebullience irrepressible, the high spirits inimitable. She/he is all things to all men and enjoys every moment of this androgynous ventriloquist's carnival, the more especially since, unlike her sisters in disguise, Julia and Viola, she has the relief of candid self-exposure to her confidante Celia as well: 'O coz, coz, coz, my pretty little coz, that thou didst know how many fathom deep I am in love! But it cannot be sounded; my affection hath an unknown bottom, like the bay of Portugal' (IV. i. 205–8). 'You have simply misus'd our sex in your love-prate', complains the soberer Celia, concerned for sexual solidarity. But what is sexual solidarity to her is to her chameleon cousin sexual solipsism and she will have none of it.

She provokes preposterously, and so exorcizes (in this a double for Orlando) the paranoia of male anti-feminism with her dire threat:

> I will be more jealous of thee than a Barbary cock-pigeon over his hen, more clamorous than a parrot against rain, more new-fangled than an ape, more giddy in my desires than a monkey. I will weep for nothing, like Diana in the fountain, and I will do that when you are disposed to be merry. I will laugh like a hyen, and that when you are inclin'd to sleep.
>
> (IV. i. 149–56)

only to reveal herself with utter if inadvertent candour the next moment: 'Alas, dear love, I cannot lack thee two hours' (IV. i. 178) and then, to cover her slip, immediately dissimulates again in the mock tirade of an abused and long-suffering wife: 'Ay, go your ways, go your ways; I knew what you would prove; my friends told me as much, and I thought no less. That flattering tongue of yours won me. 'Tis but one cast away, and so come death! Two a'clock is your hour?' (IV. i. 185–6).

Her double role is a triumph of characterization through impersonation, inconsistency, not consistency, being the key to dramatic verisimilitude if a complex and dynamic individual is to be represented. More, Rosalind, the girl, in whom natural impulse is finely cultivated and worldly wisdom cohabits with a passionate nature, together with her own 'twin' Ganymede, in whom a youth's beauty and a youth's jaunty irreverence combine, provides the double indemnity of comedy with lavish generosity. The duality of her masculine and feminine roles—itself an abolition of disjunction—gratifies our craving both for pleasure and reality, satisfies a deep defensive need for intellectual scepticism as well as an equally deep need for impulsive and limitless abandon, provides at once for cerebration and celebration,[7] resolves the dichotomies of nature and culture, wisdom and folly, mockery and festivity.

I find in a recent study of what existential psychologists call 'peak experience', interesting confirmation of the theory of comic therapy Shakespeare's practice, particularly in this play, appears to support. 'Peak experiences', says Abraham H. Maslow, make characters in plays and their audiences more apt to feel 'that life in general is worth while, even if it is usually drab, pedestrian, painful or ungratifying, since beauty, excitement, honesty, play, goodness, truth, and meaningfulness have been demonstrated to him to exist.... Life itself is validated, and suicide and death wishing must become less likely.'[8]

Thus the make-believe courtship, invented on the pretext of furnishing a cure for Orlando's love melancholy (or at least for his versification!), provides Rosalind with a homeopathic *remedia amoris* for hers. Free to fantasize, explore, experiment, she confers upon the audience a vivid sense that the mortal coil might not be solely a curse, nor the working-day world of briars beyond transfiguring.

And even that is not all. Ganymede's undertaking to cure Orlando's love-longing passes the time entertainingly in the greenwood but it also runs Rosalind into difficulties with the native population, thus providing the canonical knot of errors through a mistaken identity, and Ganymede with more livers to wash as clean as a sound sheep's heart.

Phebe's high-handed scorn for her doleful lover's courtly style exposes the substance of her own callousness as well as the absurd affectations of courtly love:

> 'Tis pretty, sure, and very probable,
> That eyes, that are the frail'st and softest things,
> Who shut their coward gates on atomies,
> Should be called tyrants, butchers, murtherers!
> Now I do frown on thee with all my heart,
> And if mine eyes can wound, now let them kill thee.
> Now counterfeit to swound; why, now fall down,
> Or if thou canst not, O, for shame, for shame,
> Lie not, to say mine eyes are murtherers!
>
> (III. v. 11–19)

Rosalind, too, knows that 'these are all lies'; that 'men have died from time to time, and worms have eaten them, but not for love' (IV. i. 108), she, too, knows that 'men are April when they woo, December when they wed', and that maids 'are May when they are maids, but the sky changes when they are wives' (IV. i. 147–8). But her realism is of another order altogether than Phebe's callow literalism, and is vouched for by the vigour with which she scolds the pair of them, combining the swashbuckling gusto of Ganymede with the passionate sincerity of Rosalind, in a *nosce teipsum* totally free of illusion:

> 'Od's my little life,
> I think she means to tangle my eyes too!
> No, faith, proud mistress, hope not after it.
> 'Tis not your inky brows, your black silk hair,
> Your bugle eyeballs, nor your cheek of cream
> That can entame my spirits to your worship.
> You foolish shepherd, wherefore do you follow her,
> Like foggy south, puffing with wind and rain?
> You are a thousand times a properer man
> Than she a woman. 'Tis such fools as you
> That make the world full of ill-favor'd children.
> 'Tis not her glass, but you that flatters her,
> And out of you she sees her self more proper
> Than any of her lineaments can show her.
> But, mistress, know yourself, down on your knees,
> And thank heaven, fasting, for a good man's love;
> For I must tell you friendly in your ear,
> Sell when you can, you are not for all markets.
> (III. v. 43–60)

Ralph Berry takes a counterview of *As You Like It*, and especially of this incident.[9] He finds unease, irritation and hostility—the groundswell of a power struggle latent or overt—to be the dominant motif of the play. This, however, is a view as over-selective as Jaques' seven ages speech. What it leaves out is the fun. But it is also not strictly accurate. Berry accounts, for instance, for the 'quite astonishing warmth' of Rosalind's diatribe—'thirty odd lines of vulgar abuse' he calls it—in terms of Phebe appearing to Rosalind as a subtly threatening parallel or caricature of herself. 'Phebe is a domineering woman who ... has mastered her man; so is Rosalind.' But when the incident occurs Rosalind has mastered no one. She has merely suggested to Orlando that they meet again. Phebe is, to be sure, the phantom Ganymede conjures to cure Orlando of just such love-longing as Silvius'.

The caricature double surely provides a foil to the hidden Rosalind; and the comedy arising from the idea of Rosalind meeting a 'real' embodiment of Ganymede's fantasy is quite lost in Berry's reductive reading.[10]

It is no wonder that Phebe, whose dejected lover Silvius is clearly not manly enough for his imperious mistress, falls head over heels in love with this high-spirited outspokenness, thus hoisting Rosalind/Ganymede with his/her own epicene petard. Ganymede has in his face that which Phebe would feign call master, it seems, and this is a tangle not easy to untie. A remedy for deadlock, however, is provided by the very occurrence which virtually exhausts the Ganymede device. The arrival of Oliver, reformed by his experience of courtly treachery, with the tale of his brother's heroic rescue (a recapitulation of the native *virtu* of the wrestling exploit on a higher moral level) provides not only proof that Orlando is no tame snake like Silvius, but also a patrimony for him and a partner for Celia. The exhaustion of the comic device is neatly dramatized by the emotional collapse of Rosalind at the sight of the bloodied handkerchief, and there is now nothing in the world to prevent the trickster heroine from undoing the turmoil she has caused. Her power to do this is beautifully 'masqued' by the chiming quartet of Act V, scene ii: Love is 'to be made of sighs and tears'—

> *Silvius* And so am I for Phebe.
> *Phebe* And I for Ganymede.
> *Orlando* And I for Rosalind.
> *Rosalind* And I for no woman. (V. ii. 85–93)

and so on, until Rosalind begs, 'Pray you no more of this, 'tis like the howling of Irish wolves against the moon' (V. ii. 109–10). This is the ironic voice which ends the play with the classic plea for applause in the epilogue, and it is worth a moment's further reflection. That Rosalind is still dressed as Ganymede has been convincingly argued in terms of the scarcity of time available at that point for a boy to change into elaborate women's clothing.[11] But there is a cogent argument to be drawn from the play's own dialectical resolution. If she is still Ganymede in the epilogue, then 'If I were a woman' is spoken out of her saucy lackey role, as the man-of-the-world bawdy of 'that between you and the women the play may please' seems to suggest. She is thus drawing the audience, too, into her transvestite trickster's net, prolonging the duplicity of self-discovery and self-concealment, the enchanting game of both/and. But if she is dressed as Rosalind, then 'If I were a woman' is spoken over the heads, so to speak, of characters and play, by the boy-actor of Shakespeare's company, and this will *collapse* the dramatic illusion of 'real' make-believe from which the whole play draws its dynamic power. Shakespeare, I submit, is not calling attention to his play as play, as opposed to reality: he is calling attention to Rosalind's 'play' as a component reality would do well to absorb.

At the end of *As You Like It* dukes are restored to their dukedoms, sons to their inheritances. Wickedness has burst, like a boil, by some mysterious spontaneous combustion, leaving not a rack behind. But not all Jacks have their Jills. Jaques is unassimilated. But he is by nature a solitary and continues his travels, happily sucking melancholy out of all occasions as a weasel sucks eggs, on the outer edge of remedy.

There is also unaccommodated William at the marriage feast. But there's hope even there, if Touchstone's fidelity can be relied upon; Jaques gives him two months (V. iv. 192). For though 'wedlock', in the view of that philosopher of life's most minimal expectations, 'will be nibbling', what of it?

> But what though? Courage! As horns are odious, they are necessary. It is said, 'Many a man knows no end of his goods'. Right! many a man has good horns and knows no end of them. Well, that is the dowry of his wife, 'tis none of his own getting. Horns? even so. Poor men alone? No, no, the noblest deer hath them as huge as the rascal. Is the single man therefore bless'd? No, as a wall'd town is more worthier than a village, so is the forehead of a married man more honorable than the bare brow of a bachelor ... (III. iii. 51–61)

If this is a mockery of 'romance' it is also a mockery of 'reason'. A protuberance is a protuberance, whether it be the bastion of a walled town or the horned frontlet of a married man. To Touchstone, logic is a bagatelle. All is immaterially interchangeable: court and country, culture and nature, fact and fiction, sense and folly, wedlock and non-wedlock, for that matter, too. Earthly things made even atone together in Touchstone's anti-logic as well as in Hymen's conjuration. Touchstone's courtship has been a mocking parody of the affectations of the mid-level characters Phebe and Silvius; but he is also a mocking foil to Rosalind's superior synthesis of culture and nature, just as his bawdy 'prick' song (if a hart do lack a hind [III. ii. 100–12]) is foil to her own frank naturalism. In this matter she can give as good as she gets, too, in Mercutio's very vein (III. ii. 117–20).

*

'Rosalind, Viola, and, to a less extent Beatrice', says Charlton (forgetting, however, Julia and Hippolyta),

> have entered into the possession of spiritual endowments which, if hitherto suspected to exist at all, had either been distrusted as dangerous or had become moribund through desuetude ... they have claimed the intuitive, the subconscious, and the emotional as instruments by which personality may bring itself to a fuller consciousness of and a completer harmony with the realities of existence. They have left Theseus far behind; they have also outgrown Falstaff.[12]

It is perhaps, as I have tried to show, less a matter of outgrowing Falstaff, than of replacing him, by a new combination: the Lady and the Fool. Touchstone is a professional jester,[13] not a bumbling village constable or a Bacchic life-force. He is not a merry fool, either. He is too Ecclesiastes-wise; and besides his feet hurt. But his burlesque fool's wisdom serves throughout most excellently to mediate our recognition of the Erastian higher folly of his ebullient mistress. When Wylie Sypher speaks of 'the unruliness of the flesh and its vitality', he characterizes the buffoon nature in all its manifestations. 'Comedy', Sypher continues, 'is essentially a carrying away of Death, a triumph over mortality by some absurd faith in rebirth, restoration, salvation.'[14] Perhaps we could say that Touchstone epitomizes the absurdity, and Rosalind the faith; and that it is the interlocking and paradoxical partnership of the two that characterizes this second, and second last of Shakespeare's post-Falstaffian comedies.

Shakespeare is not done with the wayward and unruly erotic passions. Nor will he be, needless to say, until the last word he contributes to *Two Noble Kinsmen*. But his romantic comedy treatment of them does come to an end with his next play *Twelfth Night*, in which the rivalries and duplicities, twinnings and doublings of the battle of the sexes are further extended into the ambivalent twinnings, duplicities and doublings within the lovers' own individual identities.

Notes

1. C. L. Barber, 'The Use of Comedy in *As You Like It*', *PQ*, vol. XXI (1942), p. 353.

2. Harold Jenkins, '*As You Like It*', *Shakespeare Studies*, vol. 8 (1955) pp. 40–1.

3. Unless, of course, we choose to invert the play entirely, and make the solitary, melancholy Jaques our Diogenes, and the rest mere mortal, convivial fools.

4. As D. J. Palmer puts it in 'Art and Nature in *As You Like It*', *PQ*, Vol. XLIX (1970), pp. 33–5 : 'the forest brings its inhabitants face to face with their own shadows everyone becomes more fully himself in the forest'. I find several of my observations anticipated by Palmer in this important essay, but his argument is meshed into discussion of the theme of Art and Nature and the bearing of his remarks therefore somewhat oblique to my own concerns.

5. Theobald emended 'not' to 'but': 'Here feel we but the penalty Adam, / The seasons' difference ...' etc., and many editors follows the eminent good sense of the emendation.

6. Peter V. Marinelli, *Pastoral* (London: Methuen, 1971), p. 37.

7. The neat opposition comes from Michael McCanles' excellent account in *Dialectical Criticism and Renaissance Literature* (Los Angeles: University of California Press, 1975).

8. Abraham H. Maslow, *Towards a Psychology of Being* (New York: Van Nostrand Reinhold, 1968), pp. 101–2. Quoted by Michael Payne in *SRO*, edited by W. R. Elton, nos. 7–8 (1972/4), p. 76.

9. 'No Exit from Arden', *Shakespeare's Comedies* (Princeton University Press, 1972), pp. 175–95.

10. Phebe and Silvius are a particularly fine example of the subtle effects Shakespeare derives from his middle-level mirror image characters. Richard Levin, *The Multiple Plot in English Renaissance Drama* (Chicago: Chicago University Press, 1971), has noted the social stratification in the play and points out that it is marked by appropriate emblematic animals: the stag for the courtiers, sheep for Phebe the shepherdess and the lowly goat for Audrey.

11. Maura Slattery Kuhn, 'Much Virtue in If', *Shakespeare Quarterly*, vol. 28 (Winter, 1977).

12. H. B. Charlton, *Shakespearean Comedy* (London: Methuen, 1938), p. 283.

13. Robert Armin had by this time replaced Will Kempe for the fool's roles in Shakespeare's company, a circumstance which no doubt played its part in the Shakespearean transformation here described.

14. Wylie Sypher, 'The Meaning of Comedy' in *Comedy* (New York: Doubleday, 1956), p. 220.

PETER ERICKSON

Sexual Politics and Social Structure in As You Like It

The dramatic and emotional effect of Shakespearean comedy can be defined as a process of making manifest "a tough reasonableness beneath the slight lyric grace."[1] This comic toughness derives in part from Shakespeare's ability to mix genres, an ability that helps to account for his artistic power.[2] In exploring Shakespeare's use of genre, we must be concerned as much with overlapping as with differentiation. The father–son motif, for example, provides a specific point of contact between *As You Like It* and *Henry V*. The analogous relationships between Duke Senior and Orlando in the first play and Henry IV and Hal in the second help to cut across an oversimplified generic distinction that says history plays deal with political power (implicitly understood as male power) whereas comedies treat love. Rosalind's androgynous allure can appear so attractive, her linguistic virtuosity so engaging, that all our attention becomes focused on her, as if nothing else happened or mattered. Her talking circles around Orlando seems sufficient proof of her complete triumph. Yet this line of response is deficient because it ignores important parts of the play; that is, political power is a significant element in *As You Like It*.

The transmission of paternal heritage, announced at the outset in Orlando's lament, begins to receive fulfillment when Orlando fashions an alliance with Duke Senior in the forest when no women are present. After his initial complaint about being deprived of a "good education" (1.1.67–68), Orlando is educated twice: once by Rosalind's father and then by Rosalind. The exiles in the forest can indulge in the pleasures of melancholy because the play can amply satisfy the need for true versions of debased human relationship: "Most friendship is feigning, most loving mere folly" (2.7.181). We relish the platitude of this general rule in order to appreciate the magic of the exceptions. But the question still remains: how are the twin themes of friendship and loving coordinated with each other? And an exclusive focus on Rosalind prevents our asking it. Male friendship, exemplified by the reconciliation of Duke Senior and Orlando, provides a framework that diminishes and contains Rosalind's apparent power. My point is not that *As You Like It* is a history play in disguise or that there are no differences between genres. The pastoral feast in the forest of Arden is far less stressful than the feast of Crispian that Henry V imagines as an antidote to the disturbing memory of his inheritance through "the fault / My father made in compassing the crown" (*H5*, 4.1.293–94). Unlike Henry V, Orlando is never made to confront a paternal fault. However, an exaggerated contrast between history and comedy is misleading. Concentration on Rosalind to the neglect of other issues distorts the overall design of *As You Like It*, one that is governed by male ends.

I

The endings of *Love's Labor's Lost* and *As You Like It* present a striking contrast. In the earlier play, Berowne comments explicitly on the absence of marriage and closure, for which, in his frustration, he holds the women responsible: "Our wooing doth not end like an old play: / Jack hath not Gill. These ladies' courtesy / Might well have made our sport a comedy" (5.2.874–76). *Love's Labor's Lost* culminates in the failure of courtship, but *As You Like It* reaches a fully and flamboyantly festive conclusion with the onstage revelation of the symbol of marital union, Hymen, who presides over a quadruple wedding. The prevailing mood of sourness at the end of *Love's Labor's Lost* is held in check in the later play by confining the potential for bitterness and disruption to Jaques, the nonparticipant. But even Jaques generously acknowledges the validity of love when he gives his blessing to Orlando, whom he had formerly mocked as "Signior Love" (3.2.292): "You to a love, that your true faith doth merit" (5.4.188).

In the final scene of *Love's Labor's Lost*, festivity is short-circuited. The concluding masques and songs are no more helpful in facilitating the happy ending than the men's poetry had been earlier. The masques of the Muscovites and of the Nine Worthies are farcical artistic performances that precipitate discord. "More Ates, more Ates! stir them on, stir them on!"

(5.2.688–89), cries Berowne in an enthusiastic effort to provoke violence between Costard and Armado. Nor do the companion songs of the cuckoo and the owl dispel the awkward atmosphere. The songs act as a conspicuously inadequate substitute for the consummation that has failed to occur among the main characters. The alternative presented by the songs twits the anxiety it ostensibly seeks to mitigate by invoking the larger perspective of the natural cycle:

> The cuckoo then on every tree
> Mocks married men; for thus sings he,
> "Cuckoo;
> Cuckoo, cuckoo"—O word of fear,
> Unpleasing to a married ear!
> (5.2.898–902)

This apparently blithe epilogue mirrors the men's situation in the play proper by restating women's power to make or break men. It recapitulates but does not relieve the humiliation of men as helpless victims of female caprice.[3]

By contrast, *As You Like It* creates a context in which the efficaciousness of art is affirmed rather than denied. The masque of Hymen anticipates the sanctified unity of a late romance by appealing to the trope of "wonder":

> Whiles a wedlock-hymn we sing,
> Feed yourselves with questioning;
> That reason wonder may diminish
> How thus we met, and these things finish.
> (5.4.137–40)

The equation of wedding with formal closure is indicated by Hymen's ostentatious use of words like "finish" and "conclusion": "Peace ho! I bar confusion, / 'Tis I must make conclusion" (125–26). This gratifying happy ending is convincing, however, because Hymen's role is not just a matter of external *deus ex machina*. In presenting Rosalind undisguised, the god of marriage claims that "Hymen from heaven brought her" (112), but we are entitled to feel that the reverse is true: Rosalind has brought Hymen. The character of Rosalind, the real coordinator of the final scene, stands behind the metaphor of magic she invokes for the play's resolution: "Believe then, if you please, that I can do strange things. I have, since I was three year old, convers'd with a magician, most profound in his art, and yet not damnable" (5.2.58–61). Rosalind has explored the limits of the magic that her male costume has afforded her in the forest of Arden. Like Prospero, she now gives up this magic, but she has earned her final throwaway use of it.

This comparative sketch of the endings of *Love's Labor's Lost* and *As You Like It* raises questions. How do we account for the difference between the two endings? How is the resolution of *As You Like It* achieved? A partial answer lies in Shakespeare's use of pastoral. In *Love's Labor's Lost*, pastoral applies only to the setting and general atmosphere but does not extend to the dramatic structure. The play sets up a contrast between two worlds: the court in which the men take refuge versus the field which the women insist on making their residence. However, the relationship between the two worlds is one of simple opposition. The static quality of this relationship leaves too little room for interplay between the worlds and leads directly to the stalemate of the conclusion. *As You Like It* dramatically expands the contrast and the possibilities for interaction between the two worlds of court and forest. The sharply differentiated landscapes unfold in sequence, making it possible for men to enter the green world and creating the dynamic three-part process identified by Barber and Northrop Frye.[4] This full realization of pastoral form in *As You Like It* gives Shakespeare an artistic leverage on his material that helps to make possible the final resolution.

While useful, this kind of structural comparison can take us only so far. Formal description is insufficient as a total explanation of the differences between *Love's Labor's Lost* and *As You Like It* because the respective uneasiness and confidence of their endings is a matter of the relations between men and women as well as of aesthetic form. Hence it becomes imperative to look at the plays from the perspective of sexual politics. From this perspective, Shakespeare's development from *Love's Labor's Lost* to *As You Like It* does not emerge as the unqualified advancement it might otherwise appear to be. The ending of *As You Like It* works smoothly because male control is affirmed and women are rendered nonthreatening whereas in *Love's Labor's Lost* women do not surrender their independence and the status of patriarchy remains in doubt. Harmony and disharmony have as much to do with the specific content of male–female relations as with aesthetic form.

In both *Love's Labor's Lost* and *As You Like It*, love brings out a disparity between male and female intelligence and power. Orlando, like the four lords, is transformed in a way that makes him look humorously but embarrassingly naive and helpless. Falling in love is experienced as incapacitation:

My better parts
Are all thrown down, and that which here stands up
Is but a quintain, a mere liveless block....

> O poor Orlando! thou art overthrown
> Or Charles, or something weaker, masters thee.
> (1.2.249–51, 259–60)

His sense of being mastered helps to create a one-sided relationship in which the woman has control. Again like the four lords, Orlando equates being in love with the reflex gesture of producing huge quantities of poetry, and he follows a poetic convention that further increases the woman's power:

> Thus Rosalind of many parts
> By heavenly synod was devis'd
> Of many faces, eyes, and hearts,
> To have the touches dearest priz'd.
> Heaven would that she these gifts should have,
> And I to live and die her slave.
> (3.2.149–54)

The mechanical and impersonal nature of this elevation of the woman to divine status is demonstrated by the way Orlando's poem invents her through an amalgamation of fantasized "parts." Worship of the woman that is supposed to pay homage creates an inhuman pastiche that demeans her and inhibits genuine contact. Such obeisance also belittles the man since Orlando's poem defines a sharply hierarchical relationship in which his idealization of Rosalind as the perfect goddess leaves him with the role—exaggerated in the opposite direction—of "slave."[5] The servility implied by poetic worship is taken a step further in the case of Silvius, whose "holy" and "perfect" love make him content "To glean the broken ears after the man / That the main harvest reaps" (3.5.99, 102–3). Rosalind's observation that Orlando's verse is "lame" (3.2.168) refers not only to the poem's execution but also to the psychological stance Orlando adopts toward her.

Rosalind is thus placed in a position parallel to that of the ladies in *Love's Labor's Lost*. Like them, she is strong and manipulative as she uses her superior wit along with the advantages given to her by circumstance to disabuse Orlando of his stock notions of male and female roles in love. There is, however, a vast difference in the outcome of this process in the two plays because Rosalind proves to be more flexible and accommodating than the women of *Love's Labor's Lost*. Her response to Phebe and Silvius is an attack on sonnet convention that implicitly involves a self-education for Rosalind. In upbraiding the two for their enactment of the stereotype of female scorn and male abasement, she is as critical of Silvius (3.549–56) as of Phebe. Rosalind's effort to put Phebe in her place is accompanied by her attempt to bring Silvius up to his place. This double lesson has an application to her own behavior since Rosalind's decision to "speak to him like a saucy lackey, and under that habit to play the knave with him" (3.2.295–97) carries the danger that she will allow herself to be as "proud and pitiless" (3.5.40) as she accuses Phebe of being, while Orlando languishes in Silvius-like submissiveness. Observing this dynamic at work in another relation alerts her to the potential Phebe in herself. Rosalind thus proves a more "busy actor in their play" (3.459) than she had anticipated; her fervent effort to convince Phebe to adopt more tractable behavior becomes an argument that she must accept her own advice. Rosalind's capacity to give up this pride is what allows *As You Like It* to extricate itself from the poetic postures of male subservience and female omnipotence in which *Love's Labor's Lost* remains fixed to the bitter end.

If Rosalind's flexibility is the key reason that *As You Like It* ends "like an old play" with "Jack having his Gill," we must go on to ask: what is the nature of this flexibility? and is the absence of it in *Love's Labor's Lost* entirely in *As You Like It*'s favor? The standard approach stresses that Rosalind has a larger emotional range than the ladies of *Love's Labor's Lost*. She is more impressive because more complex and more humane. The encounter between Rosalind and Jaques at the beginning of act 4, scene 1, makes clear her rejection of his detachment: "I fear you have sold your own lands to see other men's; then to have seen much, and to have nothing, is to have rich eyes and poor hands" (22–25). Her direct experience and involvement distinguish her from the women of *Love's Labor's Lost*, who in the end "have nothing." But a second approach sees Rosalind as a woman who submits to a man who is her inferior.[6] The power symbolized by her male costume is only temporary, and the harmonious conclusion is based on her willingness to relinquish this power. Thus Rosalind's passionate involvement has a significant negative side since involvement means co-option and assimilation by a society ruled by men. She escapes the female stereotype of the all-powerful woman created by lyrical inflation only at the price of succumbing to another stereotype: the compliant, essentially powerless woman fostered by practical patriarchal politics.

Before entering the forest of Arden, Rosalind's companion Celia/Aliena redefines this pastoral space to mean opportunity rather than punishment: "Now go we in content / To liberty, and not to banishment" (2.3.137–38). This "liberty" implies overcoming the restrictions of the female role. The idea of the male disguise originates as a strategy for avoiding the normal vulnerability to male force: "Alas, what danger will it be to us, / Maids as we are, to travel forth so far! / Beauty provoketh thieves sooner than gold" (108–10). Rosalind's male costume, as it evolves, expands her identity so that she can play both male and female roles. Yet the costume is problematic. Though it gives her freedom of action and empowers her to take the initiative with Orlando, it simultaneously serves as a protective device, which temptingly offers excessive security, even invulnerability. In order to love, Rosalind must reveal herself directly to Orlando, thereby making herself vulnerable. She must give up the disguise and appear—as she ultimately promises Orlando—"human as she is" (5.2.67). But in giving up the disguise, she also gives up the strength it symbolizes. As the disguise begins to break down before its official removal, Rosalind's transparent femininity takes the form of fainting—a sign of weakness that gives her away: "You a man? / You lack a man's heart" (4.3.163–64). This loss of control signals that Rosalind can no longer deny her inner feminine self. The capacity for love that we find so admirable in Rosalind is compromised by the necessity that she resume a traditional female role in order to engage in love.

This traditional image has been resent all along. Rosalind willingly confides to Celia that she remains a woman despite the male costume: "in my heart / Lie there what hidden woman's fear there will—/ We'll have a swashing and a martial outside" (1.3.118–20); "Good my complexion, dost thou think, though I am caparison'd like a man, I have a doublet and hose in my disposition?" (3.2.194–96); and "Do you not know I am a woman?" (249). By virtue of the costume, Rosalind does have access to both male and female attributes, but the impression she conveys of androgynous wholeness is misleading. Neither Rosalind nor the play questions the conventional categories of masculine and feminine. She does not reconcile gender definitions in the sense of integrating or synthesizing them. Her own insistence on the metaphor of exterior (male) and interior (female) keeps the categories distinct and separable. The liberation that Rosalind experiences in the forest has built into it the conservative countermovement by which, as the play returns to the normal world, she will be reduced to the traditional woman who is subservient to men.

Rosalind is shown working out in advance the terms of her return. Still protected by her disguise yet allowing herself to come closer to the decisive moment, she instructs Orlando to "woo me" (4.1.68) and subsequently tells him what to say in a wedding rehearsal while she practises yielding. Though she teases Orlando with the wife's power to make him a cuckold and then to conceal her duplicity with her "wayward wit" (160–76), this is good fun, and it is only that. It is clear to the audience, if not yet to Orlando, that Rosalind's flaunting of her role as disloyal wife is a put-on rather than a genuine threat. She may playfully delay the final moment when she becomes a wife, but we are reassured that, once married, she will in fact be faithful. Her humor has the effect of exorcising and renouncing her potential weapon. The uncertainty concerns not her loyalty but Orlando's, as her sudden change of tone when he announces his departure indicates: "Alas, dear love, I cannot lack thee two hours!" (178). Her exuberance and control collapse in fears of his betrayal: "Ay, go your ways, go your ways; I knew what you would prove" (182–83). Her previous wit notwithstanding, for Rosalind the scene is less a demonstration of power than an exercise in vulnerability. She is once again consigned to anxious waiting for her tardy man: "But why did he swear he would come this morning, and comes not?" (3.4.18–19).

Rosalind's own behavior neutralizes her jokes about cuckoldry, but this point is sharply reinforced by the brief account of the male hunt that immediately follows act 4, scene 1. The expected negative meaning of horns as the sign of a cuckold is transformed into a positive image of phallic potency that unites men. Changing the style of his literary response to deer killing, Jaques replaces his earlier lament (2.1.26–66) with a celebration of male hunt and conquest: "Let's present him to the Duke like a Roman conqueror, and it would do well to set the deer's horns upon his head, for a branch of victory" (4.2.3–5).[7] The rousing song occasioned by this moment suggests the power of an all-male activity to provide a self-sufficient male heritage, thus to defend against male insecurity about humiliation by women.

The final scene, orchestrated by Rosalind, demonstrates her power in a paradoxical way. She is the architect of a resolution that phases out the control she has wielded and prepares the way for the patriarchal status quo. She accedes to the process by which, in the transition from courtship to marriage, power passes from the female to the male: the man is no longer the suitor who serves, obeys, and begs but is now the husband who commands. Rosalind's submission is explicit but not ironic, though her tone may be high-spirited. To each of the two men in her life she declares: "To you I give myself, for I am yours" (5.4.116–17). Her casting herself in the role of male possession is all the more charming because she does not have to be forced to adopt it: her self-taming is voluntary. We may wish to give Rosalind credit for her cleverness in forestalling male rivalry between her father and her fiancé. Unlike Cordelia, she is smart enough to see that in order to be gratified, each man needs to feel that he is the recipient of all her love, not half of it. Yet Rosalind is not really in charge here because the potential hostility between the younger and older man has already been negotiated in the forest in act 2, scene 7, a negotiation that results in the formation of an idealized male alliance. Rosalind submits not only to two individual men but also to the patriarchal society that they embody. Patriarchy is not a slogan smuggled in from the twentieth century and imposed on the play but an exact term for the social structure that close reading reveals within the play.

II

We are apt to assume that the green world is more free than it actually is. In the case of *As You Like It*, the green world cannot be interpreted as a space apart where a youthful rebellion finds a refuge from the older generation. The forest of Arden includes a strong parental presence: Duke Senior's is the first voice we hear there. Moreover, the green world has a clear political structure. Freed from the constraints of courtly decorum, Duke Senior can afford to address his companions as "brothers" (2.1.1), but he nonetheless retains a fatherly command. Fraternal spirit is not equivalent to democracy, as is clarified when the duke dispenses favor on a hierarchical basis: "Shall share the good of our returned fortune, / According to the measure of their states" (5.4.174–75).

Although interpretations of *As You Like It* often stress youthful love, we should not neglect the paternal context in which the love occurs. Both Rosalind and Orlando acknowledge Duke Senior. Rosalind is aware, as she finds herself attracted to Orlando, that "My father lov'd Sir Rowland [Orlando's father] as his soul" (1.2.235) and hence that her affection is not incompatible with family approval. Orlando, for his part, does not go forward in pursuit of love until after he has become friends with Duke Senior. Rosalind and Orlando approach the forest in strikingly different ways. Rosalind's mission is love. Upon entering the forest, she discovers there the love "passion" she has brought with her: "Alas, poor shepherd, searching of thy wound, / I have by hard adventure found mine own" (2.4.44–45). Orlando, by contrast, has two projects (though he does not consciously formulate them) to complete in the forest: the first is his quest to reestablish the broken connection with his father's legacy; the second is the quest for Rosalind. The sequence of these projects is an indication of priority. Orlando's outburst—"But heavenly Rosalind!" (1.2.289)—is not picked up again until he opens act 3, scene 2, with his love poem. The interim is reserved for his other, patriarchal business.

In the first scene of the play, Orlando makes it clear, in a melodramatic but nonetheless poignant way, that he derives his sense of identity from his dead father, an identity that is not yet fulfilled. In protesting against his older brother's mistreatment, Orlando asserts the paternal bond: "The spirit of my father grows strong in me, and I will no longer endure it" (1.1.70–71). His first step toward recovery of the connection with his lost father is the demolition of Charles the wrestler: "How dost thou, Charles?" / "He cannot speak, my lord" (1.2.219–20). This victory earns Orlando the right to proclaim his father's name as his own:

DUKE F. What is thy name, young man?
ORL. Orlando, my liege, the youngest son of
Sir Rowland de Boys....
I am more proud to be Sir Rowland's son.
(221–22, 232)

Frederick's negative reaction to Orlando's statement of identity confirms the concept of heritage being evoked here: "Thou shouldst have better pleas'd me with this deed / Hadst thou descended from another house" (227–28). The significance of the wrestling match is that Orlando has undergone a traditional male rite of passage, providing an established channel for the violence he has previously expressed by collaring Oliver in the opening scene. Yet aggression is the epitome of a rigid masculinity that Shakespeare characteristically condemns as too narrow a basis for identity. Orlando's aggressiveness is instantly rendered inappropriate by his falling in love. Moreover, his recourse to violence simply mirrors the technique of the tyrannical Duke Frederick. As it turns out, Orlando must give up violence in order to meet the "good father."

While Rosalind's confidante Celia provides the opportunity to talk about love, Orlando is accompanied by Adam, who serves a very different function since he is a living link to Orlando's father. The paternal inheritance blocked by Oliver is received indirectly from Adam when he offers the money "I sav'd under your father, / Which I did store to be my foster-nurse" (2.3.39–40) The motif of nurturance implied by the "foster-nurse" image is continued as Orlando, through Adam's sudden collapse from lack of food, is led to Duke Senior's pastoral banquet. Treating this new situation as another trial of "the strength of my youth," Orlando imagines an all-or-nothing "adventure" (1.2.172, 177) similar to the wrestling match: "If this uncouth forest yield any thing savage, I will either be food for it, or bring it for food to thee" (2.6.6–8). In act 2, scene 7, he enters with drawn sword. Unexpectedly finding a benevolent father figure, Orlando effects as gracefully as possible a transition from toughness to tenderness: "Let gentleness my strong enforcement be, / In the which hope I blush, and hide my sword" (118–19). This display of nonviolence is the precondition for Orlando's recovery of patriarchal lineage. Duke Senior aids this recovery by his recognition of the father's reflection in the son and by his declaration of his own loving connection with Orlando's father. This transaction concludes the scene:

If that you were the good Sir Rowland's son,
As you have whisper'd faithfully you were,

And as mine eye cloth his effigies witness
Most truly limn'd and living in your face,
Be truly welcome hither. I am the Duke
That lov'd your father.
(191–96)

The confirmation of Orlando's identity has the effect of a ritual blessing that makes this particular father–son relation the basis for social cohesion in general. There is much virtue in Orlando's "If":

ORL. If ever you have look'd on better days,
If ever been where bells have knoll'd to church,
If ever sate at any good man's feast,
If ever from your eyelids wip'd a tear,
And know what 'tis to pity, and be pitied....
DUKE S. True is it that we have seen better days,
And have with holy bell been knoll'd to church,
And sat at good men's feasts, and wip'd our eyes
Of drops that sacred pity hath engend'red.
(2.7.113–17, 120–23)

The liturgy of male utopia, ruthlessly undercut in *Love's Labor's Lost*, is here allowed to stand. Virgilian piety, founded on ideal father–son relations and evoked visually when, like Aeneas with Anchises, Orlando carries Adam on his back, can achieve what Navarre's academe with its spurious abstinence could not. Orlando's heroic language as he goes off to rescue Adam is as clumsy as any he uses in the poems to Rosalind, but whereas the play pokes fun at the love poetry, the expression of duty to Adam is not subject to irony: "Then but forbear your food a little while, / Whiles, like a doe, I go to find my fawn, / And give it food" (127–29). We are invited simply to accept the doe–fawn metaphor that Orlando invokes for his obligation to reciprocate Adam's "pure love" (131).

Just as there is an unlimited supply of food in this scene, so there seems to be more than enough "pure love" to go around, Jaques excepted. Love is expressed in terms of food, and men gladly take on nurturant roles. Duke Senior's abundant provision of food and of "gentleness" creates an image of a self-sustaining patriarchial system. The men take over the traditional female prerogative of maternal nurturance, negatively defined by Jaques: "At first the infant, / Mewling and puking in the nurse's arms" (2.7.143–44). Such discomfort has been purged from the men's nurturance as it is dramatized in this scene, which thus offers a new perspective on Duke Senior's very first speech in the play. We now see that it is the male feast, not the biting winter wind, that "feelingly persuades me what I am" (2.1.11). "Sweet are the uses of adversity" because, as Orlando discovers, adversity disappears when men's "gentleness" prevails, "translating the stubbornness of fortune / Into so quiet and sweet a style" (12, 19–20). This sweetness explains why "loving lords have put themselves into voluntary exile" with the duke and why "many young gentlemen flock to him every day" (1.1.101–2, 117).

The idealized male enclave founded on "sacred pity" in act 2, scene 7, is not an isolated incident. The power of male pity extends beyond this scene to include the evil Oliver, who is threatened by a symbol of maternal nurturance made hostile by depletion: "A lioness, with udders all drawn dry" (4.3.114) and "the suck'd and hungry lioness" (126). The motif of eating here creates a negative image that might disturb the comfortable pastoral banquet, but the lioness's intrusion is quickly ended. Responding with a kindness that can be traced back to his meeting with Duke Senior, Orlando rescues his brother: "But kindness, nobler ever than revenge, / And nature, stronger than his just occasion, / Made him give battle to the lioness" (128–30). Oliver's oral fulfillment follows: "my conversion / So sweetly tastes" (136–37). The tears "that sacred pity hath engend'red" (2.7.123) are reiterated by the brothers' reconciliation—"Tears our recountments had most kindly bath'd" (4.3.140)—and their reunion confirmed by a recapitulation of the banquet scene: "he led me to the gentle Duke, / Who gave me fresh array and entertainment, / Committing me unto my brother's love" (142–44). Again the pattern of male reconciliation preceding love for women is seen in Oliver's confession of his desire to marry Celia (5.2.1–14) coming after his admission to the brotherhood.

The male community of act 2, scene 7, is also vindicated by the restoration of patriarchal normalcy in the play's final scene. In the end, as Rosalind's powers are fading, the relationship between Duke Senior and Orlando is reasserted and completed as the duke announces the inheritance to which marriage entitles Orlando: "A land itself at large, a potent dukedom" (5.4.169). Like the "huswife Fortune" who "doth most mistake in her gifts to women" (1.2.31–32, 36), Rosalind plays her part by rehearsing the men in their political roles:

ROS. You say, if I bring in your Rosalind,
You will bestow her on Orlando here?
DUKE S. That would I, had I kingdoms to give with her.
ROS. And you say you will have her, when I bring her.
ORL. That would I, were I of all kingdoms king.
(5.4.6–10)

The reference the two men make to kingdoms is shortly to be fulfilled, but this bounty is beyond Rosalind's power to give. For it is not her magic that produces the surprise entrance of Jaques de Boys with the news of Duke Senior's restoration. In completing the de Boys family reunion, the middle brother's appearance reverses the emblematic fate of the three sons destroyed by Charles the wrestler: "Yonder they lie, the poor old man, their father, making such pitiful dole over them that all the beholders take his part with weeping" (1.2.129–32). The image of three de Boys sons reestablishes the proper generational sequence, ensuring continuity.

III

C. L. Barber has shown that the "Saturnalian Pattern" that gives structure to festive comedy is intrinsically conservative since it involves only "a temporary license, a 'misrule' which implied rule."[8] But in *As You Like It* the conservatism of comic form does not affect all characters equally. In the liberal opening out into the forest of Arden, both men and women are permitted an expansion of sexual identity that transcends restrictive gender roles. Just as Rosalind gains access to the traditional masculine attributes of strength and control through her costume, so Orlando gains access to the traditional female attributes of compassion and nurturance. However, the conservative countermovement built into comic strategy applies exclusively to Rosalind. Her possession of the male costume and of the power it symbolizes is only temporary. But Orlando does not have to give up the emotional enlargement he has experienced in the forest. Discussions of androgyny in *As You Like It* usually focus on Rosalind whereas in fact it is the men rather than the women who are the lasting beneficiaries of androgyny. It is Orlando, not Rosalind, who achieves a synthesis of attributes traditionally labeled masculine and feminine when he combines compassion and aggression in rescuing his brother from the lioness.

This selective androgyny demands an ambivalent response: it is a humanizing force for the men, yet it is based on the assumption that men have power over women.[9] Because androgyny is available only to men, we are left with a paradoxical compatibility of androgyny with patriarchy, that is, benevolent patriarchy. In talking about male power in *As You Like It*, we must distinguish between two forms of patriarchy. The first and most obvious is the harsh, mean-spirited version represented by Oliver, who abuses primogeniture, and by Duke Frederick, who after usurping power holds on to it by arbitrary acts of suppression. Driven by greed, envy, suspicion, and power for power's sake, neither man can explain his actions. In an ironic demonstration of the consuming nature of evil, Duke Frederick expends his final rage against Oliver, who honestly protests: "I never lov'd my brother in my life" (3.1.14). In contrast to good men, bad men are incapable of forming alliances. Since Frederick's acts of banishment have now depopulated the court, he himself must enter the forest in order to seek the enemies so necessary to his existence (5.4.154–58). But of course this patriarchal tyranny is a caricature and therefore harmless. Oliver and Frederick are exaggerated fairy-tale villains whose hardened characters are unable to withstand the wholesome atmosphere of the forest and instantly dissolve (4.3.135–37; 5.4.159–65). The second, more serious version of patriarchy is the political structure headed by Duke Senior. To describe it, we seek adjectives like "benevolent," "humane," and "civilized." Yet we cannot leave it at that. A benevolent patriarchy still requires women to be subordinate, and Rosalind's final performance is her enactment of this subordination.

We can now summarize the difference between the conclusions of *Love's Labor's Lost* and *As You Like It*. In order to assess the sense of an ending, we must take into account the perspective of sexual politics and correlate formal harmony or disharmony with patriarchal stability or instability. Unlike Rosalind, the women in *Love's Labor's Lost* do not give up their independence.[10] The sudden announcement of the death of the princess's father partially restrains her wit. But this news is a *pater ex machina* attempt to even the score and to equalize the situation between the men and the women because nothing has emerged organically within the play to challenge the women's predominance. The revelation that the "decrepit, sick and bedred" father (1.1.138) has died is not an effective assertion of his presence but, on the contrary, advertises his weakness. The princess submits to the "new-sad soul" (5.2.731) that mourning requires, but this provides the excuse for going on to reject the suitors as she has all along. Her essential power remains intact, whereas patriarchal authority is presented as weak or nonexistent. The death of the invalid father has a sobering impact because it mirrors the vacuum created by the four lords' powerlessness within the play. There is no relief from the fear that dominant women inspire in a patriarchal sensibility, and this continuing tension contributes to the uneasiness at the play's end.

Like the princess, Rosalind confronts her father in the final scene. But in her case paternal power is vigorously represented by Duke Senior and by the line of patriarchal authority established when Senior makes Orlando his heir. Festive celebration is now possible because a dependable, that is, patriarchal, social order is securely in place. It is Duke Senior's voice that legitimates the festive closure: "Play, music, and you brides and bridegrooms all, / With measure heap'd in joy, to th' measures fall" (5.4.178–79). Orlando benefits from this social structure because, in contrast to the lords of *Love's Labor's Lost*, he has a solid political resource to offset the liability of a poetic convention that dictates male subservience. *As You Like It* achieves marital closure not by eliminating male ties but rather by strengthening them.[11]

A further phasing out of Rosalind occurs in the Epilogue when it is revealed that she is male: "If I were a woman I would kiss as many of you as had beards that pleas'd me" (18–19). This explicit breaking of theatrical illusion forces us to reckon with the fact of an all-male cast. The boy-actor convention makes it possible for males to explore the female other (I use the term *other* here in the sense given by Simone de Beauvoir in *The Second Sex* of woman as the other). Vicariously taking on the female role enables male spectators to make an experimental contact with what otherwise might remain unknown, forbidden territory. Fear of women can be encountered in the relatively safe environment of the theater, acted out, controlled (when it can be controlled as in *As You Like It*), and overcome. A further twist of logic defuses and reduces the threat of female power: Rosalind is no one to be frightened of since, as the Epilogue insists, she is male after all; she is only a boy and clearly subordinate to men in the hierarchy of things.

The convention of males playing female roles gives men the opportunity to imagine sex-role fluidity and flexibility. Built into the conditions of performance is the potential for male acknowledgment of a "feminine self" and thus for male transcendence of a narrow masculinity. In the particular case of *As You Like It*, the all-male cast provides a theatrical counterpart for the male community at Duke Senior's banquet in act 2, scene 7. This theatrical dimension reinforces the conservative effect of male androgyny within the play. Acknowledgment of the feminine within the male is one thing, the acknowledgment of individual women another: the latter does not automatically follow from the former. In the boy-actor motif, woman is a metaphor for the male discovery of the feminine within himself, of those qualities suppressed by a masculinity strictly defined as aggressiveness. Once the tenor of the metaphor has been attained, the vehicle can be discarded—just as Rosalind is discarded. The sense of the patriarchal ending in *As You Like It* is that male androgyny is affirmed whereas female "liberty" in the person of Rosalind is curtailed.

There is, finally, a studied ambiguity about heterosexual versus homoerotic feeling in the play, Shakespeare allowing himself to have it both ways. The Epilogue is heterosexual in its bringing together of men and women: "and I charge you, O men, for the love you bear to women (as I perceive by your simp'ring, none of you hates them), that between you and the women the play may please" (14–17). The "simp'ring" attributed to men in their response to women is evoked in a good-natured jocular spirit; yet the tone conveys discomfort as well. In revealing the self-sufficient male acting company, the Epilogue also offers the counterimage of male bonds based on the exclusion of women.

Though he is shown hanging love poems on trees only after achieving atonement with Rosalind's father, Orlando never tries, like the lords of *Love's*

Labor's Lost, to avoid women. The social structure of *As You Like It*, in which political power is vested in male bonds, can include heterosexual love because marriage becomes a way of incorporating women since Rosalind is complicit in her assimilation by patriarchal institutions. However, in spite of the disarming of Rosalind, resistance to women remains. It is as though asserting the priority of relations between men over relations between men and women is not enough, as though a fall-back position is needed. The Epilogue is, in effect, a second ending that provides further security against women by preserving on stage the image of male ties in their pure form with women absent. Not only are women to be subordinate; they can, if necessary, be imagined as nonexistent. Rosalind's art does not, as is sometimes suggested, coincide with Shakespeare's: Shakespeare uses his art to take away Rosalind's female identity and thereby upstages her claim to magic power.

We can see the privileged status accorded to male bonds by comparing Shakespeare's treatment of same-sex relations for men and for women. Men originally divided are reunited as in the instance of Oliver and Orlando, but women undergo the reverse process. Rosalind and Celia are initially inseparable: "never two ladies lov'd as they do" (1.1.112); "whose loves / Are dearer than the natural bond of sisters" (1.2.275–76); "And whereso'er we went, like Juno's swans, / Still we went coupled and inseparable" (1.3.75–76); and "thou and I am one. / Shall we be sund'red? shall we part, sweet girl? / No, let my father seek another heir" (97–99). Yet the effect of the play is to separate them by transferring their allegiance to husbands. Celia ceases to be a speaking character at the end of act 4, her silence coinciding with her new role as fiancée. The danger of female bonding is illustrated when Shakespeare diminishes Rosalind's absolute control by mischievously confronting her with the unanticipated embarrassment of Phebe's love for her. Rosalind is of course allowed to devise an escape from the pressure of this undesirable entanglement, but it is made clear in the process that such ardor is taboo and that the authorized defense against it is marriage. "And so am I for no woman," Rosalind insists (5.2.88). A comparable prohibition is not announced against male friendship.[12]

In conclusion, we must ask: what is Shakespeare's relation to the sexual politics of *As You Like It*? Is he taking an ironic and critical stance toward the patriarchal solution of his characters, or is he heavily invested in this solution himself? I think there are limits to Shakespeare's critical awareness in this play. The sudden conversions of Oliver and Duke Frederick have a fairy-tale quality that Shakespeare clearly intends as an aspect of the wish fulfillment to which he calls attention in the play's title. Similarly, Jaques's commentary in the final scene is a deliberate foil to the neatness of the ending that allows

Shakespeare as well as Jaques a modicum of distance. However, in fundamental respects Shakespeare appears to be implicated in the fantasy he has created for his characters.

As You Like It enacts two rites of which Shakespeare did not avail himself in *Love's Labor's Lost.* First, Shakespeare has the social structure ultimately contain female energy as he did not in *Love's Labor's Lost.* We have too easily accepted the formulation that says that Shakespeare in the mature history plays concentrates on masculine development whereas in the mature festive comedies he gives women their due by allowing them to play the central role.[13] *As You Like It* is primarily a defensive action against female power rather than a celebration of it. Second, Shakespeare portrays an ideal male community based on "sacred pity." This idealized vision of relationships between men can be seen as sentimental and unrealistic, but in contrast to his undercutting of academe in *Love's Labor's Lost*, Shakespeare is here thoroughly engaged and endorses the idealization. These two elements—female vitality kept manageable and male power kept loving—provided a resolution that at this particular moment was "As Shakespeare Liked It."

*

This chapter began with the suggestion that *Henry V* and *As You Like It* have in common a concern with father–son ties. The two plays are also connected by their treatment of mothers. Both plays deal with the problem of the mother simply by excluding it. The Henry IV–Henry V relationship occurs in a maternal vacuum; the absent mother enables Henry V to become "the motherless man."[14] Management of female vitality in *As You Like It* includes specific avoidance of women as mothers.[15] In Northrop Frye's view: "There is something maternal about the green world, in which the new order of the comic resolution is nourished and brought to birth."[16] But there is no effective maternal presence in *As You Like It.* The maternal force is confined to the emblematic angry lioness and summarily disposed of, thereby allowing the action of the play to unfold in an environment kept free of maternal interference. Rosalind contributes to this effect because she lacks sexual maturity: she is a prematernal and hence nonmaternal figure. Her transvestism hinges on the merging of "boys and women" (3.2.414) in the preadolescent moment prior to sharp gender differentiation. The occasional allusions to becoming pregnant (1.3.11; 3.2.204; 4.1.175) are only witty anticipations that have no immediate impact. The future in which the imagined pregnancy might become a reality is sufficiently distanced for us to feel that it is firmly held outside the bounds of the play. This defense against encroachment by the maternal through virtual exclusion of it serves to link *As You Like It* with *Henry V.*

Notes

1. I borrow this phrase from T. S. Eliot's essay "Andrew Marvell" (1921), in *Selected Essays: 1917–1932* (New York: Harcourt, Brace, 1932), p. 252. My essay on *As You Like It*, which forms the basis of this chapter, was presented at the 1979 Modern Language Association convention at the session on "Marriage and the Family in Shakespeare," where I received valuable commentary from Shirley Garner and Carol Neely, chair and respondent, respectively, for the session. After completing my work on the play, I discovered Louis Adrian Montrose's "'The Place of a Brother' in *As You Like It*: Social Process and Comic Form," *Shakespeare Quarterly* 32 (1981): 28–54, whose approach I regard as complementary to my own.

2. Recent studies by Marilyn French and Linda Bamber suffer from a tendency to invest too much energy in abstract definitions of genre categories, as though Shakespeare managed each genre as a strictly separate Platonic form, and too little energy in close interpretation of individual variations. In *Shakespeare's Division of Experience* (New York: Simon & Schuster, 1981), French pursues her thesis that each genre has its own gender to a formulaic, literalistic extreme, as I have noted in my review of her study in *Women's Studies* 9 (1982): 189–201. Bamber's *Comic Women, Tragic Men: A Study of Gender and Genre in Shakespeare* (Stanford: Stanford University Press, 1982) is far more subtle but nonetheless echoes French's project in stressing a rigid generic division in Shakespeare's artistic labor. Bamber's brief discussion of comedy (Ch. 5) creates intrageneric difficulty because she overrides differences among individual plays in her effort to assimilate them to a common mold, while intergenerically she emphasizes differences at the expense of continuities. For a full discussion of Bamber's approach, see my review of her book in *Women's Studies* 10 (1984): 342–49.

3. I find unconvincing C. L. Barber's argument in *Shakespeare's Festive Comedy* (Princeton: Princeton University Press, 1959) that the songs convey the missing positive note: "They provide for the conclusion of the comedy what marriage usually provides: an expression of the going-on power of life" (p. 118). Barber works too hard to create this festive closure, overstating the affirmation produced by the songs while glossing over the full force of the discomfort caused by the lack of marriage among the central characters. I draw attention to my disagreement here because it illustrates in microcosm my departure from Barber's use of festive comic form. Although he distinguishes the two phases of "release" and "clarification," Barber's practice nonetheless blurs them because the final communal celebration of "the going-on power of life" retains a wishful element characteristic of the earlier stage of festive release. The result is often to make the comic clarification more genial than the evidence warrants. My experience of *As You Like It* differs from Barber's because I see the reality that qualifies and places festivity as a more stringent one. The "resistance" (p. 88) or "tension" (p. 224) against which the festive release pushes off frequently returns in a new, more subtle form in the final moment of clarification, one major source of this renewed tension being relations between men and women and the social structure that organizes them. Yet, as the present chapter makes clear, it is Barber's comic paradigm itself that has made me see these plays differently. I am heavily indebted to the festive concept of dramatic action, but I modify it in order to be more responsive to the gap between ideal festive expectations and actual result. What makes Shakespeare's comic endings compelling is their dramatization of this gap, however muted, rather than of simple fulfillment. Thus, for example, the songs that conclude *Love's Labor's Lost*, while aiming to invoke the resources of festivity, in fact contribute to the overall mood of thwarted festivity.

4. Barber's formulation for this movement in *Shakespeare's Festive Comedy* is "through release to clarification" (p. 6). In "The Argument of Comedy" (in *English Institute Essays*,

1948, ed. D. A. Robertson, Jr. [New York: Columbia University Press, 1949], pp. 58–73), Northrop Frye uses Keats's "green world" (*Endymion*, I, 16) to describe the middle phase, which mediates between an obstructionist society dominated by people "who are helplessly driven by ruling passions, neurotic compulsions" (p. 61) and "a new social unit" (p. 60) that conveys "the birth of a renewed sense of social integration" (p. 61). This comic structure is elaborated in Frye's *A Natural Perspective: The Development of Shakespearean Comedy and Romance* (New York: Columbia University Press, 1965), pp. 73–79.

5. In "The Failure of Relationship Between Men and Women in *Love's Labor's Lost*," *Women's Studies* 9 (1981): 65–81, I show how the men's poems appeal to conventions of female domination and male humility in love poetry and how these conventions shape the dramatic action, creating a fixed barrier that blocks love.

6. See Clara Park, "As We Like It: How a Girl Can Be Smart and Still Popular," *American Scholar* 42 (1973): 262–78; reprinted in *The Woman's Part: Feminist Criticism of Shakespeare*, ed. Carolyn Ruth Swift Lenz, Gayle Greene, and Carol Thomas Neely (Urbana: University of Illinois Press, 1980), pp. 100–16.

7. Norman O. Brown employs this passage in his own celebration of the horn: "Metamorphoses II: Actaeon," *American Poetry Review* 1 (1972): 38–40.

8. Barber, *Festive Comedy*, p. 10.

9. Adrienne Rich provides a critique of the conservative use of the concept *androgyny* and a summary of recent writing on the subject in *Of Woman Born: Motherhood as Experience and Institution* (New York: W. W. Norton, 1976), pp. 62–63. Rich's poem "The Stranger," in *Diving into the Wreck* (New York: W. W. Norton, 1973), declares proudly: "I am the androgyne" (p. 19). But the revaluation of androgyny in her prose work leads Rich to disavow the term in "Natural Resources," in *The Dream of a Common Language* (New York: W. W. Norton, 1978): "There are words I cannot choose again: / *humanism androgyny*" (p. 66).

10. I do not mean to suggest that this is a positive ending in the sense of being the best possible outcome, but the women's continued assertion of independence is a valid response to the less-than-ideal circumstances with which they must deal. It allows them to retain their integrity—an alternative preferable to capitulation.

11. In Anne Barton's judgment, *As You Like It* "stands as the fullest and most stable realization of Shakespearean comic form" ("'As You Like It' and 'Twelfth Night': Shakespeare's Sense of an Ending," in *Shakespearean Comedy: Stratford-Upon-Avon Studies* 14, ed. Malcolm Bradbury and David Palmer [New York: Crane, Russak & Co., 1972], p. 161). Barton speaks of Shakespeare's loss of "faith" in comic endings after the perfection of *As You Like It* and of the "renewed faith" made possible by his "readjustment of form" in the late romances (pp. 179–80). Both the loss and the recovery of faith involve Shakespeare's changing attitudes toward the viability of benign patriarchy. In particular, *The Winter's Tale* restores this faith (after its shattering in the tragedies) by reestablishing patriarchal harmony in a believable form.

12. In this regard *The Merchant of Venice* offers a useful contrast. The conclusion of *Love's Labor's Lost* presents a three-way stalemate. Marital bonds, male bonds, and female bonds are all sources of vague discomfort: none can be affirmed. *As You Like It* affirms marriage by strengthening male bonds and eliminating female bonds. *The Merchant of Venice* breaks the stalemate in a different way. Marriage is achieved by disrupting the bond between Antonio and Bassanio, but the alliance between Portia and Nerissa remains in effect, as their comparatively sharp deployment of the cuckold motif attests. The source of uneasiness in *The Merchant of Venice*, however, is Portia's defeat of a Jewish father in the earlier court scene and, in particular, her problematic speech about Christian bounty (4.1.184–202), problematic partly because her own behavior toward Shylock fails to exhibit the mercy she recommends to him.

13. For an example of this contrast between comedies and histories, see R. J. Dorius, "Shakespeare's Dramatic Modes and *Antony and Cleopatra*," in *Literatur als Kritik des Lebens: Festschrift zum 65. Geburtstag von Ludwig Borinski* (Heidelberg: Quelle & Meyer, 1975), pp. 83–96. Dorius's overview is useful but overdrawn in the way I have suggested.

14. The use of "motherless man" is from Leslie Fiedler's discussion of Shakespeare in *Love and Death in the American Novel* (New York: Criterion Books, 1960), p. 26.

15. The existence of a need to avoid mothers can be demonstrated by two subsequent plays, *All's Well That Ends Well* and *Measure for Measure*. Both plays, in explicitly confronting procreation, testify to the difficulty of assimilating it. Part of the reason they are problem plays is the unresolved ambivalence about the sexuality evidenced in the pregnancies of Helena and Juliet. However necessary procreation is acknowledged to be in theory, its actual practice is often in Shakespeare made to appear suspect, troubling, or forbidding, as Venus's argument for procreation illustrates (*Venus and Adonis*, 168). In *The Comedy of Errors* at the beginning of Shakespeare's career, birth is evoked in passing in an equivocal, infelicitous line as "The pleasing punishment that women bear" (1.1.46); not until *Pericles*, in the final phase of Shakespeare's career, is procreation dignified, its integrity persuasively dramatized. And not until *The Winter's Tale* does he begin to approach the reconciliation of art and procreation hypothesized in sonnets 15–17.

16. Frye, "Argument of Comedy," p. 69.

MARJORIE GARBER

The Education of Orlando

When Rosalind learns from Celia that Orlando is in the Forest of Arden, she cries out in mingled joy and consternation, "Alas the day, what shall I do with my doublet and hose?" (3.2.219–20).[1] Members of the audience might perhaps be pardoned were they to answer her, not in the "one word" she demands, but with the familiar chant of the burlesque house, "Take it off!"—either literally (if she has been provident enough to bring a change of clothing with her to Arden) or figuratively, by identifying herself to him at once as Rosalind, rather than continuing the fiction that she is a youth named Ganymede, a native of the forest. Indeed Celia makes a suggestion along these lines, when she hears Rosalind—as Ganymede—abusing the reputations of women when she talks to Orlando about the nature of love. "You have simply misus'd our sex in your love-prate," says Celia. "We must have your doublet and hose pluck'd over your head, and show the world what the bird hath done to her own nest" (4.1.201–4). There is in fact very little risk to her should she do so, except perhaps from a blast of the "winter wind" about which Amiens sings so feelingly (2.7.174). She is perfectly safe. Clearly there are no outlaws in the forest, or other predatory men; they have all been left behind at court. Moreover, she is assured of Orlando's love for her, since both she and Celia have read the poems with which he has festooned Arden's otherwise blameless trees. In short, there is apparently no reason for her to remain clad as a boy. Why then does she do so?

In other Shakespearian comedies, women dressed as men have compelling reasons for remaining in disguise. Julia in *The Two Gentlemen of Verona* is trapped in her male attire because of the perfidy of her erstwhile lover, Proteus. She initially disguises herself for the same reason Rosalind gives: "for I would prevent / The loose encounters of lascivious men" (2.7.40–41), but she fully intends to reveal herself once she reaches her "loving Proteus" (7). When to her chagrin she finds him in the act of offering his love to Silvia instead, she retains her male guise, enlists herself in Proteus's service, carries his love tokens to Silvia, and only reveals her true identity in the final scene, when she fears that Valentine will make good on his extraordinary promise to give Proteus "all that was mine in Silvia" (5.4.83). At this point Julia swoons (or pretends to swoon), produces a ring given her by Proteus, and acknowledges that her "immodest raiment" is a "disguise of love" (106–7). Her costume is essential to the working out of the plot. The same is true in *Twelfth Night*. Shipwrecked in Illyria, Viola initially wishes to gain employment with the Countess Olivia in her own shape as a woman; though without disclosing her name and station. "O that I serv'd that lady," she tells the sea captain who rescues her, "And might not be delivered to the world / Till I had made mine own occasion mellow, / What my estate is" (*Twelfth Night*, 1.2.41–44). It is only because Olivia's mourning makes a suit to her impossible that Viola determines to "conceal me what I am" (53) and seek service with Duke Orsino in the guise of the youth Cesario. Like Julia she is then trapped in her disguise when she falls in love with the man she serves and is sent by him to plead his love to Olivia. Here the disguise is even more central to the plot than in *Two Gentlemen*, since it is the means by which Olivia meets and marries Sebastian, and Orsino discovers his own love for Viola.

Portia is not trapped in her role as the wise young judge Balthasar, but it is essential that she should be dressed as a man in order to free Antonio, confound Shylock, and—ultimately—teach her husband a lesson about the nature of generosity and love. And Imogen, too, is forced by circumstance to retain her male disguise. Dressed as a boy, and fleeing like Julia after her departed lover, she thinks she has found him dead and therefore enlists as "Fidele" in the service of the Roman general. Her disguise and subsequent adventures lead directly to the restoration of Cymbeline's sons, as well as to her reunion with her beloved Posthumus.

All these women must retain their disguises because of exigencies of the plot. But what is Rosalind's rationale? What if she were to step forward in act 3, scene 2, not like a "saucy lackey" (296) but like herself, and declare that she is the "Heavenly Rosalind" Orlando has been seeking? There would of course be one unfortunate repercussion, since the play would effectively come to an end in the middle of the third act (as would have occurred if Cordelia had answered at once when Lear asked her how much she loved him). But beyond that, would anything be lost? Can Shakespeare be keeping Rosalind in disguise merely to prolong his play, or is there another purpose in her decision not to unmask herself?

Many reasons have been advanced for the continued existence of Ganymede after Orlando comes on the scene. G. L. Kittredge quotes one Lady Martin, writing in *Blackwood's Magazine* for October, 1884, who offers the opinion that "surely it was the finest and boldest of all devices, one of which only a Shakespeare could have ventured, to put his heroine into such a position that she could, without revealing her own secret, probe the heart of her lover to the very bottom, and so assure herself that the love which possessed her own being was as completely the master of his." In a rather ungentlemanly fashion Kittredge then goes on to demolish Lady Martin: "This amiable and eloquent observation," he notes, "is typical of many that have been mistakenly made upon details of Shakespeare's plots. The 'device' is not Shakespeare's, but Lodge's."[2] Subsequent critics have been willing to recognize that Shakespeare was capable of changing what he did not wish to retain from his sources and have tended to theorize somewhat along Lady Martin's lines. C. L. Barber, for example, remarks that when disguised "Rosalind is not committed to the conventional language and attitudes of love, loaded as these inevitably are with sentimentality,"[3] and Anne Barton suggests that as Ganymede "she learns a great deal about herself, about Orlando, and about love itself which she could not have done within the normal conventions of society."[4] A recent feminist critic, Clara Claiborne Park, carries the argument for Rosalind's independence and self-knowledge a step further, pointing out that "male garments immensely broaden the sphere in which female energy can manifest itself. Dressed as a man, a nubile woman can go places and do things she couldn't do otherwise, thus getting the play out of the court and the closet and into interesting places like forests or Welsh mountains. Once Rosalind is disguised as a man, she can be as saucy and self-assertive as she likes."[5] Those critics interested in the question seem in general to agree that disguise is a freeing action for Rosalind and that her double role allows her to be at once caustic and caring, tender and tough.

I do not wish to quarrel with these sensible observations, but I would like to suggest a slight change of emphasis. As the lessons she gives to Orlando immediately testify, Rosalind does not have to learn much, if anything, about love, or about the quality and depth of her own feelings. Nor, as I have already mentioned, does she really need assurance (*pace* Lady Martin) that Orlando loves her. What she does need, and what the play needs, is an Orlando who knows "what 'tis to love" (5.2.83). He is the one who has immersed himself in a pseudo-Petrarchan fantasy world, hanging "tongues ... on every tree" (3.2.127) in unconscious fulfillment of Duke Senior's attitudinizing ("tongues in trees, books in the running brooks, / Sermons in stones, and good in every thing" [2.1.16–17]). What Barber calls the "conventional language and attitudes of love," with their attendant "sentimentality," are pitfalls for Orlando much more than for Rosalind.

H. B. Charlton comments that "Rosalind, disguised as Ganymede, pretends to be herself in order to teach Orlando to woo."[6] This is certainly true, but it is not, I think, the whole truth. For what Rosalind is teaching is not so much technique as substance. Her disguise as Ganymede permits her to educate him about himself, about her, and about the nature of love. It is for Orlando, not for Rosalind, that the masquerade is required; indeed the play could fittingly, I believe, be subtitled "The Education of Orlando." Whether we agree with Ms. Park that "she is twice the person he is" or not,[7] it seems clear that in *As You Like It*, as in so many of Shakespeare's comedies, the woman is superior to her man in self-knowledge and in her knowledge of human nature. The degree to which Orlando is successfully educated, and the limits of his final understanding, can be seen by examining their various encounters in the court and in the forest and by considering what happens as a result of those encounters.

In act 1, scene 2 Rosalind and Orlando meet at the wrestling match and fall in love at first sight. The following scene, which begins with Rosalind's acknowledgment of her passion to Celia, ends with her banishment, and Celia's resolution to accompany her to the Forest of Arden. The two events are psychologically related; Rosalind's advancement toward maturity by falling in love is in a sense the same act as her banishment from the palace of Duke Frederick. Banishment is a rite of passage here, a threshold moment that leads both lovers to the forest. The whole scene is beautifully modulated, as the young women's discussion of Orlando leads naturally into some playful observations on the paternal generation and the relationship between his father and theirs.

ROSALIND: The Duke my father lov'd his father dearly.
CELIA: Doth it therefore ensue that you should love his son dearly?
By this kind of chase, I should hate him, for my father hated his father dearly; yet I hate not Orlando.
ROSALIND: No, faith, hate him not, for my sake.
CELIA: Why should I not? Doth he not deserve well?
Enter DUKE [FREDERICK] *with* LORDS.

ROSALIND:	Let me love him for that, and do you love him because I do.
	Look, here comes the Duke.
CELIA:	With his eyes full of anger.
DUKE FREDERICK:	Mistress, dispatch you with your safest haste, And get you from our court.
	(1.3.29–43)

The shift from prose to verse with Duke Frederick's first speech underscores the sudden change from intimacy to formality. Rosalind's act of falling in love is itself a rebellion against patriarchal domination and the filial bond. Since she is living under the foster care of her jealous and unloving uncle, her sundering from his protection is abrupt and harsh, but some such separation would have been inevitable. Her love, as much as his hatred, banishes her to Arden.

Meanwhile Orlando, who has also fallen in love, is likewise banished from home. His tyrannical older brother, Oliver, has usurped his patrimony and stands in a relationship to him that is structurally analogous to that between Duke Frederick and Rosalind. Although he is the youngest son, Orlando bears his father's name ("Rowland de Boys" translates readily as "Orlando of the forest"), and in the play's opening scene he asserts that "the spirit of my father, which I think is within me, begins to mutiny against this servitude" (1.1.22–24). Orlando's banishment, like Rosalind's, is a step toward independence and maturity. It is interesting to note that in the first scene he complains about the quality of his upbringing; Oliver, he says, "mines my gentility with my education" (21). The education he does not receive at home he will find in the forest, with "Ganymede" for his teacher. Carrying old Adam on his shoulders like Aeneas bearing his father Anchises, Orlando enters the forest (where, as he matures, the father-figure Adam disappears from the plot), and shortly begins to post his love poems on the trees.

When she learns that it is indeed Orlando who has written these poems in her praise, Rosalind asks Celia a crucial question: "But doth he know that I am in this forest and in man's apparel?" (3.2.229–30). Deception is already in her mind. If he does not know who she is, she will not at this time reveal herself to him. Instead she declares her intention to "speak to him like a saucy lackey, and under that habit play the knave with him" (295–97).

What is her motivation for doing so? In seeking to answer this question, we should note that there are three distinct stages in Orlando's development as a lover. When he first meets Rosalind after the wrestling match he is tongue-tied, unable to speak. She has presented him with a chain, but he can find no words to acknowledge her gift: "Can I not say, 'I thank you'? My better parts / Are all thrown down, and that which here stands up / Is but a quintain, a mere lifeless block" (1.2.249–51). Rosalind abandons maidenly modesty to approach him ("Did you call, sir?" [253]), but he remains speechless, struck dumb by love: "What passion hangs these weights upon my tongue? / I cannot speak to her, yet she urged conference" (257–58). This is the first stage, that of ineffability; for the match to succeed he must somehow learn to communicate his feelings.

He does this initially through the medium of his love poems, but while the poems are an advance upon total speechlessness, they do not constitute a wholly satisfactory mode of communication. For one thing, they are one-sided, mono-vocal; Orlando has no reason to expect that Rosalind will ever see or hear of them. For another thing, as Touchstone drily points out, they are simply not very good poems. "The very false gallop of verses" (3.2.112) is his sardonic verdict, and even Rosalind acknowledges that they offer a "tedious homily of love" (155–56) with "more feet than the verses would bear" (165–66), and lame ones at that. Hackneyed, conventional, derivative, ineloquent, Orlando's poems announce an emotion but fail to go further than that; they do not attain the condition of discourse. One of Rosalind's tasks, therefore, will be to make him speak to her in the natural language of men and women. The method she adopts to do so—remaining in a disguise that will make him less ill at ease than he was at their first meeting—is somewhat comparable to the plot of Goldsmith's *She Stoops to Conquer*, in which the bashful young Marlow is able to make love to Miss Hardcastle because he thinks she is a servant in a country inn, not the well-bred daughter of a wealthy man. Rosalind, too, stoops to conquer, by retaining her doublet and hose.

Orlando's love poems also suggest a psychological state of self-absorption that accords with Erik Erikson's description of adolescent love: "an attempt to arrive at a definition of one's identity by projecting one's diffused self-image on another and by seeing it thus reflected and gradually clarified."[8] The first time Rosalind sees him in the forest he is deep in conversation with Jaques, the play's epitome of self-love, and there are resemblances between them, despite their mutual antipathy (and perhaps contributing to it). Both are obsessed with their own feelings. Orlando successfully teases Jaques with the old joke of the fool in the brook, but there is a sense in which he himself is also a Narcissus, seeking his own reflection. His mock-Petrarchan poetry, like that of the lords in *Love's Labour's Lost*, indicates a lack of maturity and a failure of other-directedness. Like Phebe, he is in love with love and with the image of himself as a lover. Rosalind seems to sense this when, in the character of Ganymede, she points out that he is not dressed in the true lover's traditional disarray: "you are no such man; you are rather point-device in your accoustrements, as loving yourself, than seeming the lover of any other" (3.2.381–84). Orlando needs time—time to grow from an infatuated youth to a man who knows the real nature of love, from a boy who pins poems on trees to a man whose love token is a "bloody napkin" (4.3.138). By not revealing her true identity Rosalind gives him that time. From their first encounter in the forest she becomes his teacher.

Time is, indeed, the first subject that they touch upon in the course of that encounter—time and its relativity. Pretending she does not know who he is, Rosalind is able to mention the hypothetical presence of a "true lover in the forest" (3.2.302) and to comment upon the eagerness of "a young maid between the contract of her marriage and the day it is solemniz'd" (313–15). She thus usurps and desentimentalizes the topic of love that Orlando has elaborately established as his own. Jaques had addressed him contemptuously as "Signior Love," and I think we may see his insistence on playing the part of the lover as an aspect of his adolescent posturing. He will now be required to prove his love by acts of constancy and by the quick use of his wits—very different from the self-glorifying practice of posting love poems for all to see. Dialogue and interplay have already begun to replace the sterile and stereotypical intercourse between a man and his pen. Orlando is no longer in command of the love theme—if, indeed, he ever was. The focus and the creative energy are instead to be found in "Ganymede"—or rather, in "Ganymede" as "he" will take up the part of "Rosalind."

It is a convention of Shakespearian comedy that husbands and lovers do not recognize their ladies when those ladies are dressed in male attire. Bassanio fails to see through Portia's disguise, and Posthumus cannot recognize Imogen. But both of these men are distracted by important events taking place concurrently. Bassanio is overwhelmed with gratitude by the salvation of Antonio, and Posthumus is convinced that his wife is dead and that he has found her murderer. Orlando, by contrast has his mind wholly on Rosalind, yet he does not see her as she stands before him. "Let no face be kept in mind," he wrote, "But the fair of Rosalind" (3.2.94–95). He is now gazing into that face and does not recognize it. This is particularly striking because of the nature of the dialogue that takes place between them. Consider some of the peculiarities of diction in the following exchange:

ORLANDO: Where dwell you, *pretty* youth?
ROSALIND: With this shepherdess, my sister; here in the *skirts* of the forest, like fringe upon a *petticoat*.
ORLANDO: Are you native of this place?

ROSALIND: As the *cony* that you see dwell where *she* is kindled.
(334–340; emphasis mine)

Given the dramatic situation, such a collection of sex-linked words is bound to call attention to itself. Orlando's word "pretty" probably carries the primary meaning, now obsolete, of "clever, skillful, apt" (OED 11.2a), referring to the witty conversation that has just taken place. But the word *pretty* in Shakespeare is almost always used to describe either women or children; it is interesting to note that the only reference to a "pretty youth" in any of Shakespeare's other plays is addressed to Julia in *Two Gentlemen* when she is masquerading as a boy (4.2.58). Moreover, a few scenes later in *As You Like It* the infatuated shepherdess Phebe also uses the phrase "pretty youth" (3.5.113). She is cataloguing "Ganymede's" verbal and physical charms, and her word "pretty" could refer to either, though she will shortly speak of "a pretty redness in his lip" (120). The phrase "pretty youth" is not conclusive evidence that Orlando somehow senses the woman beneath the doublet and hose, but it is suggestive, especially in view of what follows. For Rosalind's key words in this exchange are unambiguously female: "skirts" and "petticoat"—both garments she is not wearing but should be—and the image of a female rabbit rather than a male one with whom to compare herself. "Skirts" meaning "borders" is a word in common usage, appearing both later in this play (5.4.159) and in *Hamlet* (1.1.97), as well as in the works of many of Shakespeare's contemporaries, but in combination with "petticoat" it is plainly mischievous, a witty and pointed literalizing of the implicit metaphor. "Petticoat" itself is often a synonym for woman, as in Rosalind's own earlier exclamation as the travelers entered the Forest of Arden: "I could find it in my heart to disgrace my man's apparel and to cry like a woman; but I must comfort the weaker vessel, as doublet and hose ought to show itself courageous to petticoat" (2.4.4–7). As to "cony," which in the forest context means "rabbit," in Shakespeare's time it was also a term of endearment for a woman. For Orlando as well as for the audience these words are clues to her real identity, though clues he is too dense to follow up. This part of the scene should, I think, be extremely funny on the stage—but funny at Orlando's expense.

Since the Elizabethan actor playing Rosalind would of course have been a boy, presenting the Chinese box syndrome of a boy playing a girl playing a boy playing a girl (actor–Rosalind–"Ganymede"–"Rosalind"), some periodic hints or asides would have been dramaturgically helpful in keeping the audience cognizant of what they were supposed to be seeing. *As You Like It* is particularly playful in this regard, ringing the changes on these changes throughout the play and especially in the epilogue. But the proliferation of such sly hints in the first conversation between Orlando and the disguised Rosalind is of considerable interest. "I thank God I am not a woman," she remarks (347–48), and again there is a broad wink to the audience—but perhaps also a small nudge in the ribs to Orlando. Yet he is so determined to be lovesick that he does not recognize the object of his love.

> ORLANDO: Fair youth, I would I could make thee believe I love.
> ROSALIND: Me believe it? You may as soon make her that you love believe it, which I warrant she is apter to do than to confess she does: that is one of the points in the which women still give the lie to their consciences.
>
> (385–91)

Here Rosalind is wrestling with the same maidenly dilemma that troubled Juliet and Cressida—what are the social risks for a woman who tells her love? But like those women, she is in a sense telling her love now—if only Orlando had the wit to listen. Yet by the end of the scene he is still addressing her as "good youth" (433). "Nay," she replies, "you must call me Rosalind" (434).

Their fictive courtship, with its badinage, wooing lessons, and play-acted "marriage," threatens to go on forever in the timelessness of Arden. Under the guise of Ganymede, Rosalind teaches Orlando not only the rules of love and its nature, but the uses of language—and even, to her everlasting credit, the gentle arts of irony and self-deprecation. But two events intervene to bring the fiction to an end: Orlando's rescue of his brother Oliver from a lioness, and the instant mutual passion of Oliver and Celia.

I have elsewhere discussed at length the incident of the lioness and the "bloody napkin" Orlando sends as a love token "unto the shepherd youth / That he in sport cloth call his Rosalind" (4.3.155–56).[9] Let me merely say briefly here that I regard this as an initiation ritual, both in martial and in sexual terms, and that I see the gift of the bloody napkin as a curiously but appropriately displaced version of the ceremonial "showing of the sheets" by which in some cultures a newly married woman demonstrates her virginity and fidelity to her husband. The napkin is thus a love token of a very different kind from the superficial love poems Orlando has earlier sent to Rosalind in testimony of his love. For the education of Orlando, however, the love match between his brother and Celia is even more germane, because it brings an end to the fictional world in which Orlando has lived with his "Rosalind." "O, how bitter a thing it is to look into happiness through another man's eyes!" he exclaims (5.2.43–45), and Rosalind asks, "Why then, tomorrow I cannot serve your turn for Rosalind?" (48–49). Orlando's reply is the single most important turning point in his development: "I can live no longer by thinking" (50). In the language of education we have been using, this is both a graduation and a commencement, a change and a new beginning. Imagination and play, which have brought him to this point, are no longer enough to sustain him. And as if he has said the magic words—as indeed he has—Rosalind now promises to produce his true beloved, "to set her before your eyes tomorrow, human as she is, and without any danger" (66–68). The significant phrase here is "human as she is." The real Rosalind is not the paper paragon of Orlando's halting sonnets but a woman of complexity, wit, and passion. This will be Orlando's final lesson.

Readers of the play are occasionally as nonplussed as Orlando by the rapidity with which Oliver and Celia fall in love.[10] "Is't possible that on so little acquaintance you should like her? that but seeing, you should love her? and loving, woo? and wooing, she should grant? And will you persever to enjoy her?" (5.2.1–4). Our amazement is the more because all of this wooing takes place offstage, between acts 4 and 5. Compared with the protracted courtship of Orlando and Rosalind, which has constituted virtually the entire action of the play, this manifestation of betrothal-at-first-sight is potentially unsettling, especially because we have no particular reason to like Oliver before he appears in the forest and because we have been led by Rosalind to believe that some extended education is necessary to develop a true and enduring love. Orlando, too, liked and loved at first sight, but he is still learning "what 'tis to woo," and is—or so he thinks—very far from having his lady grant his suit.

Oliver describes his transformation from tyrant to lover as a "conversion." "I do not shame / to tell you what I was," he explains to Celia, "Since my conversion / So sweetly tastes, being the thing I am" (4.3.135–37). His is the alternative path to Rosalind's gradualist mode of education, an instantaneous Pauline reversal that fills the erstwhile nay-sayer with the spirit of love. Oliver's "conversion" accords with the Christian doctrine of salvation; like the late-arriving laborers in the vineyard (Matt. 20:1–16) his reward is made equal to that of his apparently more deserving brother, and the two courtships, one so lengthy and the other so swift, are, in Hymen's words, "earthly things made even" (5.4.109).

Conversion is in fact a recurrent theme in the final scene of the play. We learn that Duke Frederick, advancing on the forest with malign intent, has encountered "an old religious man" and "after some question with him, was converted / Both from his enterprise and from the world" (5.4.160–62). Like Oliver he offers to abdicate his lands and position in favor of the brother he had formerly sought to kill. At this point Jaques decides to join him, observing that "Out of these convertites / There is much matter to be heard and learn'd" (184–85). The emphasis upon instruction and discourse here is significant, offering a pertinent analogy to the love lessons Rosalind has been giving Orlando. But while Duke Frederick's conversion removes him from society, Oliver's socializes him. Learning to love his brother, he finds himself, more or less in consequence, capable of falling in love with Celia.

As we have seen, the lightning love affair of Oliver and Celia acts as a catalyst for Orlando, moving him to make the crucial transition from play acting to reality. His declaration, "I can live no longer by thinking," makes possible Rosalind's change of roles, from teacher to "human" lover. The lessons, and the need for them, are over. But how much has Orlando really learned? Throughout the play Rosalind has offered clues to her real identity, double-edged hints that she is in fact the very woman she is pretending to be. Orlando's failure to take those hints was, for the audience as well as Rosalind, an indication that he was not yet prepared to have the truth thrust upon him. When he finally feels ready to choose the real, despite its inherent dangers, over the make-believe, we have some reason to think that he has profited from the unsentimental education he has received. Yet even after "Ganymede" promises to set Rosalind before his eyes, Orlando makes one significant error in interpretation that makes it clear he is, in one sense at least, no match for Rosalind. The issue is subtle—some might say finical—but it is also, as is Rosalind's way, instructive, for the audience in the theater if not for Orlando.

In the course of that same first conversation in the forest with which we have been so much concerned, Orlando inquires as to whether the "youth" he addresses is native to the forest. "Your accent," he observes, "is something finer than you could purchase in so remov'd a dwelling" (3.2.341–42). Once again he hovers on the brink of discovery. But Rosalind has a ready reply, one that touches on "Ganymede's" own education. "An old religious uncle of mine taught me to speak, who was in his youth an inland man; one that knew courtship too well, for there he fell in love" (345–47). The former courtier who finds purity and peace in the countryside is a commonplace of pastoral literature; Spenser's Melibee is only one member of a hoary and numerous tribe, who, had they all inhabited England's forests in Elizabeth's time, would have jostled one another uncomfortably for lack of room. Rosalind's invention thus has just the right degree of verisimilitude to take in Orlando, and just the right degree of triteness to amuse the listening audience. Orlando readily accepts this explanation, moving eagerly on to the more tempting topic of love, and the matter is dropped. Or so it seems.

Much later in the play, when the spectacle of Celia and Oliver in love has incited him to abjure "thinking" for action, Orlando is vouchsafed another item of information about the supposed education of "Ganymede." "Believe then if you please," the disguised Rosalind tells him,

> that I can do strange things. I have, since I was three years old, convers'd with a magician, most profound and yet not damnable. If you do love Rosalind so near the heart as your gesture cries it out, when your brother marries Aliena, shall you marry her. I know into what straits of fortune she is driven, and it is not impossible to me, if it appear not inconvenient to you, to set her before your eyes tomorrow, human as she is, and without any danger.
>
> ORLANDO: Speak'st thou in sober meanings?
>
> ROSALIND: By my life, I do, which I tender dearly, though I say I am a magician.
>
> (5.2.58–71)

Orlando accepts this windfall without question and confides his good luck to Duke Senior, who willingly agrees to give Rosalind to him in marriage. On the following day "Ganymede" approaches both Orlando and the Duke to make sure their minds are constant. Receiving the appropriate assurances, "he" exits the stage, and the Duke turns immediately to Orlando to offer one of those observations that so often herald the clearing of the skies at the close of Shakespearian comedy: "I do remember in this shepherd boy / Some lively touches of my daughter's favor" (5.3.26–27). We are very close to the truth here. Yet Orlando, characteristically, confuses rather than clarifies the matter, so sure is he that he is in possession of the facts.

> My lord, the first time that I ever saw him
> Methought he was a brother to your daughter.
> But, my good lord, this boy is forest-born,
> And hath been tutor'd in the rudiments
> Of many desperate studies by his uncle,
> Whom he reports to be a great magician,
> Obscured in the circle of the forest.
>
> (28–34)

It is Orlando himself who is obscured here, in the circle of the forest. For notice what he has done. He has conflated the two tales Rosalind told him, identifying the "old religious uncle" who ostensibly taught young Ganymede to speak, with the profound magician with whom Ganymede has conversed from the age of three. This inference makes perfect sense, but it is wrong, and wrong in an important way. "I am a magician," she told him, plainly. And plainly the magician with whom Rosalind has conversed from the voluble age of three is no one but Rosalind herself, the only begetter of the magic that will produce Orlando's beloved before his eyes and reveal to the Duke and all the lovers her true identity, and their true partners.

Rosalind's role as a magician is emphasized in the epilogue, when she announces to the audience "My way is to conjure you" (Epilogue, 10–11). As she herself remarks, "It is not the fashion to see the lady the epilogue" (1–2), but in this play the lady has earned her place. Hand in hand with Orlando she danced in celebration of her wedding, and then, with the other couples, departed the stage. But she returns, and she returns alone. Her reappearance underscores the degree to which she has directed events in Arden from her first encounter with Orlando to the successful performance of four marriages. "Human as she is" she has played two parts throughout the play and, in the process, transformed Orlando from a tongue-tied boy to an articulate and (relatively) self-knowledgeable husband. If he is not entirely her equal, it is hard to fault him for that. For Rosalind stands alone among Shakespeare's comic heroines as clearly as she stands alone on the stage for the Epilogue. Like Prospero, whom in many ways she prefigures, she tempers her magic with humanity, and were she to divest herself of her doublet and hose, she might justifiably address them as Prospero addresses his "magic garment": "Lie there, my art" (*Tempest*, 1.2.24).

Notes

1. References are to *The Riverside Shakespeare*, ed. G. Blakemore Evans et. al. (Boston: Houghton Mifflin, 1974).

2. *As You Like It*, ed. George Lyman Kittredge (Boston: Ginn and Co., 1939), pp. 149–50.

3. C. L. Barber, *Shakespeare's Festive Comedy* (Princeton: Princeton University Press, 1959), p. 233.

4. Anne Barton, Introduction to *As You Like It*, in *The Riverside Shakespeare*, ed. Evans, p. 366.

5. Clara Claiborne Park, "As We Like It: How a Girl Can Be Smart and Still Popular," in *The Woman's Part: Feminist Criticism of Shakespeare* (Urbana: University of Illinois Press, 1980), p. 108.

6. *Shakespearian* Comedy (1938: reprint, London: Methuen, 1973), p. 282.

7. Ibid., p. 109.

8. Erik Erikson, *Identity: Youth and Crisis* (New York: W. W. Norton, 1968), p. 132.

9. Marjorie Garber, *Coming of Age in Shakespeare* (London: Methuen, 1981), pp. 145–48.

10. I say "readers" because audiences in the theater tend to be so swept up by the energies of the plot that they do not stop to analyze the improbability here. My students, however, have occasionally been perturbed by it.

RENÉ GIRARD

Mimetic Rivalry in As You Like It

When we think of those phenomena in which mimicry is likely to play a role, we enumerate such things as dress, mannerisms, facial expressions, speech, stage acting, artistic creation, and so forth, but we never think of desire. Consequently, we see imitation in social life as a force for gregariousness and bland conformity through the mass reproduction of a few social models.

If imitation also plays a role in desire, if it contaminates our urge to acquire and possess, this conventional view, while not entirely false, misses the main point. Imitation does not merely draw people together, it pulls them apart. Paradoxically, it can do these two things simultaneously. Individuals who desire the same thing are united by something so powerful that, as long as they can share whatever they desire, they remain the best of friends; as soon as they cannot, they become the worst of enemies.

The perfect continuity between concord and discord is as crucial to Shakespeare as it was to the tragic poets of Greece, serving as a rich source of poetic paradox as well. If their work is to outlast fleeting fashionability, dramatists as well as novelists must discover this fundamental source of human conflict,—namely mimetic rivalry—and they must discover it alone, with no help from philosophers, moralists, historians, or psychologists, who always remain silent on the subject.

Shakespeare discovered the truth so early that his approach to it seems juvenile, even caricatural, at first. In the still youthful *Rape of Lucrece*, his potential rapist, unlike the original Tarquin of the Roman historian Livy, resolves to rape a woman he has never actually met; he is drawn to her solely by her husband's excessive praise of her beauty. I suspect that Shakespeare wrote this scene just after discovering mimetic desire. He was so taken with it, so eager to emphasize its constitutive paradox, that he created this not entirely unbelievable but slightly disconcerting monstrosity, a totally blind rape, just as we say a "blind date."

Modern critics intensely dislike this poem. As for Shakespeare, he quickly realized that to wave mimetic desire like a red flag in front of the public is not the sure road to success (as I myself have never managed to learn, I suppose). In no time at all, Shakespeare became sophisticated, insidious and complex in his handling of desire, but he remained consistently, even obsessively, mimetic.

Shakespeare can be as explicit as some of us are about mimetic desire, and has his own vocabulary for it, close enough to ours for immediate recognition. He says "suggested desire," "suggestion," "jealous desire," "emulous desire," and so forth. But the essential word is "envy," alone or in such combination's as "envious desire" or "envious emulation."

Like mimetic desire, envy subordinates a desired *something* to the *someone* who enjoys a privileged relationship with it. Envy covets the superior *being* that neither the someone nor something alone, but the conjunction of the two, seems to possess. Envy involuntarily testifies to a lack of *being* that puts the envious to shame, especially since the enthronement of metaphysical pride during the Renaissance. That is why envy is the hardest sin to acknowledge.

We often brag that no word can scandalize us anymore, but what about "envy"? Our supposedly insatiable appetite for the forbidden stops short of envy. Primitive cultures fear and repress envy so much that they have no word for it; we hardly use the one we have, and this fact must be significant. We no longer prohibit many actions that generate envy, but silently ostracize whatever can remind us of its presence in our midst. Psychic phenomena, we are told, are important in proportion to the resistance they generate toward revelation. If we apply this yardstick to envy as well as to what psychoanalysis designates as repressed, which of the two will make the more plausible candidate for the role of best-defended secret?

Who knows if the small measure of acceptance that mimetic desire has won in academic circles is not due, in part, to its ability to function as a mask and a substitute for, rather than as an explicit revelation of, what Shakespeare calls envy. In order to avoid all misunderstanding, I have chosen the traditional word for the title of this study, the provocative word, the astringent and unpopular word, the word used by Shakespeare himself—envy.

Does this mean that no legitimate use remains for mimetic desire? Not quite. All envy is mimetic, but not all mimetic desire is envious. Envy suggests a single static phenomenon, not the prodigious matrix of forms that conflictual imitation becomes in the hands of Shakespeare.

DO YOU LOVE HIM BECAUSE I DO!

The Pastoral Genre in *As You Like It*

Are there works by Shakespeare to which the law of mimetic desire does not apply? A most promising candidate seems to be *As You Like It*, the comedy that follows *Much Ado About Nothing*. In this pastoral comedy, the relations between the protagonists seem as conventionally idyllic as required by the genre.

Celia is the only child of Duke Frederick, a villain, who has usurped the place of his older brother, duke Senior, now living with some followers in Arden, the land of the pastoral. Rosalind, the exile's only child, has remained at court because of her cousin Celia. The two girls were raised together and are the closest of friends:

We still have slept together,
Rose at an instant, learned, played, eat together;
And wheresoe'er we went, like Juno's swans,
Still we went coupled and inseparable.
(I, iii, 73–76)

We know that this perfect intimacy of school friends or close relatives is the breeding ground par excellence of mimetic rivalry. Celia and Rosalind should be especially vulnerable to it, since both of them are the sole heirs of rivalrous fathers, and yet they never become rivals.

Shakespeare has Celia's father, a villain, try to infect his daughter with his villainy. Duke Frederick chides his daughter for not being envious enough of her cousin, as required by the mimetic facts of life:

She is too subtile for thee; and her smoothness,
Her very silence and her patience,
Speak to the people and they pity her.
Thou art a fool. She robs thee of thy name,
And thou wilt show more bright and seem more virtuous
When she is gone....
Thou art a fool.
(I, iii, 75–85)

Our mimetic rivals always seem superior to us, so the duke tries to give his daughter the "inferiority complex" that, in his view, the situation demands. Celia should agree to the expulsion of Rosalind, whose popularity endangers her political future: "Thou art a fool."

Early in the play an even more redoubtable occasion of mimetic rivalry arises between the two cousins. The charming Orlando has challenged the undefeated wrestling champion of Duke Frederick, Charles, a formidable opponent who seems like an emanation of his master's villainy. The two cousins fear greatly for the frail young man but would not miss the fight for anything. Orlando wins with the greatest of ease, and the two girls, after almost fainting from dread, swoon with delight, especially Rosalind, who announces to Celia that she is in love with Orlando.

In *The Two Gentlemen of Verona* and *The Rape of Lucrece*, Shakespeare has the character already in love urge the character not yet in love, his future rival, to follow his example. The success of this mimetic incitement is the principal cause of the disastrous rivalry that follows. Since mimetic rivalry is a priori excluded from *As You Like It*, there is no point in having Rosalind try to inculcate her desire for Orlando upon her cousin Celia. A scene of mimetic incitement makes no sense in this play and yet, amazingly, Shakespeare has one:

[*Celia*]: Is it possible on such a sudden that you should fall into so strong a liking with old Sir Rowland's youngest son?
Rosalind: The Duke my father loved his father dearly.
Celia: Doth it therefore ensue that you should love his son dearly? By this kind of chase, I should hate him, for my father hated his father dearly; yet I hate not Orlando.
Rosalind: No, faith, hate him not, for my sake.
Celia: Why should I not? Doth he not deserve well?
Rosalind: Let me love him for that, and do you love him because I do!

(I, iii, 26–39)

This last line is a superb definition of the *double bind* characteristic of mimetic rivalry. All desires that display themselves in the manner that Rosalind's do send two contradictory messages to the hearer: first, *Do love him because I do*; second, *Do not love him because I do.*

The innocent Rosalind is a diabolical temptress. To Celia, to Rosalind herself, and to their common friendship, she is a much greater peril than even the most villainous duke and father. The parallel with the works already examined is striking; once again the mimetic heroine tries to camouflage her desire behind the respect that is due to *fathers*, and this bad faith is ironically criticized by the perceptive Celia.

Fathers are always less important than children and psychoanalysts claim. I have tried to show that this was already the true message of *A Midsummer Night's Dream*, and this time it is so explicit that we cannot doubt its Shakespearean pertinence. When Rosalind coyly tries to explain her love for Orlando by her obedience to her father, and to Orlando's father, Celia humorously challenges her hypocritical excuse.

One of the two fathers is dead and the other is absent; Rosalind's passion has nothing to do with either one. Quite explicitly this time, Shakespeare mocks the favorite myth of youthful desire, fatherly omnipotence. When he was writing, this myth was not quite as ludicrously deceptive as it is today, but it was ludicrous enough, it seems, to justify the Shakespearean satire. The paternalistic system, if it ever really existed in the Christian West, had already disintegrated.

For the purpose of the present book, this little scene is marvelous: Shakespeare himself recapitulates admirably the two points I attributed to him in my analysis of earlier comedies, the point about fathers and the point about mimetic conflict between close friends. But the earlier works are no reliable guide to what actually happens in *As You Like It*. Celia will never fall in love with Orlando; the friendship of the two girls will remain cloudless. Here is a play, finally, to which the mimetic law does not apply.

Does Shakespeare want to depict in Celia a true heroine, a genuine saint of mimetic renunciation? Has the playwright finally decided to create one human being truly immune to the mimetic plague? I do not think so. It would be a mistake to speculate about Celia. Her role is minor; she possesses only minimal existence. It is not she who is impervious to the mimetic temptation: the genre of the pastoral is impervious for her.

Since Rosalind falls in love first, Celia politely abstains from doing the same. If Celia had been first, Rosalind would have returned the courtesy; she would not have cast even a single glance in the direction of Orlando. Regardless of how tempestuous and unruly love is supposed to be, pastoral heroes and heroines never have the bad taste of falling in love out of turn. For the avoidance of mimetic rivalry, the most elaborate kinship rules of the Australian aborigines are less effective than pastoral literature.

The play reflects the blindness of *superficial* literature. The rule of the pastoral genre forbids conflict between two nice heroines such as Rosalind and Celia, and Shakespeare conforms to this rule most obediently. He simply wants to show what this obedience entails. To poke fun at the pastoral, he makes sure that all indicators point to massive trouble between the two girls, the maximum trouble imaginable; but no trouble will erupt.

In the Celia–Rosalind relation, if not elsewhere in *As You Like It*, Shakespeare keeps his promise of being a pastoral writer. Nothing is easier to achieve. All it takes is to suspend the application of a law the existence of which most people never suspect anyway. To appreciate the parodic dimension of *As You Like It*, we must first perceive the potential for trouble between Celia and Rosalind.

"Do you love him because I do!" belongs in the same category as *love by hearsay* and *love by another's eyes*; it is impossible to believe that these marvelously ironic lines were never understood by anyone at all, that they were written in vain! More than ever we must assume that the original public included an inner circle of initiates to whom, from time to time, the author is sending signals that they alone can understand.

After building up the dramatic possibilities inherent in his plot structure, Shakespeare fails to exploit them; he discards the conflict toward which the play was moving, though not without a word. As a rule, the pastoral genre will do this sort of thing unthinkingly, automatically, because it knows nothing of the mimetic crisscrossing of desires. Shakespeare wants to show that he, at least, is aware of what he is doing. His satire is discreet, perceptible only to those spectators who are not likely to be offended by it.

By the time of *As You Like It*, the knowledgeable few must have regarded mimetic interaction as highly characteristic of Shakespearean art. If we do not grasp the mimetic law, we cannot decipher the author's allusions to it. They operate like a coded message, but the code is not arbitrary. "Do you love him because I do!" is Shakespeare's personal signature written across a most un-Shakespearean relationship. Shakespeare signals that he has not forgotten what real conflicts are about.

If we had found "Do you love him [or, rather, her] because I do!" in *The Two Gentlemen of Verona*, *The Rape of Lucrece*, *A Midsummer Night's Dream*, or *Much Ado About Nothing*, this formula would have helped our analysis of these works. Paradoxically, it cannot help with *As You Like It*. It makes little sense where it should make most, in the context of its own play. Its real context is a Shakespearean intertextuality that embraces the whole oeuvre.

What we know about the previous works makes it impossible to believe that "Do you love him because I do!" is an inconsequential turn of phrase, rhetorical in the trivial sense, a meaningless combination of words; it is too pertinent to mimetic friendship and rivalry not to reflect the author's continued preoccupation with this subject, yet it is not pertinent to *As You Like It*. In order to see its overall indirect pertinence, a detour through the more explicitly mimetic plays is necessary. The critics who insist on dealing with each play as an autonomous work of art cannot discover what we are talking about. A whole dimension of Shakespearean wit escapes them.

If we interpret each play in isolation from its neighbors, in deference to some principle of aesthetic formalism, we will never perceive the network of allusions crucial to a real intelligence not only of what binds the plays together but of each play considered separately. Aesthetic formalism has been a great extinguisher of Shakespearean satire. The enjoyment of satiric literature rests on a feeling of reader-author complicity incompatible with the notion of an "intentional fallacy"—one of the deadliest of our critical fallacies, in my opinion.

The satiric nature of the play is suggested by its title, *As You Like It*. The author addresses the spectators and announces that for a change he is not writing his own kind of play, but theirs. Like all great satirists, Shakespeare must have been besieged with requests for a more uplifting view of mankind. Great mimetic writers are always asked to renounce the very essence of their art, mimetic conflict, in favor of an insipidly optimistic view of human relations, always presented as more gentle and humane, whereas in reality it reflects the cruelty of self-righteousness.

In *As You Like It* Shakespeare feigns to oblige and, to a certain extent, really does. "Here is a play," he says, "that paints the world not as I see it, not as it really is, but *as you, my public, like it*, without ambivalent sentiments, without ambiguous conflicts, a play full of characters clearly designated as "heroes" and "villains."

A drama that evacuates mimetic entanglements needs some substitute source of conflict or it will not be dramatic at all. It can only turn to what is sometimes called the "Manichaean" perspective. If it does not attribute conflict to the antagonists' identical desires, it must postulate some intrinsic difference between them, the difference of good and evil. Instead of facing up to envy and jealousy such as they are, namely, as two-sided, slippery phenomena, the pastoral genre systematically portrays some characters as intrinsically good, and other characters as intrinsically bad.

The conflicts that we do not want to attribute to the process of mimetic rivalry must be given some cause external to the goodness of the hero or heroine, and it can only be the evil disposition of some clearly designated villain. This official troublemaker will have no other purpose in life than to make the lives of noble-minded heroes and heroines miserable. He will be the indispensable scapegoat, thanks to whom the noble-minded people are able to wash their hands of whatever unpleasantnesses the plot requires.

Idealistic literature reflects what may be called the normal paranoid structure of human relations. It systematically transforms mimetic doubles into highly differentiated aggressors and "aggressors." This structure belongs to mimetic rivalry itself; it expresses the reluctance of this rivalry to acknowledge itself as such. We had a good example of it in the scene where Helena and Hermia each projects on the other the sole responsibility of a discord that is paradoxically based on too much concord. Shakespeare alludes to this paradox, I believe, in *A Midsummer Night's Dream* when, after reading the announcement of *Pyramus and Thisbe*, a play no less deluded in principle than *As You Like It* is supposed to be, Theseus asks incredulously:

> How shall we find the concord of this discord?
>
> (V, i, 60)

In *As You Like It* Shakespeare makes all the stereotyped oppositions that indirectly reflect mimetic rivalry as visibly false as he can. He makes the hatred of Oliver for Orlando completely gratuitous. In Lodge's *Rosalynde*, the source of the play, there are the same two brothers as in the comedy, but the discontented one has objective reasons for discontent; he is the dispossessed brother, whereas in *As You Like It* it is the reverse. Systematically, Shakespeare does away with realism in his play. Among all available possibilities, he always chooses the most far-fetched, the one most contaminated with romantic illusion.

The play loudly advertises its opposition to common sense, but never takes itself seriously; in the conclusion, the cardboard villains all undergo an instantaneous conversion to the pastoral good. This too is part of the pastoral tradition. Thus as soon as Orlando's bad brother, Oliver, and Duke Frederick have acquitted themselves of their villainous business, which does not amount to much anyway, they decide to settle in Arden and are immediately cleansed of all evil propensities.

The bad duke Frederick,

> ... hearing now that every day
> Men of great worth resorted to the forest.
>
> (V, iv, 154–55)

comes to Arden at the head of a large army, full of murderous thoughts, but on his arrival there,

> ... meeting with an old religious man,
> After some question with him, was converted
> Both from his enterprise and from the world,

His crown bequeathing to his banish'd brother,
And all their lands restor'd to them again
That were with him exil'd. This to be true,
I do engage my life. (160–66)

The sole desire of a converted villain is "to die a shepherd." All former exiles, however, must return to the bad old world in order to marry the good women, of which there is a surplus, inevitably, since all villains belong to the male gender.

Oliver is an example. He was asleep in the forest and was saved by Orlando from a lioness and a serpent that threatened his life. Greatly moved by the kindness of the brother he had always persecuted, Oliver too turns good in a single instant and can therefore provide Celia with the type of husband that her considerable patience certainly deserves. Ultimately, the only people left in the pastoral world are a few unmarriageable ex-villains who spend the rest of their lives expiating their sins in ecologically healthy surroundings, while the heroes and heroines, having no sins to expiate, rush back to the bad old world swiftly to appropriate the estates and dignities conveniently vacated by the reformed villains.

The pastoral genre gives free rein to our tendency to deny the possibility of acute conflict among close relatives and friends, which is the substance of tragedy according to Aristotle. The pastoral world can be regarded as the anti-tragic world par excellence, and an amused Shakespeare discreetly underscores the most outrageous features of its self-deception. All who suffer from mimetic desire would like to see it abolished by decree. They feel about it the way they feel about their rivals, associating the latter with such desire and regarding their dislike for both as incontrovertible proof that they have nothing to do with either. The problem always seems to lie with "them," the *others*, never with ourselves.

Only mimetic desire would dream of escaping from itself through physical means, by moving to some distant land still untouched by the plague of contagious rivalry, a more pristine and "natural" world, perhaps—an old-fashioned, less urbanized country, an unspoiled nature with inhabitants more innocent and fresh than our distressingly competitive neighbors. If we moved there, we could enjoy the company of delightful *others* with no fear of ever getting embroiled in the mimetic entanglements of the bad old world.

At the time of Shakespeare, the main literary version of this eternal dream was the pastoral genre. *As You Like It* gives it a Shakespearean twist that ironically points to the mimetic urge as the hidden source of the dream itself. Take the main story of the plot: Orlando and Rosalind have both taken refuge in the pastoral world, far from the fiercely mimetic relatives who have forced them into exile. They love each other; between them, no obstacle remains—they could get married immediately. What a fine ending that would make! Unfortunately there are three acts to go and the lovers have reached this happy moment too early. All that remains for them to do is to enjoy each other until death do them part—a most uncertain prospect.

The ultimate fulfilment must be deferred; we do not want to confront the disenchantment that it might bring. Shakespeare wards off this threat through a trick highly typical of pastoral literature, a device so transparent in its absurdity that it lays bare the real raison d'être of all such fictional tricks. Rosalind has the bright idea of making herself unrecognizable to her lover. She decides to retain in the company of Orlando the masculine disguise that she had put on to ensure her safe travel. Under the name of Ganymede she persuades her lover, who of course never suspects her real identity, that he needs some coaching in the art of courting his absent mistress, a certain Rosalind, whom she offers to impersonate. What could be more natural?

This kind of nonsense is typical of pastoral literature. Mimetic desire is always yearning for the *presence* of the beloved and yet, at a deeper level, this presence is anathema, because of the disenchantment that goes with it. Whenever the lovers have unobstructed access to each other, they are in imminent danger of falling out of love; their passion depends on the metaphysical transcendence of each partner in the eyes of the other, and this in turn requires a more or less permanent separation.

When the manuals of "true love" and the French *precieux* present the various impediments as an indispensable and preferably interminable phase of the mystique, they manipulate mimetic desire more cleverly than our advocates of "sexual gratification," who apply their principle of consumerism even to human relations, with the most dismal results. If Rosalind consented to be wooed openly, in her own name, by her own lover, her constant availability would rapidly squander the metaphysical capital that has accumulated during the phase of separation. Under her masculine disguise, Rosalind can enjoy her lover's presence without losing the benefit of absence. She makes herself accessible, yet keeps reaping the fruit of inaccessibility. She can have her mimetic cake and eat it, too.

This artificial scheme is typical of what pastoral literature is really after. Presence must be deferred, at least until the curtain falls. Pastoral literature never openly acknowledges the dreadful truth, of course, but it devises the most artificial tricks to postpone gratification as long as possible.

'TIS NOT HER GLASS, BUT YOU THAT FLATTER HER
Self-Love in *As You Like It*

Even though spectacularly absent at the center, mimetic desire proliferates on the margins of *As You Like It*, especially in the story of Phebe and Silvius. These two young people are not exiled courtiers; they have lived all their lives in Arden, it seems, and know nothing of its antimimetic properties. The pastoral magic has no effect on them; wherever home is, the land of the pastoral is not.

Silvius resembles a slave more than a lover; his devotion to Phebe is so meek and sheepish that she takes shameless advantage of him. The more tyrannical she becomes, the more his docility increases. Then Rosalind accidentally overhears Phebe mistreating the unfortunate Silvius. A little quixotically, she intervenes on his behalf, warning him that his worshipful attitude defeats his own interest. Thanks to her lover, Phebe imagines herself more beautiful than she really is, and concludes that she deserves a better husband than poor Silvius. Rosalind assures this young man that he is much more attractive than his beloved:

> You are a thousand times a properer man
> Than she is a woman. (III, v, 51)

Phebe uses Silvius as a deceptive mirror because she *imitates* his desire for her, she sees herself in the same flattering light as he does:

> 'Tis not her glass, but you that flatter her,
> And out of your eyes, she sees herself more proper
> Than any of her lineaments can show her.
> (54–56)

The force that shapes the relation is not an objective appreciation of their respective merits by the two partners, but the one-sidedness of Silvius's desire, which displays itself too openly and contaminates Phebe. She avidly absorbs this idolatrous fawning of Silvius and as a result can love only herself.

The pathetic Silvius not only provides Phebe with the desire that enables her to reject him, but he in turn imitates this reflected desire, the desire that comes originally from him, and so becomes more enslaved than ever. This vicious spiral keeps increasing the pride of Phebe and the self-contempt of Silvius. The coproduction of self-contempt and self-love is a mimetic reproduction of Silvius's initial desire for Phebe, a potentially infinite process of reciprocal imitation. Both partners are simultaneously models and imitators of the same desire and, inside this circular system of imitation, there is no room for a second desire, an independent desire of Phebe for Silvius, for instance. In a world of rampant mimetic contagion, no good reciprocity is possible.

All mimetic desire yearns for the object of its model. If my model's object is myself, I will desire myself and will try to keep my model (who is also my imitator) from possessing the object we both desire, myself. This recoiling of desire upon itself is a mimetic rivalry in which the winner cannot win without strengthening the initial impulse that caused his or her victory in the first place. The system becomes more and more imbalanced, creating a false impression of immutability, of natural necessity.

The extreme self-love of one lover and the extreme self-contempt of the other are interdependent phenomena that keep regenerating and reinforcing each other with no need for outside intervention. There may be outside factors, no doubt—"objective differences" that initially contributed to the launching of the system in one direction or the other—but they are more or less fortuitous; the slightest difference in the starting point might have produced the opposite result. That is the reason why, in *Much Ado About Nothing*, Beatrice and Benedick both refuse to be the first to say, "I love you." They both fear they will end up at the wrong end of the relationship, in the unenviable position of Silvius.

If the configuration of desire had gone the other way, everything would be the same, but all relative positions inside the system would be reversed: a starry-eyed Phebe would be enslaved to an insufferably pretentious Silvius. This reversal seems unthinkable only because the existing situation, once solidified, shapes reality in such a persuasive way that it seems to possess the attributes of a natural phenomenon.

What a mimetic effect has erected, another mimetic effect can destroy. With great bluntness, Rosalind warns Phebe that she should not mistake her present luck for the permanent effect of some deterministic cause. She may not always find a meekly obedient Silvius in front of her:

> But, mistress, know yourself, down on your knees,
> And thank heaven, fasting, for a good man's love;
> For I must tell you friendly in your ear,
> Sell when you can, you are not for all markets.
>
> (57–60)

The financial metaphor in this last line corresponds neatly to what quite a few economists have theorized in recent years about the mimetic nature of financial speculation. Jean-Pierre Dupuy, André Orléan, and others have interpreted some of Keynes's observations mimetically. In a free market, values fluctuate not according to the law of supply and demand but according to each speculator's evaluation of what the overall evaluation will be in regard to this same law. This is a far cry from the objective law itself, which can never determine the situation directly, since it is always subject to interpretation, and all interpretations are mimetic and self-referential. These interpreters are not interested in the objective facts but in the forces that actually shape the market, the forces of public opinion, which really means the dominant interpretation.[1]

Economists are dealing with a mimetic game that most of them overlook in their fetishistic belief in so-called "objective data." Mathematical calculations can apprehend objective data, but they cannot take interpretations into account; that is why no amount of objective information will ever make prediction foolproof.

Only a mimetic effect can place a mediocre Phebe at the very top in some kind of ideal beauty contest; this illusion may continue forever if there are only Silviuses around, but it may be as short-lived as a speculative bubble in the stock market. After moving upward and upward, the spiral of mutual imitation can reverse itself or disappear altogether. If the holders of the stock—in this case Phebe alone—do not sell when the selling is good, they may lose their entire investment.

At the very instant when Rosalind warns Phebe of this possibility, her prophecy comes true. Rosalind is disguised as a young man, and Phebe falls in love with her on the spot:

> Sweet youth, I pray you, chide a year together,
> I had rather hear you chide than this man woo.
>
> (64–65)

What has happened? In order to perpetuate itself, self-love, or self-desire, needs to subjugate all the desires exposed to its presumably irresistible charm. Any desire that remains unimpressed and does not join the unanimous cult threatens the very existence of that cult. The dissident desire is perceived by the current idol, Phebe, as a more attractive model than herself, a stronger self-love, an invulnerable autonomy, and this is what Phebe's love at first sight for Rosalind really means.

By speaking as she does, Rosalind designates herself as both a model and an object of desire. Phebe's desire moves away from herself, it irresistibly gravitates toward the higher divinity. Self-love is never genuine self-centeredness in Shakespeare; it is really other-centered, but its false superiority may endure forever and therefore go forever unrecognized, if no one shows up who proves capable of resisting the mimetic pull of the dominant model. Phebe's self-love is a Silvius-centeredness in disguise; it vanishes when Rosalind reveals the disguise.

To a great majority of Elizabethans who speak of self-love, this expression means something different from what it does to Shakespeare; it means substantial self-love, a permanent feature of an individual's personality, truly endowed with the necessary stability of being. This illusion of substantial self-love is shared by the traditional critics who take for granted that creative writers always have the portrayal of permanent *characters* as their goal when they write a play or a novel.

If we interpret Phebe in terms of character, we will describe her as "cold," "haughty," "authoritarian," "egotistical," and so forth. We will add up these traits and call the sum total Phebe's "character." But her sudden passion for Rosalind contradicts this so-called character. In order to preserve our "psychology," our belief in characters, we will have to assume that Phebe acts *out of character* when she falls in love with Rosalind. The problem with this implicit theory is that those who adopt it without realizing that they adopt a theory at all—as a rule, they regard themselves as immune to all theory—really dismiss as inconsequential the major point of the Phebe episode, the truly Shakespearean point: the role of *others* in triggering this revolution in Phebe's attitude, the impermanence and ultimate unreality of what passes for our "character."

The word *narcissism* is popularly used nowadays as a synonym for Elizabethan self-love. It sounds more "scientific" than self-love but means exactly the same thing. The word does not designate a natural attribute, as "character" does, but it is hardly less misleading, since it still implies a more or less permanent feature in our psychic makeup. This notion can only hinder our understanding of Shakespeare.

Faith in the genuineness and intrinsic durability of narcissism is characteristic of subjugated desires; Silvius, for instance, is sincerely convinced that Phebe is as autonomous as Jupiter himself. If we read the essay that launched the modern career of the word "narcissism," Freud's *Introduction to Narcissism*, we will see that the mistake of the good Silvius is also the mistake of good old Sigmund Freud.

Unlike Freud and other theoreticians of the self, the literary masters of mimetic desire see through the illusion of self-love and reveal the mimetic nature of its composition and decomposition. In an earlier essay I tried to show that Proust is more lucid than Freud with respect to the mimetic fragility of narcissism.[2]

I have been criticized for neglecting the later developments of narcissism in Freud, which take into account the acute lack of true self-sufficiency that may suddenly characterize the so-called narcissist. Freud was too good an observer, indeed, not to discover in the end that the most extreme narcissism, so-called, is often associated with the very opposite symptoms, extreme dependency on others. This much I will concede. If you read the relevant texts, however, you will quickly see that Freud never discovers the mimetic link between the two opposites; as a result, he never satisfactorily accounts for the "paradox" of their juxtaposition in the same individual. He keeps thinking in terms of a strictly individual desire rooted entirely in family history and uninfluenced by other desires in the vicinity. He never unraveled the crucial mystery of two or more desires that violently disagree because they agree too much, because they imitate each other.

To the critic of Shakespeare, the main problem is not whether such phenomena as intrinsic self-centeredness or permanent character really exist; up to a point, they certainly do, but their existence is irrelevant to a playwright interested in dramatic effects. He is not writing philosophical or psychological treatises, but comedies and tragedies of desire.

When a playwright sits down to write a play, he does not have "characters" or eternal humanistic truths in mind, but comic and tragic possibilities that invariably amount to some misunderstood mimetic interaction. Mimetic patterns seem elusive and even unreal to people who are not used to thinking in these terms. That is why these patterns are systematically misunderstood; the misunderstanding can be either comic or tragic according to its consequences, or the viewpoint of the observer. The mimetic patterns are many, but they are all interrelated because they generate one another. They keep evolving from play to play. First, during the opening years of Shakespeare's career, they move toward more complexity, and then, in the later comedies, they become harsher, seeming to announce the great tragic period.

The whole triangular relation of Silvius, Phebe, and Rosalind is not too different from the relations between the four lovers in *A Midsummer Night's Dream*—in particular, the enslavement of Helena by Demetrius—but the genders are reversed. It is Silvius in this case who plays the role of the spaniel. In *A Midsummer Night's Dream*, however, the mimetic games include such rapid reversals and substitutions that no single moment becomes the same focus of sustained attention as the Phebe–Silvius episode in *As You Like It*. All configurations retrospectively look like fleeting moments in a process that remains dynamic and fluid at all times. In *As You Like It* the relationship of enslavement is unstable as well since Phebe, in the end, falls in love with Rosalind. The self-love or pseudonarcissism of Phebe is not absolutely new, therefore, yet something has changed.

In the later comedies, beginning with *As You Like It*, it seems as if the process of desire that is present as a whole in *A Midsummer Night's Dream* has been dislocated and fragmented. Only one of the fragments, a certain length of the total chain, is under scrutiny, but one distinctive enough to constitute a relatively independent configuration with a status of its own, including features that were implicit in the earlier plays but never observed in detailed fashion.

The fragile self-sufficiency of false narcissism can be understood neither as an objective reality, in terms of cause and effect, nor as a merely "subjective" illusion, since it exists both for Phebe and for Silvius. This is true of all relations of desire, but self-love has a great importance for the later comedies of Shakespeare, not only in the erotic but in the political domain, especially in *Troilus and Cressida*, as we shall see later.

The emphasis on self-love and on the corresponding enslavement of one or more desires is part of a general evolution that leaves less and less room for any middle ground between a grotesquely inflated self-love and the extreme depression of self-contempt. The struggle between the selves becomes more acute with time; it tends to turn into an all-or-nothing proposition. The enslaved desires that "prop up" self-love are not merely the flying buttresses that sustain an independently existing edifice; they are this edifice itself and, if they are withdrawn, nothing is left.

Notes

1. Jean-Pierre Dupuy, "Le Signe et l'envie," in Paul Dumouchel and J.-P. Dupuy, *L'Enfer des choses* (Paris: Editions du Seuil, 1979), 85–93. André Orléan, "Monnaie et spéculation mimétique," in *Violence et vérité* (Paris: Editions Grasset et Fasquelle, 1985), 147–58.

2. René Girard, "Narcissism: The Freudian Myth Demythified by Proust," in *Psychoanalysis, Creativity and Literature*, ed. Alan Roland (New York: Columbia University Press 1978), 293–311; also in *Literature and Psychoanalysis*, ed. Edith Kurzweil and William Phillips (New York: Columbia University Press, 1983), 363–77. See also: *Things Hidden Since the Foundation of the World* (Stanford, Calif.: Stanford University Press, 1988), 367–92; Sarah Kofman, "The Narcissistic Woman: Freud and Girard," *Diacritics* 10:3 (Fall 1980), 419–24; Toril Moi, "The Missing Mother: the Oedipal Rivalries of Rene Girard," *Diacritics* (Summer 1982), 21–31.

TED HUGHES

Active Ritual Drama and As You Like It

The deeper understanding, the instinctive prompting, of ritual drama recognizes, presumably, that a human being is only half alive if their life on the realistic, outer plane does not have the full assent and cooperation of their life on the mythic plane. The whole business of art, which even at its most naturalistic is some kind of attempt at 'ritualization', is to reopen negotiations with the mythic plane. The artistic problem is to objectify the mythic plane satisfactorily—so that it produces those benefits of therapeutic catharsis, social bonding and psychological renewal—without becoming unintelligible, and without spoiling the audience for adaptive, practical life on the realistic plane. The human problem is that life evolves at different speeds on the two planes. Only where the two planes are synchronized can there be fully effective ritual drama. This obtains in static societies, before they enter the historical torrent. And it obtains in those societies where the mythic plane itself tilts and pours down the historical cataract, as in religious revolutions. The society then seems to be changing very fast, but it is still controlled by the mythic plane. When evolution on the outer, realistic plane wrenches a society away from its allegiance to the mythic plane there is a psychological explosion—ritual drama goes into convulsions: as in fifth-century BC Athens and Elizabethan/Jacobean England. Once the dissociation is complete, and the mythic plane makes demands which the individual life

From *Shakespeare and the Goddess of Complete Being.*

on the realistic plane refuses to meet, ritual drama becomes difficult. Perhaps this is another way of describing what Eliot called the 'dissociation of sensibility' that occurred, according to the testimony of art and literature, in seventeenth-century England. After that, ritual art, in any medium, becomes more and more fragmentary, experimental, provisional, primitive, as it searches deeper and deeper into the primordial levels of the psyche for any scraps of mythic experience that still might be shared, and that might still produce a trickle of the old benefits.

The second kind of ritual drama, active ritual drama, works on the same premise as the first, but with a different purpose. This is the kind of drama relevant to *As You Like It* and *All's Well that Ends Well*. It is invented by proselytizing religions, or Hermetic societies, or magicians, as a large-scale application of the technology of making a spell, working on the assumption (archetypal and instinctive) that a deliberately shaped ritual can reactivate energies on the mythic plane so powerfully that they can recapture and reshape an ego that seems to have escaped them on the realistic plane.

The familiar example of this kind of sympathetic magic as actively manipulative ritual drama is the Mass. Materialists grant the technique some validity and explain it by hypnosis. However its functioning was understood, Hermetic alchemical ritualists, which is to say Occult Neoplatonist ritualists, went to work just as mystery religions always have done in the past, and as orders such as the Golden Dawn have done in the present, attempting to transform the personality by manipulating the mind or 'soul' on the mythic plane.

Various aspects of *As You Like It* suggest that, on one level, it is a manipulative ritual of this kind. Active ritual drama always begins with a psychic malaise, usually a failure in the link between the personality on the realistic plane and the spiritual self or soul on the mythic plane. This breakdown of communications between ego and soul is always brought about by a 'sin'—usually some more or less extreme form of the ego's neglect or injury to the soul. The result is like the primitive's 'loss of the soul'. In this sense, active ritual drama begins where the traditional shaman's healing drama begins, and its purpose is the same: to recover the soul and reconnect it to the ego. The basic mythical form of its operation is also the same.

It is on this level that *As You Like It* begins, with Shakespeare's ailing ego personified by the dispossessed Orlando. The play dismantles his entire being into its component parts, rearranges them correctly, as if rearranging disordered chromosomes, then reassembles the whole, with ego and soul reunited in perfect love. This means: with ego illuminated and transfigured by new spiritual understanding and in harmony with the universe—of which the elemental soul is an emanation.

In effect, two different dramas are being performed simultaneously. One for the public who wants to be entertained, and one for Shakespeare himself—and, it may be, a small circle of initiates. The first audience enjoys a romantic comedy and accepts the confusing details (the fact that there are two characters called Jaques, for instance) as part of the rich complexity of general effect. The second audience watches an active ritual in which a shattered individual is put back together again on the realistic plane, and is simultaneously, on the mythic plane, committed to the spiritual quest.

As You Like It: the ritual pattern

Assuming for a little while longer that Jaques is something of a self-portrait (not so much a self-portrait as a way of Shakespeare having a self-representative in the ritual) in *As You Like It*, and Prospero the same in *The Tempest*, one looks for a connection between them. But though the theme of the Rival Brothers shapes both plays, Prospero's place in the pattern is obviously very different from that of Jaques, or at least it seems so. Prospero, at the end of the tragic series, is the banished Duke, as if Shakespeare were making some statement about his career in general (and, as James Joyce has suggested, about his brother in particular). But Jaques, on the threshold of the tragic series, seems quite unrelated to either of the Dukes in *As You Like It*. To make 'ritual' sense of Jaques, one needs, as I say, to read *As You Like It* as a 'double' play: the outer entertainment, the comedy, conceals (yet reveals) the inner soul-drama, the ritual.

There is another Jaques. In all Shakespeare's work there appear only two characters called Jaques, and for some peculiar reason or by some unimaginable oversight (not corrected in many performances?) both are in this play. He found neither of them in his sources.

In the dance of the two pairs of brothers, the two Dukes keep to the background, while the foreground is taken up by Oliver and Orlando, the heirs of a rich estate. In the second sentence of the play, Orlando describes a third brother: Jaques. This Jaques, older than Orlando, younger than Oliver, is still at school, where 'report speaks goldenly of his profit'. But this brainy Jaques is not the Jaques who later ruminates in the Forest of Arden, and is no relation of his either. He seems to have no link with him whatsoever except that they happen to appear in the same play and share that unusual name.

In such a polished and musically shaped drama, it is not easy to imagine that Shakespeare could duplicate such an odd name, except to secure, very carefully, a meaning which was important for him. He can only have intended that if his audience did notice the duplication of the name they would be alerted to some shared identity in the two characters. Which is what happens. The listener who does register that first use of the name, and that particular relationship, and that scholarly prowess, automatically assumes, when Melancholy Jaques first appears in the forest, that this is the aforementioned brother of Orlando, now playing truant, his academic precocity sunk into moody contemplation of the corruption and pathos of man. He sounds a little more travelled and seasoned than might have been expected. But at this point in the play that is a gnat easily swallowed. Generally, there is no confusion, because few have registered the first fleeting mention of the name, or if they have, they put it down, perhaps, to Shakespeare's carelessness. Likewise, at the very end of the play, where that student brother of Oliver and Orlando finally emerges on to the stage, for the very first time, to make an announcement, there is still no confusion, because he is not introduced by name. He specifically avoids using his name Jaques (at this point it certainly would be confusing). The audience merely hears that he is the 'second son of old Sir Rowland'. It is only the close reader of the text of the play who, seeing the stage directions, is sharply reminded that this is no other than Jaques de Boys, that mysterious third brother, apparently even more superfluous to the play than Melancholy Jaques, and never mentioned since that first scene's second sentence. And now one looks again at the curious surname of the three brothers, de Boys.

Like the name Jaques, that de Boys is also Shakespeare's invention. Here again, he presumably picked the surname 'of the Forest' because in a play set in the Forest of Arden he wanted to indicate something in particular—namely that these three de Boys brothers are intimately and internally linked with Arden Forest, which, as I suggested, can only mean the 'Mother' Forest. That they are lineally somehow hers. Their names are virtually Oliver, Orlando and Jaques (i.e. Shax-père) Arden. (Maybe it's a coincidence that in this same year, 1599, Shakespeare was applying for the right to impale his mother's family arms with the Shakespeare arms that he had procured in 1596.)

It now becomes possible to see the framework of verbal connections and parallel circuits by which Shakespeare conducted the current of meanings to illuminate his coded ritual. Externally, his purposeful ingenuity seems purely architectonic, without metaphysical intent, because the ritual which he so carefully constructs is one whose existence no casual theatre audience could possibly divine, if only because such details as the name *de Boys*, and the fact that the Jaques are synonymous, hardly break into consciousness and have no function, except on that covert level of the esoteric ritual. Different names would not damage in the slightest the popular appreciation of the play as a charming confusion of romantic changes of fortune which seem, somehow, mysteriously, inevitable and right. In other words, the two Jaques become the key to the inner ritual only to an audience of initiates.

In alchemical allegories of this kind (as in Gnostic narratives or dramas) the theme of the Rival Brothers is a standard motif. The ruling principle, because it is weakened in some way, is violently displaced by an immoral impulse, which takes the throne. Suffering and calamity result, in which the dislodged ruling principle, exposed to the primitive elements, is spiritually enlightened, by divine help, whereupon order is restored in greater understanding and strength.

In *As You Like It*, the central figure, the figure who contains, as it were, all the others, Orlando, is morally the natural, virtuous sovereign of himself—but in trouble. His trouble is that he is divided from his soul no less. At least he is so according to the ritual. This makes sense, obviously, only in terms of the ritual, only in terms of the movement of the figures in the ritual game or dance.

Orlando's lack weakens him and exposes him to takeover from the inside, by his 'dark' brother. In this 'primal, eldest' crime the evil, usurping brother, who is a composite of all that the rational principle, the lawfully ruling brother, has necessarily rejected, is, in Freudian terms, Lord of the Id and of all misrule. As Lord of the Id he is prince of the Underworld, consort of the Goddess of Hell. In this way, he is always a kind of Tarquin. Claudius in *Hamlet*, Macbeth (where King Duncan is his 'kinsman'), Edmund in *King Lear*, Antonio in *The Tempest*, are only four. Each of these Tarquins commits a rape on the soul of order, i.e. displaces the ruling figure violently. The displaced brother collapses into the abyss, the infernal darkness, the blasted heath, the islet in the ocean, the Mother Forest, where he disintegrates. Eventually, reconstituted in some superior, enlightened, avenging form, he returns. Murdered King Hamlet returns as Prince Hamlet, Duncan returns as Banquo's ghost plus Macduff, Edgar returns as Edgar invincible, Prospero returns as Master of the Elements.

Orlando's double emerges into dramatic, realistic form as his ruthless brother Oliver. Oliver is 'older' because, though morally inferior, he is temporarily, circumstantially stronger. Orlando, disinherited by his brother and banished, falls into the abyss—the Mother Forest. The conflict between the two human brothers—the two selves of Orlando—cannot be resolved on the human or realistic plane because that is where it is entrenched. It can be resolved only by resort to the mythic plane: their brotherhood—Orlando's unity—can only be repaired where they might find mythic, supernatural help.

Their conflict is itself projected on to the mythic plane. In this way the two Dukes appear as the mythic selves of Oliver and Orlando (royalty, sanctity of rule, etc., being phenomena of the mythic plane, hieroglyphic symbols, invented spontaneously on the mythic plane and operating there, manipulating transcendent solutions to what is happening on the realistic plane).

Older Oliver's family cruelty exercised against younger Orlando is expressed, on the mythic plane, by Duke Frederick's (mythically younger because morally less evolved) usurping and banishing of his brother the lawful Duke Senior. (Shakespeare establishes his position in the mythic pattern by what would be otherwise a feebly perfunctory name.) The revolutionary coup and displacement of Duke Senior is therefore the same event, on the mythic plane, as Oliver's usurping and disinheriting of Orlando on the realistic plane. Displaced, Duke Senior falls, like his real self, Orlando, on to the dance floor of the mythic plane, the maze of the Mother Forest, where real and mythic selves meet. This makes the role of Rosalind clear. She is the Lucrece figure corresponding to the soul of lawful rule: the spirit of the Crown of order. (More about this a little later.) She remains with (or rather quickly rejoins) her banished father Duke Senior as inevitably as Miranda grew up beside the banished lawful Duke Prospero. According to this, she is the feminine aspect of Orlando's mythic self—which is to say, she is Orlando's 'soul'. She is what Orlando was lacking at the beginning of the play. The two recognize each other automatically, on first sight. The end of the play and the mending of all the other fractures will come when Orlando and Rosalind are betrothed.

Celia is clearly subordinate to Rosalind, but her closest friend. She is the feminine aspect of the usurping Duke, who is Oliver's mythic self. She is therefore Oliver's 'soul', as Rosalind is Orlando's. As I say, the quarrel of the two Dukes reflects in passive, mythical representation the quarrel of the two brothers or Orlando's two selves. But the mutual loyalty of the two women expresses the deeper mythic circumstance that the two selves of Orlando belong together in mutual support and love.

The play opens with every relationship falling apart or in difficulties (and the lower characters are figures in the same dance). Orlando is separated from his soul and therefore from Oliver, Duke Senior from Duke Frederick, Rosalind from her father, then Celia from her father, and both women from their sex. But the moment that Rosalind and Orlando begin to move, indirectly, towards each other, all these relationships begin to move, somehow, towards unity and enlightenment, though with apparent reversals and new delays, which nevertheless all have their mythic logic according to the mechanism of the pattern. This process makes up the body of the play.

The two Jaques still have to be accounted for. The closed square of the two pairs of brothers left that middle brother, Jaques de Boys, as the odd man out. Between Orlando and Oliver he seems to be the invisible third, belonging equally to both. Because such pointed emphasis was placed on his mental ability, one supposes that he is a factor of understanding. He is the principle of the single awareness, in some way, of Orlando's divided mind.

In a system of such tidy symmetry one looks towards the two Dukes for some equivalent of this intermediate brother. And of course the moment the banished Duke Senior enters the play, in the Forest of Arden, there he is—Melancholy Jaques. After an introductory word or two, the Duke will hear of nobody but Jaques. And he leaves the stage only to search for Jaques and to learn what he can from him:

> I love to cope him in these sullen fits,
> For then he's full of matter.
> *As You Like It*, ii. i. 67–8

Melancholy Jaques, it appears, occupies a position between the two Dukes, in some way a counterpoise to that of Jaques de Boys between Oliver and Orlando. And like Jaques de Boys he is the mental type. He is a summarizing, unifying intelligence. But he is not, like his namesake, wrapped in abstract studies. His study is the world. He suffers the usurper's conscience as keenly as he suffers the pains of the usurped. He is the interrogator of the real nature and cost of the quarrel of brothers. The anomalous and in a way disruptive aspect of Jaques is that he seems not to belong to the mythic world of the Dukes. And he is no part of the healing dance in the Mother Forest. He is a gloomy wallflower there, a gatecrasher from the real world, who has brought the real world with him. Pondering the mythic quarrel of the Dukes, he makes it real. He belongs, rather, to the world of the opening scene, the hard-edged realism of the conflict between Oliver and Orlando, and Charles the Wrestler.

Now it is possible to find a place for him in the design. Still considering the worlds of the two pairs of brothers as two distinct planes, one can see that Melancholy Jaques, the unifying intelligence from the human or realistic plane, is operating, as a kind of investigator, on the mythic plane. And Jaques de Boys, though he is positioned on the realistic plane (as brother of Oliver and Orlando) never actively operates there: he is buried in studies (like young Prospero, perhaps), which is to say that he actually belongs to the mythic plane. The realistic intelligence is on the mythic plane: the mythic intelligence is on the realistic plane. Jaques de Boys, in other words, is the mythic double of Melancholy Jaques, and this mortise-and-tenon interlocking joint of the mythic and the realistic intelligence binds the two planes together. The exchange expresses the accessibility of each plane to the other, and is what makes it possible—in a mythic sense—for Orlando on the realistic plane to find Rosalind on the mythic plane. That is presumably why Jaques de Boys and his cleverness is almost the first thought that occurs to Orlando in the play.

When all the fractured relationships, except one, have been repaired, suddenly from the depths of the Mother Forest comes the news that the usurping Duke Frederick, en route to find his banished brother and put him 'to the sword', has met an old religious man in the forest and has been converted, on the spot, to such extraordinary effect that he has relinquished his crown to his banished brother, its rightful owner Duke Senior, has 'Thrown into neglect the pompous court' and has 'put on a religious life' (V. iv. 188–9).

According to the play as a romantic comedy, this news, which solves every last problem, could as well be brought by almost anybody. It might have looked much neater, for instance, if Monsieur le Beau had brought it. We know him, though not very well, as Duke Frederick's man, and he is otherwise left dangling somewhere at a loose end. But le Beau's role bears no load in the ritual structure. According to the play as a ritual structure, only one person can bring good news from the mythic plane: it has to be the mythic intelligence, Jaques de Boys.

Once that news has arrived, it is inevitable that it should be Melancholy Jaques, the unifying intelligence of the realistic dimension, who solemnizes the repair of Orlando's whole being, returning the Duke to his dukedom and each of the selves to his soul, and all to Orlando, in a formal ceremony. This small but very clear instance indicates just how it is the mythic pattern alone which dictates the moves of the pieces in the ritual game. The human motivation may often seem arbitrary or inexplicable, but that is because the characters are moving in this way, according to mythic, not human, logic. But maybe this is how a surface effect of apparent confusion and irrational sequences, resembling life, nevertheless completes a pattern that seems, on the deepest level, inevitable and right.

But now, as far as the play's position in relationship to the tragic sequence is concerned, the most important thing of all happens. The pattern of the play is complete, but, as in a Persian carpet, at the end of the pattern a thread leaks out into a great mystery—the unpatterned.

Orlando and Oliver, the divided mind, like an ego of consciousness and another in subconsciousness, are both intent on the life struggle, and the play has temporarily healed their division. But if the two Dukes are the same divided mind on the mythic level, and if Duke Senior, corresponding to Orlando, has now returned to a sovereign control, which corresponds to Orlando's healed unity of mind, what about Duke Frederick?

If one now shifts the whole play on to the stage of autobiography, as if it were a visionary dream that Shakespeare happened to write out in dramatic form, one might say the following. Jaques de Boys, the invisible student, represents the mythic intelligence, alias the unifying, healing intelligence of the Mother Forest, alias the creative intelligence or spiritual intellect. This figure now brings news that the mythic, irrational self, the former usurper (Duke Frederick), has abjured all earthly ambitions and committed himself to the spiritual quest. If this were indeed happening in a visionary dream, the dreamer would have to take this news seriously. What the rational self decides depends on the support of the irrational self and the precarious apparatus of the conscious will. What the irrational self decides is generally a foregone conclusion, and will be carried out whether the conscious rational self approves or not, as a rule. But in this case, it seems, Shakespeare's rational self approves: Melancholy Jaques, the unifying intelligence of his rational consciousness, determines to join the convertite Duke. In other words, Shakespeare commits himself consciously to the quest on which his irrational self has already decided. Melancholy Jaques dismisses the pursuit of social happiness:

> So, to your pleasures:
> I am for other than for dancing measures.
> V. iv. 199–200

This solemn playfulness at the end of *As You Like It* might seem like the truest poetry which is the most feigning if it were not immediately followed by *All's Well that Ends Well*, *Troilus and Cressida*, *Measure for Measure*, *Hamlet*, *Othello*, *Macbeth* and *King Lear* all within the next five or six years.

Jaques de Boys, then, appears as a kind of Hermes, the guide to the mysteries of the Underworld. He is the voice of the mouth of the Underworld which opens through the cave in the Mother Forest. He has announced the call. And Shakespeare, as Melancholy Jaques, has answered and willingly started towards it. One sees that the two Jaques coalesce like the diver entering his image. And the two pairs of warring brothers, and the two daughters who are now to be wives, coalesce into each other and into the Jaques who sinks into the Underworld as (twelve years before *The Tempest*) Prospero climbs, with his baby daughter, into 'the rotten carcass of a butt'.

And Jaques is Shakespeare himself, thirty-five years old, *nel mezzo del cammin*, awake in the depth of the Mother Forest, about to enter (there is even a lion!) his *Divina Commedia*.

ANDREW BARNABY

The Political Consciousness of Shakespeare's As You Like It

> the purpose of playing ... [is] to hold as 'twere the mirror up to nature: to show virtue her feature, scorn her own image, and the very age and body of the time his form and pressure.
>
> —*Hamlet* (III.ii.20–4)

When in *As You Like It* the courtier-turned-forester Jacques declares his desire to take up the vocation of the licensed fool, he is immediately forced to confront the chief dilemma of the would-be satirist: the possibility that his intentions will be ignored and his words misconstrued as referring not to general moral concerns—the vices of humankind, for example—but rather to specific realities, persons, events (II.vii.12–87).[1] Given that Jacques has just demonstrated a laughable inability to grasp the barbs of a true practitioner of the satiric craft (Touchstone), we must be wary of taking him as a reflexive figure of Shakespeare's own vocation. But the lines undoubtedly show Shakespeare's discomfort with the recent censoring of satiric material (including a well-publicized burning of books in June of 1599),[2] and his own earlier experience with *Richard II*, as well as Ben Jonson's recent jailing for the "seditious and slanderous" content of the *Isle of Dogs*, had certainly made him familiar with the danger posed by those readers who misread the typical as the straightforwardly topical. Despite his simple-mindedness, then,

From *SEL Studies in English Literature 1500–1900* 36, no. 2 (Spring 1996).

Shakespeare's Jacques does in some way reflect a working playwright's continual anxiety that his works might be misconstrued as deriving meaning not from his intentions but from ideas and events beyond the signifying scope of his labors.

The modern equivalent of this reader–writer conflict resides not in the competing interpretations of author and court censor but in those of author and scholar-critic. But the necessity of facing up to such interpretative discrepancies has for the most part been obscured by the reigning critical methodology in Renaissance studies, New Historicism, and in particular by its inability to formulate a convincing explanatory model for the processes of acquisition by which texts come both to represent and to participate in the larger discursive systems that determine them. Although it would be counterproductive to dismiss the very impressive critical achievements of New Historicism, we might yet need to consider what we are to make of writing itself as a purposeful and perspectivally limited activity: what of writers as the agents of meaning within their own textual compositions? what do we do when what we can reconstruct of authorial intention runs counter to "cultural" evidence? and, more broadly, how precisely can any literary work be understood to signify historical reality?

In taking up these issues, Annabel Patterson has recently argued that it has become necessary to "reinstate certain categories of thought that some have declared obsolete: above all the conception of authorship, which itself depends on our predicating a continuous, if not a consistent self, of self-determination and, in literary terms, of intention." And she adds specifically of poststructuralist criticism of Shakespeare that the "dismissal of Shakespeare as *anybody*, an actual playwright who wrote ... out of his own experience of social relations" has shown itself to be both incoherent methodologically and reductive at the level of historical understanding.[3] Such out-of-hand dismissal precludes the possibility of understanding how the early modern period actively conceptualized and debated its cultural forms or how an individual writer may have sought to engage in those debates.

The remainder of this essay will focus on how *As You Like It* (and so Shakespeare himself) does consciously engage in debate concerning the crises points of late-Elizabethan culture: the transformation of older patterns of communal organization under the pressures of new forms of social mobility, an emergent market economy, and the paradoxically concomitant stratification of class relations; the more specific problems of conflict over land-use rights, the enclosure of common land and its attendant violence, poverty and vagrancy.[4] In considering how modern historical understanding might itself seek to articulate this engagement, moreover, I shall be arguing that the play's meditation on the unsettled condition of contemporary social relations is precisely, and nothing more than, an interpretative response to the perceived nature of those conditions.

To recognize that what we have in Shakespeare's play can never be anything but a rather one-sided dialogue with social conditions then current is not to deny that the play is, in crucial ways, at once topical and discursively organized. But it is to acknowledge that such topicality and discursivity are necessarily transformed by the historical condition of writing itself. What we are left with, then, is not a symbolic re-encoding of the entire sweep of current circumstances (as if the play could encompass the full historical truth of even one element of Elizabethan culture in its own tremendous complexity). Shakespeare does indeed address the peculiar historical circumstances of late-Elizabethan culture, and that engagement is evidenced in the formal elements of his play (most particularly in its pastoral form, an issue that will be examined in greater detail in subsequent sections). But if *As You Like It* is historically relevant it is so primarily because it can be read as a rhetorical (and so intentional) act in which one writer's sense of things as part of history becomes available to his readers in the purposeful design of the play. It is to an understanding both of that design and of the limitations of current critical practice that the following discussion is directed.

I

The play begins with Orlando's complaining of his mistreatment at the hands of his older brother, Oliver, who has refused to fulfill the charge of their father, Sir Rowland de Boys: it was Sir Rowland's wish that his youngest son receive both a thousand crowns and sufficient breeding to make a gentleman of himself, despite being excluded from the much greater wealth of the estate because of the law of primogeniture. But Oliver has treated Orlando as a servant instead, and, in likening himself to the prodigal son (I.i.37–9), Orlando seeks both to remind Oliver that, unlike his gospel counterpart, *he* has yet to receive his promised inheritance and to register, for the audience as well as for Oliver, the discrepancy between his noble birth and his current circumstances.

In the course of rebuking Oliver for being so remiss in his fraternal duties, Orlando violently, if briefly, seizes his brother. In his finely nuanced reading of the play, Louis Montrose has argued that, in its explosive suddenness and aggressiveness, Orlando's action captures the essential tension caused by the culturally charged nature of the sibling conflict over primogeniture in Renaissance England, where younger sons of the gentry were excluded from the greater wealth of family estates in increasing numbers.[5] Moreover, the symbolic associations of the violence complicate the political inflections of the scene. For, in context, the violence does not just move from younger brother to older brother but also from servant to master and from landless to landowner, and these associations extend the cultural scope of the already politicized conflict. As Montrose suggests, in the broader discursive contextualization of the scene, Orlando's alienation from his status as landed gentleman serves "to intensify the differences between the eldest son and his siblings, and to identify the sibling conflict with the major division in the Elizabethan social fabric: that between the landed and the unlanded, the gentle and the base."[6]

Richard Wilson has recently elaborated on this argument by suggesting that the play's central conflicts reenact the particular tensions unleashed in Elizabethan society by the subsistence crisis of the 1590s. According to Wilson, in its "discursive rehearsal" of the social hostilities generated out of the combination of enclosure and famine (especially severe in the years just prior to the play's composition and in Shakespeare's native Midlands), the play becomes complexly enmeshed in the "bitter contradictions of English agricultural revolution," a struggle played out in the various conflicting relations between an enervated aristocracy, a rising gentry, and a newly dispossessed laboring class and effected primarily by the emergence of a new market economy.[7]

As compelling and historically informed as Wilson's reading is, however, it is yet undermined by its vagueness concerning how the play actually represents these issues. That Wilson wants and needs to posit the dialogic encounter of text and context as the site of the play's (and his argument's) meaning is evidenced by his own critical rhetoric. As we have just noted, he refers to the play as a "discursive rehearsal" of a multifaceted sociocultural history; elsewhere he writes that "the play is powerfully *inflected* by narratives of popular resistance"; that "social conflict [over famine and enclosure] *sears* the text"; that Duke Senior's situation in the forest of Arden "*chimes* with actual projects" associated with the capitalist development of the woodlands; that the play "*engages in the discursive revaluation* of woodland" that emerged as part of the rise of a market economy in late-Renaissance England.[8] The problem with this type of phrasing is that it never renders intelligible the processes by which text and context come into contact. We are dealing, in short, with the theoretical problem of how precisely a literary work may be said to allude to, reflect, meditate on, or even produce the historical forces that form its enabling conditions.

To put the issue another way, Wilson's reading is stranded by its inability to assess what we might call the play's signifying capacity. While I am not disputing that the particulars of enclosure and famine (and more generally the social transformation of late-Elizabethan society) constitute the proper historical backdrop of the play, Wilson consistently scants the historical conditions of writing and reception, and he therefore has no means of assessing the work of the text as a site of meaning.[9] Eschewing any reliance on the text's own coherence or Shakespeare's possible intentions as explanatory models, Wilson's argument relies instead on the juxtaposition of select formal elements of the play (plot details, bits of dialogue, character motivation, etc.) with a dense evocation of historical details that appear circumstantially relevant to the play's action. While this mode of argumentation—what Alan Liu has recently termed a kind of critical *bricolage*[10]—yields some perceptive insights into the workings of the play, social reality, and the discursive networks connecting them, what it really produces is a series of strange allegorical encounters in which the play is said to provide shadowy symbolic re-encodings of a broad spectrum of historical realities: legal edicts, demographic statistics, anecdotes from popular culture, institutional practices, persons, events, and even vast structural changes in the organization of English culture.

To get a clearer sense of this method we might consider just a few of his more suspect interpretative findings. For example, according to Wilson, Rosalind's lack of "holiday humor" in I.ii stems not from her father's banishment but from her recognition of a broader crisis of the aristocracy (particularly centered on a new "aristocratic insolvency"), and this even though her own subsequent banishment is read as a symbol of the expulsion of tenant farmers from common lands; and later her cross-dressing becomes an "impudent challenge" both of rural poachers to "the keepers of game" and, more generally, of class and gender trespassers to the patriarchal hierarchy maintained by the Elizabethan upper orders. The "obscure demise" of Orlando's servant, Adam, figures the rising "mortality rate" in rural England due to the late-1590s dearth, even though Adam does not die (he merely disappears as a character—a point to which we shall return). Orlando's carving of his beloved Rosalind's name on the forest trees is said to symbolize a Stuart policy of marking trees as part of the surveying that preceded royal disafforestation; and this is so even though such a policy postdates the composition of the play and even after Wilson has described Orlando as a gentleman-leader of popular resistance for whom the damaging of trees was a potent sign of protest.[11] In almost all of the examples he gives, the text is so overdetermined by contradictory historical realities that it becomes virtually unreadable; despite his historicizing efforts, Wilson seems to repeat the very argument of those he terms "idealist critics" who see the play as "free of time and place."[12]

The argument's lack of coherence appears to derive primarily from

Wilson's attempt to analyze what he calls the play's "material meaning." Although he never says precisely how we are to understand the phrase, his one effort at glossing suggests that it is something known only in the negative, as that which is concealed or evaded by the text's explicit statements.[13] This is an odd notion, given the ease with which Wilson finds the text making explicit statements about the social situation;[14] indeed, given his practice, it makes more sense to take the term "material" in its traditional Marxist sense: the "historical" as located in a culture's dominant mode of production. In the case of *As You Like It* the "material" would then include the cultural struggle over agrarian rights, the conversion of woodland to arable land, and the broader movement of a regulated to a market economy (seen especially in the capitalization of land-use rights), and this "material" history would provide the base from which the manifestations of superstructure (including the play) would derive meaning.

The problem with this formulation is that it both reduces the play to a straightforward (albeit jumbled) allegory of "history as it really happened" and avoids the theoretical problem of how (or where) the play actually represents this history. Addressing precisely this hermeneutic problem in relation to the Shakespearean text (and so offering a different sense of "material meaning"), Patterson properly asks: "how do words relate to material practice?" And she notes that Shakespeare himself "used both 'abstract' and 'general' as terms to denote his own form of material practice, writing for a popular audience, the 'general,' and abstracting their experience and his own into safely fictional forms."[15] Such a critical stance depends on several related notions: that Renaissance writers were quite capable of comprehending the cultural situation of their own productions; that these productions must be read as forms, that is, as organized, fictionalized, and generically regularized abstractions of perceived realities; that any discussion of form must consider the representational practices by which historical situations are reproduced aesthetically; and that, as abstractions, forms take their meaning from a variety of interpretative exchanges—between author and world as an act of perception, author and reader/audience as a rhetorical act, reader/audience and world as an act of application—and therefore cannot be explained by recourse to the notion of a general, all-encompassing discursive field. To view fictional form as a significant material practice in its own right is to see that it at once signifies historical realities and constitutes its own reality, that it is both constantive and performative; it thus "both invite[s] and resist[s] understanding in terms of other phenomena."[16]

As texts such as Ben Jonson's Preface to *Volpone* suggest, for Renaissance writers this invitation and resistance is played out primarily (though not exclusively) in ethical terms.[17] The citation from *Hamlet* that stands as my epigraph makes a similar point: "to hold ... the mirror up to nature" is to engage in moral discrimination, distinguishing virtue from vice in acts of praise and blame. Such acts might themselves be understood as historically relevant; indeed, Hamlet's earlier assertion that actors are "the abstract and brief chronicles of the time" (II.ii.524–5) suggests that dramatic representations were expected to speak to contemporary history (albeit in "abstract and brief" form). Leah Marcus takes this point even further in her claims that "local meaning was at the center" of Renaissance literary practices, and that what contemporaries "attended and talked about" concerning a literary work was its "currency .... its ability to ... 'Chronicle' events in the very unfolding." But, as she also points out, Renaissance "poets and dramatists [typically] looked for ways to regularize and elevate topical issues so that they could be linked with more abstract moral concerns."[18] In *As You Like It* that ethical sensibility, "regularizing and elevating" a pressing cultural debate over current social conditions, is marked especially in the play's engagement with the traditions of pastoral, where pastoral must be understood as a form obsessively concerned with the related questions of social standing (the constant remarking of distinctions between gentle and base) and moral accountability.[19] It is to an attempt to assess the moral and political commitments of the play, as well as the representational strategies it employs to render these commitments intelligible, that we now turn.

II

The three plays that Shakespeare wrote in 1599—*Julius Caesar*, *Henry V*, and *As You Like It*—are all variously concerned with aristocratic identity, an issue cited, probed, redefined in late-Elizabethan culture in "a vast outpouring of courtesy books, poetry, essays, and even epics," all directed toward "the fashioning ... of the gentleman or the nobleman."[20] *Julius Caesar* looks at the issue as a crisis of aristocratic self-definition in the face of Tudor efforts at political and cultural centralization; the play examines this crisis and moralizes it in terms of a questioning of the continued possibility of aristocratic excellence (defined primarily in terms of humanist notions of virtuous civic action).[21] *Henry V* explores the relationship between aristocratic conduct and national identity in the context of militarist expansionism, but this focus is extended to an examination of the aristocratic capacity for responsible leadership of commoners and the popular response to that leadership.[22] As critics have recently argued, both plays are concerned with the nature of historical understanding itself, and especially with examining the possibilities and limits of applying knowledge of the past—already an interested rhetorical activity—to present concerns.[23] Like *As You*

Like It, then, both plays are interested at once in the vexed relation between aristocratic culture and the broader workings of political society and in the representational and interpretative practices by which fictional accounts serve as mediatory sites of informed public concern over contemporary affairs.

As You Like It returns the meditation on aristocratic conduct to the domestic sphere where, as we have seen suggested, it focuses on the related issues of inheritance practices, agrarian social structure, and the current controversy over land-use rights. Right from its opening scene, in fact, the play introduces us to its particular interest in the problem of aristocratic definition. Indeed, despite Orlando's complaints against the system of primogeniture which denies him his brother's authority, the real source of his frustration is that his "gentlemanlike qualities"—the very marks of his class, so crucial in a deferential society—have been obscured by his having been "trained ... like a peasant" (I.i.68–70). Throughout the opening scene, in fact, what Orlando is most concerned with is the possibility that his status might be taken away simply by its not being properly recognized. In its particular locating of Orlando's predicament, then, the play's opening scene initiates a line of inquiry that will both inflect the rest of the play and share in a culturally charged debate: by what markings is it possible to identify the true aristocrat?

But the issues of status and its violation, of place, displacement, and recognition—all so central to the play's comic vision—are not confined to the interactions among the upper orders. For they are raised as part of an exploration of the customary bonds between the upper and lower orders as well. And, as the relationship between landowner and landless servant depicted in the opening suggests, the play also puts in question the nature and meaning of aristocratic conduct toward social inferiors. Shakespeare, we shall see, interlaces the depiction of violated noble status with a depiction of the displacement of laboring classes (represented in the opening scenes by both Orlando and Adam) from their traditional places in the service of the rural nobility.

The play's concern with the related issues of social standing and displacement, aristocratic conduct, and the moral bonds connecting high and low, is further developed in II.iii. Upon returning from Frederick's court, Orlando is secretly met by Adam who warns him of Oliver's villainous plot:

> this night he means
> To burn the lodging where you use to lie,
> And you within it.
>
> (II.iii.22–4)

Amidst the special urgency of the moment, Adam's warning is enveloped in a broader meditation on what has happened in the wake of Sir Rowland's passing. So he addresses Orlando:

> O unhappy youth,
> Come not within these doors! Within this roof
> The enemy of all your graces lives.
> Your brother—no, no brother, yet the son
> (Yet not the son, I will not call him son)
> Of him I was about to call his father—
> ....
> This is no place, this house is but a butchery;
> Abhor it, fear it, do not enter it.
>
> (II.iii.16–28)

Marking the logical consequence of the sibling conflict set in motion in the opening scene, Oliver's "unbrotherly" act is viewed here as particularly heinous, totally unnatural, a kind of abomination; indeed, as Montrose notes, we hear in this struggle the echoes of the original fratricide, the elder Cain killing his younger brother Abel.[24] But the fratricide is clearly rewritten in the cultural context of Renaissance inheritance practices, for we note that Oliver's "sin" is figured particularly as a repudiation of the familial duties and obligations emanating from a line of inheritance between noble father and noble son. Sir Rowland's heir, in effect, perverts the very link between nature and human social order—the family—and thereby disavows the very foundation of his inheritance. Oliver's unbrotherly dealings mark the violation of more than just the person of his brother; they are symbolically broadened to assimilate the house itself, symbol of both the family and the larger estate as an extension of the family. In dishonoring his place within the family, Oliver threatens the very cultural inheritance that extends a sense of place to those outside the family. Adam thus identifies Oliver's special villainy as a violation of kinship ties that both reenacts human history's primal scene of violence and marks the loss of that "place"—the noble manor—whose very purpose is to locate the various lines of interaction defining the social order.[25]

In II.iii, then, younger brother and elder servant are linked together in their experience of the psychically disorienting effects of displacement, a loss registered particularly in the feelings of estrangement they voice over their impending exile (II.iii.31–5, 71–4). There is something extremely conservative in this nostalgic evocation of tradition, of course, but it is important to insist that the image of "proper" social relations that

Shakespeare depicts does not offer merely a moralized restoration of traditional cultural forms but provides rather an extended meditation on the political economy that should at once reveal and sustain the moral economy.

As an example of this concern, Shakespeare's complex adaptation of the gospel parable he so carefully etches into the opening scene deserves greater attention. We noted earlier that at the very outset of the play Orlando's self-figuration as the prodigal son is intended to register the discrepancy between his noble birth and his current circumstances. But the very lack of applicability of the parable to Orlando's case—unlike the prodigal son he has neither squandered his inheritance nor even received it—is even more significant within the play's moral and political vision. This discrepancy is critical primarily because it reconfigures the parable's central focus on the interaction of family members from how each of the two brothers interacts independently with the father to a direct confrontation between them. At the most obvious level, this change has the effect of politicizing the fraternal struggle by making it a conflict over the now deceased father's patrimony, whereas in the parable the fraternal conflict is less about inheritance per se than with the sibling rivalry over the attentiveness of the still-living father. Shakespeare, that is, transforms a story concerned with the nature of a future "heavenly" kingdom into a decidedly human, indeed, political affair.

More specifically, the retelling provides a completely different context for understanding the roles of the two brothers within the parable. For example, whereas the parable faults (even as it treats sympathetically) the elder brother's uncharitable attitude toward his younger brother, the play, by contrast, renders this animosity, and the behavior that attends it, unsympathetic; indeed, Shakespeare appears to conflate two different parts of the parable by rewriting the elder brother's (now perverse) behavior as the cause of the (now innocent) younger brother's degradation. Living among the hogs and eating husks with them, Orlando appears as the dutiful son, toiling long years without just recompense. Although the play never quotes the parable directly on this point, Shakespeare subtly borrows from the parable the elder brother's complaint to his father—"All these years I have slaved for you and never once disobeyed any orders of yours"—and reassigns the context to Orlando's frustration with Oliver's unfair treatment of him. And as Orlando is no longer responsible for his fallen circumstances, so his situation ceases to represent a moral failing—a lapse in personal ethical responsibility—and comes instead to mark a political and economic awareness of the social mechanisms that lead one into such penury.

Oliver's role is thereby refigured (loosely to be sure) as "prodigal." In the parable, of course, it is the elder brother who laments that while he has never "disobeyed any orders" of the father, his prodigal brother enjoys all the special privileges even after "swallowing up [the father's] property." But Shakespeare makes the true bearer of privilege appear prodigal precisely because, while he has done nothing to earn his portion of the estate (other than being the eldest son), he has enjoyed its benefits without sharing them with his hard-working brother. And even as the play merges the Judeo-Christian primal scene of violence—Cain's killing of his younger brother Abel—with the Christian parable of the difficult demands of brotherly love, it also recontextualizes the elder brother's failure of charity in the political relations not just between elder and younger sons (already politicized in Renaissance culture) but also between masters and servants, landed and landless, gentle and base. Moreover, while the opening scene stages, in the guise of Orlando's violence, a threat to the overturning of traditional authority, the subsequent scenes stage a recognition of what is more precisely in need of transformation: the aristocratic figure who fails to fulfill the obligations of status and custom, and especially to maintain cultural stability by sustaining the moral (and political) value that accrues to social place.

It is within the context of such unbrotherly dealings and their symbolic affiliation with social injustice conceived on a broader scale that Duke Senior's praise of rural life at the opening of act II has its strongest resonance:

> Now, my co-mates and brothers in exile,
> Hath not old custom made this life more sweet
> Than that of painted pomp? Are not these woods
> More free from peril than the envious court?
> Here feel we not the penalty of Adam.
>
> (II.i.1–5)

Exiled to Arden by his usurper-brother, Frederick, Duke Senior moralizes his own violated status as a paradoxically edifying experience, one in which the recovery of a communal (fraternal) ethic, in opposition to a courtly one, marks the return to a prelapsarian condition.

We must pause over such an idealization, of course. For it is possible to read the "pastoral" vision here as merely mystifying the class consciousness it appears to awaken. Montrose asserts, for example, that Renaissance pastoral typically "puts into play a symbolic strategy, which, by reconstituting the leisured gentleman as the gentle shepherd obfuscates a fundamental contradiction in the cultural logic: a contradiction between the secular claims of aristocratic prerogative and the religious claims of common origins, shared fallenness, and spiritual equality among ... gentle and base alike."[26] For a modern reader especially, the very social structure maintained in Duke Senior's Arden weakens the political force of his claims for ethical restoration. From this limited perspective, that is, Duke Senior bears a remarkable resemblance to the gentleman-shepherd of so many Elizabethan pastorals, who, "in the idyllic countryside" is most determined to "escape temporarily from the troubles of court." As Montrose adds, "in such pastorals, ambitious Elizabethan gentlemen who may be alienated or excluded from the courtly society that nevertheless continues to define their existence can create an imaginative space within which virtue and privilege coincide."[27] The duke's idealization of the leisured life of the country would then, despite its egalitarian appeal, serve to re-emphasize the division between baseness and gentility and to celebrate aristocratic values in isolation from a broader vision of how those values serve as the foundation of an entire network of social relations.

We might note further how Duke Senior's aristocratic rhetoric appears to de-radicalize its own most potent political symbol: the image of a prelapsarian fraternal community. As Montrose and others have pointed out, from the Peasants' Revolt of 1381 onward popular social protest in England often challenged class stratification by appealing to a common Edenic inheritance. Powerfully condensed into the proverb, "When Adam dalf and Eve span, who was then the Gentleman?" such protest offered a radical critique of aristocratic privilege, both interrogating the suspect essentialism inherent in the notion of "degree" and reversing the valuation of labor as a criterion of social status.[28] Duke Senior's speech, however, does neither: it never questions the "naturalness" of his rank within the fraternal community (which never ceases to be hierarchically organized) nor does it champion labor as a morally edifying and communal burden. For Duke Senior, the retreat to a prelapsarian condition becomes rather the site from which to critique court corruption and decadence.

Nevertheless, we should not underestimate the reformist, populist impulse embedded in that critique. For, as act I depicts it, the condition of fallenness that exists in Frederick's court is defined primarily by its persecution of those members of the nobility—Orlando and Rosalind—most popular with the people (I.i.164–71, I.ii.277–83). Moreover, Orlando and Rosalind are conceptually linked to Sir Rowland himself, so universally "esteemed," as Frederick tells us, and so an enemy (I.ii.225–30). Frederick's function as the play's arch-villain is registered therefore, like Oliver's before him, by a lack of respect for the memory of that overdetermined father whose recurrent, if shadowy, presence in the play provides a "local habitation and name" to a broader cultural ideal: the forms of customary obligation that link gentle and base in pastoral fraternity, an evocation of religious communion that emphasizes social dependency and reciprocity even as it does not thereby reject society's hierarchical structure.

Much of the value (both moral and political) associated with that community is symbolized in Duke Senior's phrase "old custom" and its own associations with popular protest. As Patterson remarks, even when such protest did not advocate structural changes in the social order, an appeal to the authority of "origins" (again, often condensed into the recollection of a common Edenic origin) "was integral to the popular conception of *how* to protest, as well as providing theoretical grounds for the 'demands,' for the transformation of local and individual grievances into a political program."[29] *As You Like It* makes it clear that the duke's use of the phrase cannot be seen as privileging the rights of the nobility alone; indeed, Adam's subsequent lament over his exile (II.iii.71–4) is designed to set out the meaning of "old custom" from the perspective of the rural servant. Linking together a sense both of the immemorialness of custom and of its historical embeddedness by reference to his age and associating that further with the original Edenic dispensation through his name, Adam's speech marks how an appeal to customary practices could serve the interests of the lower orders.

In the tradition of popular protest, an idealization of the past could serve as the focal point of protesters' awareness of current social injustice, even as the perception of injustice was rarely separated from an appeal to the moral economy taken to subtend the political one. This ethical evaluation of the mutual interests of the upper and lower orders is powerfully figured in the tableau that closes act II: Duke Senior, Orlando, and Adam gathered together at a life-sustaining meal. Here, the problem of rural poverty (old Adam is starving to death) is answered in the nostalgic evocation of "better days," when paupers were "with holy bell ... knoll'd to church, / And sat at good men's feasts" (II.vii.113–5). The meal, reimagined as a Sabbath-day feast, symbolizes the restoration of social communion especially as this is founded on those culturally sustaining lines of authority in which servants and masters properly recognize each other with reciprocal "truth and loyalty" (II.iii.70), the very qualities that were the hallmark of the days of Sir Rowland.[30]

In focusing on the paired plights of Orlando and Adam up through the end of act II, the play defines that perception of injustice, and of the moral obligations of the community, from the perspective of the lower orders and their first-hand experience of the effects of enclosure and eviction, dearth and hunger. Moreover, what Wilson misreads as Adam's subsequent "demise" (his disappearance from the play after act II) can be better understood as Shakespeare's attempt to give even more nuanced attention to the plight of the lower orders. In replacing Adam with the shepherd, Corin, as the play's test case, Shakespeare refocuses the issue of the condition of rural laborers in a character whose situation more obviously typifies such conditions in their particular relation to enclosure and eviction, especially in the face of the new commercialization of the land.

Significantly, Shakespeare puts the words describing the bleak prospects for rural living into Corin's own mouth; he thereby suggests a clear-sighted popular consciousness of the current situation. So Corin has earlier described his living in response to Rosalind's request for food and lodging:

> I am shepherd to another man,
> And do not shear the fleeces that I graze
> My master is of churlish disposition,
> And little reaks to find the way to heaven
> By doing deeds of hospitality.
> Besides, his cote, his flocks, and bounds of feed
> Are now on sale, and at our sheep-cote now
> By reason of his absence there is nothing
> That you will feed on.
>
> (II.iv.78–86)

Hunger is again the central issue, but the exchange subtly shifts attention away from the almost incidental hunger of disguised aristocrats (who can afford to "buy entertainment" [line 72]) to the plight of the rural laborer whose suffering derives from the very condition of his employment (significantly, in the service of an absentee landlord). As Lawrence Stone summarizes the historical situation described here:

> the aristocracy suffered a severe loss of their landed capital in the late-Elizabethan period, primarily because of improvident sales made in order to keep up the style of life they considered necessary for the maintenance of status. When they abandoned sales of land and took to rigorous economic exploitation of what was left in order to maximize profits, they certainly restored their financial position, but at the expense of much of the loyalty and affection of their tenants. They salvaged their finances at the cost of their influence and prestige.

He adds that as part of a "massive shift away from a feudal and paternalist relationship" on the land, "these economic developments were dissolving old bonds of service and obligation," a process compounded by an "increasing preference [among the nobility] for extravagant living in the city instead of hospitable living in the countryside."[31] A figure for the current destruction of the manorial economy, Corin's master is guilty of all these charges simultaneously: he is absent from the estate; he exploits the (once commonly held) land for profit; he threatens to sell the estate with no concern for his workers' future prospects; he refuses the ethical responsibilities of his class—hospitable living, the sustenance of the customary culture, leadership of the countryside. The scene's concern with the immediate need to allay hunger becomes then a stepping-stone to a broader meditation on hunger's place in the complex socioeconomic transformation of late-Elizabethan culture. From the immediate perspective of the play, moreover, this transformation threatens to become a dangerous social upheaval, the blame for which must be assigned to the moral failure of well-to-do landowners.

As idealistic as it is, then, Celia and Rosalind's offer to purchase the "flock and pasture" and "mend" Corin's wages (II.iv.88, 94) retains an element of popular political consciousness; for it suggests that it is still possible for laborers to reap the rewards of faithful service to masters who know how to nurture traditional lines of authority.[32] Shakespeare's revision of his source text, Thomas Lodge's *Rosalynde*, is particularly relevant on this point, not the least for its demonstration of the deliberateness with which Shakespeare addresses the specific issue of economic hardship among the rural poor. In Lodge's romance, the shepherd (Coridon) offers Aliena and Ganimede the simple comforts of his lowly cottage as part of a traditional extolling of pastoral content:

> Marry, if you want lodging, if you vouch to shrowd your selves in a shepheardes cotage, my house ... shalbe your harbour ... [A]nd for a shepheards life (oh Mistresse) did you but live a while in their content, you would saye the Court were rather a place of sorrowe, than of solace. Here (Mistresse) shal not Fortune thwart you, but in meane misfortunes, as the losse of a few sheepe, which, as it breeds no beggerie, so it can bee no extreame prejudice: the next yeare may mend al with a fresh increase. Envie stirs not us, wee covet not to climbe, our desires mount not above our degrees, nor our thoughts above our fortunes. Care cannot harbour in our cottages, nor do our homely couches know broken slumbers: as we exceede not in diet, so we have inough to satisfie.[33]

The fact that the sheepcote is for sale (and so, by a stroke of good fortune, available as a home for the wandering noblewomen) is only incidental to Coridon's prospects; the simple pleasures of his life will hardly be affected by a change in masters. Shakespeare, by contrast, revalues Corin's poverty by tying it explicitly to his economic vulnerability in the new commercial market: as one who, as "shepherd to another," does not "shear the fleeces" he grazes. In associating Corin's straitened circumstances—his limited supply of food is not "inough to satisfie"—with his very lack of authority over the estate (and his master's unreliable ownership practices), Shakespeare's revision of the scene emphasizes the real threat of rural dispossession; he thus makes it clear that "pastoral content" can only result from a functional economic relation between servant and landowner: hence, Corin's concern that his new masters actually "like ... / The soil, the profit, and this kind of life" (II.iv.97–8).

The conflicted relationship between leisured gentleman and base laborer is symbolically played out in the conversation between Corin and Touchstone in III.ii. Although the confrontation is humorous, it also includes a more serious evaluation of the attendant problems of social stratification, marked especially by the lack of respect shown toward common laborers. As Judy Z. Kronenfeld points out, Shakespeare here transforms the typical pastoral encounter in which an "aristocratic shepherd" (a gentleman pretending to be a shepherd) demonstrates courtly superiority by mocking the "clownish countryman" (or what is really a "burlesque version of the countryman").[34] What Shakespeare depicts instead is an encounter between a lowly court servant (now a pretended gentleman) and a sympathetically realistic shepherd. Touchstone's pretense to gentility in the scene hearkens back to his original meeting of Corin in II.iv. There, in the company of Celia and Rosalind, Touchstone responds to Corin's "Who calls" with the demeaning "Your betters, sir" (lines 67–8): the response mockingly raises Corin to the level of the gentlewomen ("sir") only to reassert the difference in social standing ("your betters") and to place Touchstone in that higher circle.

Touchstone maintains the masquerade in III.ii when he attempts to flout Corin's baseness in a condescending display of courtly sophistication (lines 11–85). But, as Kronenfeld notes, the sophistication comes off as mere "court sophistry," and the emptiness of his claims to superiority is thereby exposed as nothing more than a witty social rhetoric covering over an absence of any clearly defined *essential* differences between gentle and base. Shakespeare thus uses the tradition against itself, for the typical encounter of aristocrat (pretending to be a shepherd) and countryman—where the contrast is meant to "reaffirm the social hierarchy"—is rewritten to suggest (albeit humorously) the mere pretense of that contrast.[35] It is possible to read the scene as positing that there are no differences between gentle and base, a position which might include the more radical recognition that class standing itself is merely the result of an ideological manipulation of cultural signs. Within the context of the play as a whole, however, it perhaps makes more sense to read it as a moral commentary on class division and especially on the meaning of aristocratic identity: if gentility is as much a social construct as it is a privileged condition of birth, its maintenance requires that it be continually reconstructed through meritorious signs, and these signs are to be made legible in the virtuous conduct shown toward those whose livelihood depends on how the "gentle" fulfill the obligations of their class.

III

In discussing George Puttenham's *Arte of English Poesie* in the context of Elizabethan pastoral discourse, Montrose cites Puttenham's claim that pastoral was developed among ancient poets "not of purpose to counterfait or represent the rusticall manner of loves and communication: but under the vaile of homely persons, and in rude speeches to insinuate and glaunce at greater matters, and such as perchance had not bene safe to have beene disclosed in any other sort."[36] Puttenham's related concerns with safety and the necessity of dissimulation in a dangerous social environment, the poet's self-awareness as a cultural commentator, and the struggle to make homely fiction serve the higher ends of instruction bring us back to Patterson's contention that Shakespeare's own "material practice" purposely seeks out "safely fictional forms" to achieve its ends. In *As You Like It*, moreover, Shakespeare's practice turns explicitly to pastoral form, which, we might surmise, is deliberately deployed to "glaunce at greater matters" "cleanly cover[ed]" (as Spenser puts it in the *Shepheardes Calender*) by a "feyne[d]" story.[37]

The precise nature of those "matters" and Shakespeare's specific ends may be debated, of course. But it is hard to imagine that they are any less comprehensive than those attributed by Montrose to Puttenham. Puttenham, Montrose writes, conceives "of poetry as a body of changing cultural practices dialectically related to the fundamental processes of social life"; and his "cultural relativism and ethical heterodoxy, his genuinely Machiavellian grasp of policy, are evident ... in his pervasive concern with the dialectic between poetry and power."[38] It comes as some surprise, therefore, when Montrose later revises this estimation and gives us a Puttenham whose writing only serves the ends of personal aggrandizement within the confined circles of the court, whose sense of his culture's complexity is merely the sophistry of a "cunning princepleaser," and whose grasp of the political purposes of poetry never rises above its merely politic ends. And, as Montrose dismisses the narrowness of Puttenham's courtly orientation, so he dismisses pastoral discourse itself, whose power to "glaunce at greater matters" is suddenly reduced to courtliness in another form: thus, the "dominantly aristocratic" perspective of Elizabethan pastoral becomes but a reinscription of "agrarian social relations ... within an ideology of the country," which is "itself appropriated, transformed, and reinscribed within an ideology of the court."[39] Pastoral's "greater matters," it seems, are only the matters of the great for whom the masks of rural encomium serve their own (narrowly defined) hegemonic interests. For Montrose, that is, despite pastoral writers' own recognition that their art form is "intrinsically political in purpose," pastoral's central concern with aristocratic identity only serves to mystify the issues of class standing and social relations it appears to raise.[40] As he argues, finally, because Renaissance pastoral "inevitably involve[s] a transposition of social categories into metaphysical ones, a sublimation of politics into aesthetics," it necessarily functions as "a weapon against social inferiors."[41]

Without denying pastoral's aristocratic orientation, we might note that it is only from the reductively binary perspective of the New Historicist that an "elite community" must be opposed to all "egalitarian ideas," or that its members could have "little discernible interest" in the condition of those who serve them.[42] *As You Like It* certainly suggests that such a critical perspective fails to register the possibility of the presence of dissenting voices within the dominant culture. Indeed, if the play is not in full support of the popular voice, it is yet concerned to link an aristocratic crisis of identity to the more vexing problems of the "base." Shakespeare's pastoral world is thus less concerned with celebrating nobles as virtuous than in reexamining the precise nature of aristocratic virtue. And lest we think Shakespeare is the exception that proves the rule, it is instructive to recall the aristocratic Sidney's own brief meditation on pastoral in his *Defence of Poesy*: "Is the poor pipe disdained, which sometimes out of Meliboeus' mouth can show the misery of people under hard lords and ravening soldiers and again, by Tityrus, what blessedness is derived to them that lie lowest from the goodness of them that sit highest?"[43] That "blessedness," moreover, is not presumed to be the reality of his culture but only a symbolic idealization challenging his aristocratic readers to a kind of creative, ethically oriented imitatio.

Montrose's Historicism cannot envision this possibility because he denies to Renaissance pastoral writers any critical distance from the courtly aristocracy from which they drew support (including occasional financial support). He goes even further in denying that "the mediation of social boundaries was [even] a conscious motive in the writing of Elizabethan pastorals," let alone that a cultural critique might have been leveled "in terms of a consciously articulated oppositional culture."[44] Such a dismissal of

Renaissance writing as a purposeful, socially engaged activity is typical of New Historicist criticism more generally, which matches a methodological subordination of individual intention to larger "systems" of thought with a tonal condescension toward the capacity of earlier writers to comprehend their own cultural situations. Against this effacement of the subject, I would counter that an interest in the historical conditioning of texts is necessarily concerned with the conditions of their being written and being read, with the social processes by which meaning is formulated and communicated, with acts of knowledge as acts of persuasion, with the "rhetoricity" of texts as the essence of their historicity.[45] The reduction of historical criticism to the impersonal voice—to what Foucault once called the "it-is-said"[46]—precludes the possibility of understanding how the movement of ideas within discursive systems requires real readers and writers whose very activities help reveal to us the contours of historical existence.

Notes

1. All references to Shakespeare's plays are to *The Riverside Shakespeare*, ed. G. Blakemore Evans (Boston: Houghton Mifflin, 1974).

2. Celia's earlier remark to Touchstone—"since the little wit that fools have was silenc'd, the little foolery that wise men have makes a great show" (I.ii.88–90)—obliquely refers to this.

3. Annabel Patterson, *Shakespeare and the Popular Voice* (Oxford: Basil Blackwell, 1989), pp. 4, 24.

4. For a concise summary of these changing historical circumstances, see Lawrence Stone, *The Causes of the English Revolution, 1529–1642* (New York: Harper and Row, 1972), pp. 58–117.

5. Louis Montrose, "'The Place of a Brother' in *As You Like It*: Social Process and Comic Form," *SQ* 32, 1 (Spring 1981): 28–54.

6. Montrose, "'The Place of a Brother,'" pp. 34–5. That the exchange between Orlando and Oliver is more than just the struggle between younger and older brothers is emphasized by Orlando's response to Oliver's insulting question: "Know where you are, sir?" Orlando replies: "O sir, very well; here in your orchard" (I.i.40–1). The condition of "gentility" (marked in the mocking uses of "sir") is clearly tied to the question of who actually owns the property.

7. Richard Wilson, "'Like the old Robin Hood': *As You Like It* and the Enclosure Riots," *SQ* 43, 1 (Spring 1992): 1–19, 3–5. For a historical overview of the broader cultural, political, and economic issues conditioning this hostility, see Roger B. Manning, *Village Revolts: Social Protest and Popular Disturbances in England, 1509–1640* (Oxford: Clarendon Press, 1988).

8. Wilson, "'Like the old Robin Hood,'" pp. 4, 5, 9; my emphases.

9. Wilson's lack of interest in what the text itself does to produce the meanings he finds in it is perhaps not so surprising given his attempt, formulated elsewhere, to theorize the fundamental irrelevance of literature to the forces of history and culture that must always supersede it. See his Introduction to *New Historicism and Renaissance Drama*, ed. Richard Wilson and Richard Dutton (London: Longman, 1992), pp. 1–18. It should be noted that Wilson considers himself a "Cultural Materialist" rather than a "New

Historicist," and in that Introduction he seeks to differentiate the critical assumptions governing their respective practices. But the mode of argumentation employed in his essay on *As You Like It* does not bear out the differences he alleges.

10. Alan Liu, "The Power of Formalism: The New Historicism," *ELH* 56, 4 (Winter 1989): 721–71, 721.

11. Wilson, "'Like the old Robin Hood,'" pp. 4, 6, 9, 10–11, 13, 18.

12. Wilson, "'Like the old Robin Hood,'" p. 3 and n. 15. Liu remarks that "the limitation of the New Historicism is that in its failure to carve out its own theory by way of a disciplined, high-level study of the evolution of historically situated language, its discoverable theory has been too assimilable to the deconstructive view of rhetoric as an a–, trans–, or uni-historical figural language" (p. 756). Although his own critical practice employs precisely this kind of formalism, Wilson himself makes much the same complaint about New Historicist critics, whose elision of historical referent in favor of the "textuality of history," he asserts, aligns them with New Critics (*New Historicism and Renaissance Drama*, pp. 9–10).

13. Wilson first uses the phrase, without defining it, on p. 3 of "'Like the old Robin Hood'"; later he cites Foucault's observation that "in every society discourse is controlled and redistributed to avert its dangers and *evade its formidable materiality*." As an instance of this, Wilson notes that "pastoral discourse ... *will conceal* the real revolution in the forest economy" (p. 17; my emphases). (Inexplicably, although in his Introduction to *New Historicism and Renaissance Drama* Wilson again notes Foucault's claim for the "'formidable materiality' of all discourse" [p. 9], he does so as part of his critique of the overly abstract post-Marxist practice of Foucault and other French intellectuals, especially as this tradition has become the philosophical foundation of American New Historicism.) For discussion of the trope of revelatory "concealment" within post-structuralist criticism, see Richard Levin, "The Poetics and Politics of Bardicide," *PMLA* 105, 3 (May 1990): 491–504, 493–4.

14. One example: Touchstone's quip to the bumpkin, William, concerning their rival claims on Audrey—"to have, is to have" (V.i.40)—means, we are told, that a new concept of property ownership is now superseding traditional agrarian rights based on the notion of collective possession (Wilson, p. 18).

15. Patterson, p. 14.

16. Ibid.

17. See Preface to *Volpone*, in Ben Jonson, ed. C. H. Herford and Percy and Evelyn Simpson, 11 vols. (Oxford: Clarendon Press, 1925–52), 5:18–9. Having been jailed again in 1604, along with Chapman and Marston, for the anti-Scottish sentiments of *Eastward Ho!*, Jonson used the Preface to chastise readers for their propensity for assigning topical meanings to his plays: by substituting local for more general meanings, Jonson thought, his readers would necessarily fail to appreciate the moral lessons of his writing and so not see how his meanings were to be used for their own edification and improvement.

18. Leah Marcus, *Puzzling Shakespeare: Local Reading and Its Discontents* (Berkeley: Univ. of California Press, 1988), pp. 26, 41.

19. For discussion, see Louis Montrose, "Of Gentlemen and Shepherds: The Politics of Elizabethan Pastoral Form," *ELH* 50, 3 (Fall 1983): 415–59, esp. 425, 433.

20. Wayne A. Rebhorn, "The Crisis of the Aristocracy in Julius Caesar," *RenQ* 43, 1 (Spring 1990): 75–111, 81.

21. For discussion, see Timothy Hampton, *Writing from History: The Rhetoric of Exemplarity in Renaissance Literature* (Ithaca: Cornell Univ. Press, 1990), pp. 198–236.

22. For discussion, see Patterson, pp. 71–92.

23. Hampton, pp. 210–4; Patterson, pp. 83–90.

24. Montrose, "'The Place of a Brother,'" p. 46.

25. On the importance of the noble manor to the aristocratic ethical ideal, see Don E. Wayne, *Penshurst: The Semiotics of Place and the Poetics of History* (Madison: Univ. of Wisconsin Press, 1984).

26. Montrose, "Of Gentlemen and Shepherds," p. 432.

27. Montrose, "Of Gentlemen and Shepherds," p. 427.

28. Montrose, "Of Gentlemen and Shepherds," pp. 428–32; Patterson, pp. 39–46.

29. Patterson, p. 41.

30. For discussion of the cultural importance of the meal as a marker of "serviceable" authority in the Renaissance, see Michael Schoenfeldt, "'The Mysteries of Manners, Armes, and Arts': 'Inviting a Friend to Supper' and 'To Penshurst,'" in *"The Muses Common-Weale": Poetry and Politics in the Seventeenth Century*, ed. Claude J. Summers and Ted-Larry Pebworth (Columbia: Univ. of Missouri Press, 1988), pp. 62–79.

31. Stone, pp. 68, 72, 84.

32. The promise of increased wages for Corin recalls the 500 crowns Adam has saved under Sir Rowland (II.iii.38). Although Orlando goes on to extol Adam's virtue as "the constant service of the antique world, / When service sweat for duty, not for meed!" (lines 57–8), we see that dutiful service rightfully expects proper compensation.

33. Thomas Lodge, *Rosalynde*, in *As You Like It* (A New Variorum Edition), ed. Howard H. Furness (Philadelphia, 1890), p. 338; spelling slightly modernized.

34. Judy Z. Kronenfeld, "Social Rank and the Pastoral Ideals of As You Like It," *SQ* 29, 3 (Summer 1978): 333–48, 344.

35. Kronenfeld, pp. 345, 344.

36. Quoted in Montrose, "Of Gentlemen and Shepherds," p. 435.

37. Edmund Spenser, *The Shepheardes Calender*, "September" (lines 137–9), in *Poetical Works*, ed. J. C. Smith and E. de Selincourt (Oxford: Oxford Univ. Press, 1970), p. 453.

38. Montrose, "Of Gentlemen and Shepherds," pp. 435–6.

39. Montrose, "Of Gentlemen and Shepherds," pp. 438–44, 426, 431.

40. Montrose first makes this point in "'Eliza, Queene of shepheardes,' and the Pastoral of Power," *ELR* 10, 2 (Spring 1980): 153-82, 154.

41. Montrose, "Of Gentlemen and Shepherds," pp. 446–7.

42. Montrose, "Of Gentlemen and Shepherds," p. 427; for broader discussion, see Kevin Sharpe, *Politics and Ideas in Early Stuart England* (London: Pinter, 1989), esp. chaps. 1–2, 6, 10.

43. Quoted in Kronenfeld, p. 334.

44. Montrose, "Of Gentlemen and Shepherds," pp. 427, 432; my emphases.

45. For discussion of the promise of this kind of "rhetorical" criticism, see Liu, p. 756.

46. Michel Foucault, *The Archaeology of Knowledge*, trans. A. M. Sheridan-Smith (New York: Pantheon Books, 1972), p. 122.

PAUL ALPERS

What Is Pastoral? Mode, Genre, and Convention

Like pastoral romances, pastoral dramas are episodic, characterized by set pieces, relatively unmarked by the shapings and energies of plot. The pastoral source and the pastoral character of *As You Like It* explain its unusual dramaturgy, which has been noted by many critics:

> It is in the defectiveness of its action that *As You Like It* differs from the rest of the major comedies—in its dearth not only of big theatrical scenes but of events linked together by the logical intricacies of cause and effect.[51]
>
> *As You Like It* comes nearer in form to a discussion play or a symposium than any other of Shakespeare's comedies. Not only is the action punctuated by songs; there is much reporting of meetings and conversations, and the comparatively uneventful plot marks time while the actors talk.[52]

What seems puzzling and idiosyncratic, when we view the play as a comedy, appears explicable, even "normal," when we view it as a pastoral. Some of the scenes in Arden have a clear relation to the eclogues that are the foundation of pastoral romance and drama: the dialogue between Silvius and Corin about the pains of love (2.4, derived from a formal eclogue in Lodge); the exchange between Touchstone and Corin on the virtues of life in the court and the country (3.2); the scene between Silvius and Phebe (3.5), which Corin calls "a pageant truly play'd" between true love and scorn (3.4.52); and above all the songs, which, with one exception, are the occasion and centerpiece of separate scenes (2.5, 3.2, 5.3). Other scenes have a looser, but nonetheless real, relation to eclogues. When Rosalind persistently interrupts Celia's description of Orlando lying under a tree, in order to elaborate her own conceits on the descriptive details, Celia's impatient outburst "I would sing my song without a burthen" (3.2.247)—reveals the scene's descent from amoebean eclogues. A common eclogue-type, in which an older shepherd reproves a younger for the follies of love, lies behind Rosalind/Ganymede's first scene with Orlando, in which she attributes her antidote for love to "an old religious uncle of mine" (3.2.344). More broadly, the pastoral dramaturgy is seen in the fact that though there is a large cast of characters, one encounters them, as Harold Jenkins notes, "most often two at a time."[53]

A modal view of the dramaturgy of *As You Like It* implies not only that its scenes have a pastoral genealogy, but also that they retain a pastoral character. Many critics vindicate the play's pastoralism by connecting its variety of wit and its brilliant ease with the "golden world" imagined by the wrestler Charles and the atmosphere of the Forest of Arden. These critics usually acknowledge a certain tension between the play's critical energies and awarenesses and the idyllicism that is assumed to be of the essence of pastoral. Rosalie Colie, who was keenly aware of the generic presences in the play, says:

> *As You Like It*'s beautiful finish seems the greater achievement precisely because of the playwright's uncompromising insistence upon the problematical within pastoral thematics.... We are forced to attend to the tensions underlying even this most idealized of literary modes.[54]

There will always seem to be a conflict between Shakespearean tough-mindedness and pure pastoralism if we think that "the literary pastoral celebrates the glorious unrealities of the imagination," that "pastoral myths" offer "wish-fulfilling satisfactions," and that "the forest, then, shelters a counter-society, idyllic and playful, offering a model of possibility to the real world."[55] When the pastoral world is conceived this way, it is hard to regard it as the locale of critical wit and realistic perceptions, and hence difficult to connect the play's pastoralism with its self-consciousness and what Colie well calls its "perspectivism."

The play itself helps us understand the critical problem by offering us a choice of mottos. Critics most frequently take up the one first offered:

> They say he is already in the Forest of Arden, and a many merry men with him; and there they live like the old Robin Hood of England. They say many young gentlemen flock to him every day, and fleet the time carelessly, as they did in the golden world. (1.1.114–19)

After what we have seen of Oliver's treatment of Orlando, this speech indeed suggests "a countersociety, idyllic and playful." But it is a view from the court world, and there is something searching and impressive in Shakespeare's putting it in the mouth of the wrestler Charles. The paradox of the brutish character intuiting ease and freedom anticipates Caliban, and Charles's words have a certain pastoral authority. It is as if his own occupation at court—"low" and physical, utterly dependent yet providing an admired spectacle—gives him the capacity to see what his social superiors cannot. (We should remember that he arrives on the scene not to do Oliver's bidding but to warn him not to let Orlando wrestle that day.)

The play never denies the force of Charles's speech, but it adjusts our understanding of what it means to be "careless," i.e. without care:

> Now, my co-mates and brothers in exile,
> Hath not old custom made this life more sweet
> Than that of painted pomp? Are not these woods
> More free from peril than the envious court?
> Here feel we not the penalty of Adam
> The seasons' difference, as the icy fang
> And churlish chiding of the winter's wind,
> Which when it bites and blows upon my body
> Even till I shrink with cold, I smile and say,
> "This is no flattery: these are counsellors
> That feelingly persuade me what I am."
> Sweet are the uses of adversity,
> Which like the toad, ugly and venomous,
> Wears yet a precious jewel in his head;
> And this our life, exempt from public haunt,
> Finds tongues in trees, books in the running brooks,
> Sermons in stones, and good in every thing.
> (2.1.1–17)

These are the first words we hear in the Forest. What marks the place out is not idyllic nature but a way of life, for which the Duke can speak because he appears in the guise of—in our terminology, represents himself as—a forester, an inhabitant of the woods.[56] Hence he establishes his claims by rhetorical questions that are addressed to his "co-mates and brothers in exile" and that register a felt obviousness in values and a shared sense of life. This is a style very different from the pronouncements of a Prospero, who remains a monarch even in exile. The distinctiveness of the Duke's mode is even more striking in the sentence that follows his opening questions. The imagery of the winter's wind reminds us of *King Lear*, and the clinching line—"That feelingly persuade me what I am"—could well be imagined to come from that play, as if it incorporated into Lear's recognitions on the heath Gloucester's anguished "I see it feelingly" (4.4.149). What can make such a line so different in this context? Though it is said in the Duke's own person it is put at one remove from the present utterance, by being attributed to a characteristic scene. That scene is a pastoral encounter, between a nobleman, suspicious of flattery and used to being addressed by counsellors, and a natural force that is represented, in the phrase "churlish chiding," as a rustic interlocutor. The Duke has in effect imagined and internalized a pastoral of the type we know best from the Sixth Book of *The Faerie Queene*, where the knight Sir Calidore finds his blandishments and his gold resisted and reproved by the old shepherd Melibee. By the same token, the Duke's statement of self-knowledge is not, like Gloucester's, an utterance wrenched from experience, but is, in true pastoral fashion, made out to be the responsive iteration of something impressed upon him. Hence almost identical words can be pastoral rather than tragic in mode: they bear witness not to the individual's attempt to make sense of his own and others' suffering, but to a common condition acknowledged as obvious. In his response to the Duke's rhetorical poise, Amiens provides an alternative motto to the wrestler Charles's:

> I would not change it. Happy is your Grace,
> That can translate the stubbornness of fortune
> Into so quiet and so sweet a style.
>
> (2.1.18–20)

The claim, initiated by the double meaning of "translate," is that a style of speech is a style of life. The Duke has given an epigrammatic example in his final lines, where the translation of nature's lessons into apparently simple verbal patterns is seasoned by the wit that switches "tongues" and "books" from the natural objects to which they might be thought to belong and thus makes clear that, in pastoral, nature's meanings are uttered by man.

Amiens's praise of the Duke can be applied very widely in *As You Like It*: all the characters can be seen as dealing in a recognizable style of speech with what their lives and fortunes have imposed upon them. As so often, Touchstone gives his own formulation when he arrives in the Forest: "Ay, now am I in Arden, the more fool I. When I was at home, I was in a better place, but travellers must be content" (2.4.16–18). Commentators usually say that this disputes the "conventional" preference of country to court, but it is a thoroughly pastoral remark—less because it speaks of content (for it does so wryly, as if discontentedly) than because of the comic primness of "the more fool I," where Touchstone's self-mockery also contains the main claim for the Forest, that it enables its inhabitants to be themselves. Touchstone, of all the characters, shows us that a style of speech is a style of life, and it is this that explains why the dominance of wit and talk over action in *As You Like It* can be so satisfying. It is a pastoral phenomenon, for its ultimate model is the literary shepherd's translation of experience into song and the stylish exchanges we find in singing contests and other dialogic eclogues. But if most of the characters are from the court world and if the two characters Shakespeare added to *Rosalynde*, Touchstone and Jaques, seem resistant to Arden and critical of life in it, we need to explain how the modes of self-presentation in the play can be viewed as and assimilated to pastoral.

All the court figures in *As You Like It* can be seen as playing out Spenser's metaphor for himself as a pastoral poet: "Lo I the man, whose Muse whilome did makee, / As time her taught, in lowly Shepheards weeds" (*FQ* 1.Proem.1). It is by willingly stepping into the forester's garb that the Duke and his men accept their exile; Orlando, thus appareled, manages to stay in his suit (the pun is Rosalind's, 4.1.87); Rosalind's guise, first adopted out of necessity, allows her the freedom to play out her courtship with Orlando, and Celia's tests the integrity of Oliver's love. Surrounding these courtly pastoralists are characters in whom we see the extremes of naive and masked self-presentation. Though the natives of Arden are conspicuously stylized and associated with literary roles—as if to insure in the audience's pastoralism as much critical awareness as in the Duke's or Rosalind's—each is what he or she seems to be, in dress and in rhetoric. Touchstone and Jaques, the two characters who have not changed costume, are at the other extreme. Both are caught up in, and indeed strikingly exemplify, the problematic of pastoral masking: they self-consciously play out and test for us the relation between one's dress, one's style of speech, and one's adopted role. Their mockery and realism thus have no privileged or even separate grounds. They are as much part of life in Arden as anyone else, willy-nilly involved in the play of styles of speech.[57]

The vitality and sufficiency of roles and gestures gives *As You Like It* its characteristic tone. Not surprisingly it is Touchstone who defines this element of the play, when he teases us into looking for a statable attitude towards the pastoral world:

> Truly, shepherd, in respect of itself, it is a good life; but in respect that it is a shepherd's life, it is naught. In respect that it is solitary, I like it very well; but in respect that it is private, it is a very vild life. Now in respect it is in the fields, it pleaseth me well; but in respect it is not in the court, it is tedious. (3.2.13–19)

"Through the apparent nonsense of his witty clown," Poggioli says,

> Shakespeare seems to reply to three important questions. The first is whether he values or scorns the pastoral ideal. The second is whether this comedy is a pastoral play. The third is whether it reaffirms or denies the traditional poetics of the pastoral. The equivocal answer that the clown gives to all three on behalf of the poet amounts to an echo of the comedy's title: as you like it.[58]

This is well said, but whether truly or not, let the forest judge. Poggioli calls the play's pastoralism equivocal, because for him true pastoral is irredeemably committed to idyllic impulses and innocent needs. But the self-pleasuring performance he relishes is itself pastoral in character, the more so as Touchstone's speech, with its sophisticated redundancies, prompts the plain rustic redundancies—e.g. "the property of rain is to wet and fire to burn"—with which Corin stands up to him. Colie, for all her Schillerian assumptions, understands better the literary genealogy of *As You Like It* and therefore its modal character:

> Perspectivism is built into this play; it is the play's method, but it relies on traditional implications within the mode, by developing an inherent dialectical tendency in pastoral eclogues to an astonishing degree. Many contests question the traditions which ultimately they endorse.[59]

The role playing, the welcoming of one's situation, the satisfactions of wit and playfulness, and thus the play's pastoralism all come together in the figure of Rosalind. No one doubts her centrality to the play. It is not simply that her impulsiveness, wit, and strength of feeling can be seen to associate her with characters as different as Silvius (for romantic love), Phebe (for coyness and literalizing wit), and Touchstone (for mocking realism and willingness to perform). Her character seems so to dominate the play that one critic compares her in this respect to Hamlet.[60] The finest of the older essays argues that the play's "two polar attitudes" towards love, "romantic participation" and "humorous detachment," "meet and are reconciled in Rosalind's personality": "she possesses as an attribute of character the power of combining wholehearted feeling and undistorted judgment which gives the play its value."[61] One understands the reasons for such statements, but critics in this vein tend to confuse the authority of Rosalind's presence with dramatic and moral autonomy. As she herself recognizes—"Alas the day! What shall I do with my doublet and hose?" (3.2.219–20)—the disguise which gives her freedom is also her dilemma. She is thus in the situation of all the other pastoralists: constrained to adopt a costume, she learns to play a role that expresses her needs and nature more truly than would have been possible in the "workaday world."

Taking Rosalind at her word, critics say she administers physic to the sentimentally romantic Orlando, but the scene in which she undertakes his cure does not put them in the relation suggested by this metaphor. It is the last of the brilliant encounters in Act 3, scene 2 (Corin–Touchstone, Touchstone–Rosalind with the former's mocking verses, Celia–Rosalind, Jaques–Orlando), all of which display responsive wit and give the audience a sense of a pleasurable standoff. Rosalind prepares to meet Orlando by saying, "I will speak to him like a saucy lackey, and under that habit play the knave with him."[62] Their encounter is no less marked than the earlier ones by conscious performance and appreciative response. Orlando is not mooning about but is clearly charmed by this youth, willing to give rein to his saucy wit. Rosalind, whose vulnerability has been evident in the preceding dialogues, exercises this wit not to cure Orlando but to elicit declarations of his love and find ways of safely expressing her own: in her own way, to adapt the Duke's words of Touchstone (5.4.106), she uses her wit like a stalking horse. The structure of Rosalind's performance comes out in the exchange that follows her telling Orlando he does not look like a lover:

Orlando. Fair youth, I would I could make thee believe I love.
Rosalind. Me believe it? You may as soon make her that you
love believe it, which I warrant she is apter to do than
to confess she does.

(3.2.385–89)

This is absolutely transparent to us—it states exactly what is true of Rosalind at the moment she utters it—but quite opaque to Orlando, not simply because Rosalind is in disguise but because the statement is rhetorically disguised by the role she has adopted of mocking women.

At such moments, when acting in disguise enables her to express her love, Rosalind plays out the double meaning of Touchstone's motto for a poetics of pastoral: "The truest poetry is the most feigning" (3.3.19). But all her turns, gestures, and performances are versions of pastoral. The great set piece on dying for love (4.1.94–108)—perhaps too often regarded as the ultimate wisdom on its subject—is pastoral not only by virtue of being a performance under a mask (a motif charmingly doubled in its opening phrase, "No, faith, die by attorney"), but also because, in its youthful breeziness, it yields to the pleasures of affection and performance. It is followed by an equally splendid pastoral gesture:

> *Rosalind.* Men have died from time to time, and worms have eaten them, but not for love.
>
> *Orlando.* I would not have my right Rosalind of this mind, for I protest her frown might kill me.
>
> *Rosalind.* By this hand, it will not kill a fly.
>
> (4.1.106–11)

This both mocks Orlando's hyperbole and makes a pledge from an equally extravagant love. Its pastoralism comes from the apparent wholeheartedness and simplicity of its rhetorical form, whether we take it to be oath, promise, or asseveration. At such a moment, one can imagine that nothing more need be said, and we can understand why this scene of mock-wooing feels, to audiences and readers, like the thing itself.

But even though Rosalind can express her desires by her pretense, the play cannot leave her or us satisfied with the pastoral presence we have described. "Wedlock would be nibbling," Touchstone says (3.3.81), and Orlando will soon announce, "I can live no longer by thinking" (5.2.50). Precisely to the extent that the play of these middle acts is self-sufficient and satisfying, there will be an awkwardness felt about bringing the comedy to a close. In the concluding scenes, Barber says, "the treatment becomes more and more frankly artificial," and he speaks of it apologetically: "The lack of realism in presentation does not matter, because a much more important realism in our attitude towards the substance of romance has been achieved already by the action of the comedy."[63] There is unquestionably a problem here, as G. K. Hunter points out:

> The central episodes ... show a series of contrasting attitudes to love and to the country; these are developed through the meaningful play of Rosalind ... and Orlando. This play is a uniquely powerful way of presenting the richness and complexity

> of a relationship; but it requires a suspension of place, time and intrigue, and this becalming of the play makes it difficult to steer it to a satisfactory conclusion.[64]

Everything we have seen about pastoral as a mode suggests that it minimizes the energies of plot, and it is therefore not surprising that the pastoralism of *As You Like It* gives rise to this dilemma. What our account has not yet provided for (...) is the pastoral solution Shakespeare found.

PASTORAL CONVENTION

(...) Let us return to *As You Like It*, which we left as a play in need of a conclusion from the wrestler Charles's evocation of the young gentlemen who flock to the exiled Duke, to Jaques's discordant nonsense word "ducdame"—"a Greek invocation, to call fools into a circle" (2.5.59)—to the Duke's feast, the various pastoral encounters, and Rosalind's appointments with Orlando, until Hymen makes "earthly things ... atone [=at one] together" (5.4.109–10), the thematics of convening bear the burden of the play. But is it thereby a "conventional" pastoral? There are a number of reasons one might think it is not; one is the transformation of Montanus, in *Rosalynde*, into Silvius. Montanus is the poet of Lodge's Arden: his complaints greet Rosalind and Alinda when they come to the forest and it is he who performs for the exiled King Gerismond before the weddings that conclude the romance. One might say from Silvius's mode of speech that the gods have made him poetical, but he never performs a song or writes a poem, and therefore no special status is granted to his expression of his passion. Quite the contrary, the cool breeze of Rosalind's wit blows over him and Phebe and is one of the ways the tone of the play is established. C. L. Barber's comment suggests the way it seems to treat this pair of lovers and, with them, pastoral convention:

> Rosalind is not committed to the conventional language and attitudes of love, loaded as these inevitably are with sentimentality. Silvius and Phebe are her foils in this: they take their conventional language and their conventional feelings perfectly seriously, with nothing in reserve. As a result they seem naive and rather trivial.[60]

This may be enough to say about Silvius and Phebe as characters, but they play rather important roles in the play's patterns and dynamics. In Act II, in which all the characters except Oliver are assembled in the Forest of

Arden, it is Silvius; and Silvius alone, who lets us know that this is a locale in which love can flourish. When Rosalind and Celia arrive in the forest, weary in body and spirits, they come upon Silvius protesting the extremity of his love to Corin. In Lodge, this exchange is a formal eclogue, with Corydon reproving love in the usual manner of old shepherds. Shakespeare's Corin is quite sympathetic to Silvius's plight, but his age leaves him insufficiently attuned to his young friend's present state. Silvius therefore improvises a set speech—not a song and not a composition but half-way to being a poem and with a pseudo-refrain ("Thou hast not lov'd")—and exits calling "O Phebe, Phebe, Phebe!" Rosalind reacts precisely in the "conventional" way:

> Alas, poor shepherd, searching of thy wound,
> I have by hard adventure found mine own.
> (2.4.44–45)

Touchstone steps forward with a burlesque version of what Silvius calls the follies that love does "make thee run into," and he concludes with an aphorism that critics often treat as a motto of the play: "We that are true lovers run into strange capers; but as all is mortal in nature, so is all nature in love mortal in folly" (2.4.54–56). Rosalind endorses the sentiment—"Thou speak'st wiser than thou art ware of"—but not the tone, as she proves by a final gesture in Silvius's vein:

> Jove, Jove! this shepherd's passion
> Is much upon my fashion.
> (2.4.60–61)

The kinship Rosalind first feels with Silvius does not cease to be an element in the drama, even in the scene in which she mocks him and Phebe. Barber gives an account of the scene as we tend to remember it:

> All-suffering Silvius and his tyrannical little Phebe are a bit of Lodge's version taken over, outwardly intact, and set in a wholly new perspective. A "courting eglogue" between them, in the mode of Lodge, is exhibited almost as a formal spectacle, with Corin for presenter and Rosalind and Celia for audience. It is annou ced as
>
> a pageant truly play'd
> Between the pale complexion of true love
> And the red glow of scorn and proud disdain.
> (3.4.53–5)

> What we then watch is played "truly"—according to the best current convention.... Shakespeare lets us feel the charm of the form; but then he has Rosalind break up their pretty pageant.[61]

What Barber omits is that Rosalind has an investment in this scene even before she comes to it. Corin comes upon her when she is impatient at Orlando's failure to keep his appointed hour and Celia is teasing her for her impulsive shifts of mood. When Corin proposes to show the "pageant truly played," Rosalind replies with alacrity, in the final speech of the scene:

> O, come, let us remove,
> The sight of lovers feedeth those in love.
> Bring us to this sight, and you shall say
> I'll prove a busy actor in their play.
>
> (3.4.56–59)

In effect, she would rather watch Silvius and Phebe than be subjected to Celia's teasing. The last line is prophetic, but she cannot, at this point, know or intend what it proves to mean. Her meaning here must be that she will somehow enter into the love sports of Arden: the shepherd's passion is still much upon her fashion.

Rosalind is thus not a mere spectator of the scene between Silvius and Phebe, and the issue is therefore not whether she responds conventionally, on the one hand, or with independent wit on the other. Shakespeare has brought her to the scene by dramatizing the conventional response to the lover—the sense of sharing his plight—and her response to what she sees and hears is an equally dramatic response to the scornful mistress.

> Why, what means this? why do you look on me?
> I see no more in you than in the ordinary
> Of nature's sale-work. 'Od's my little life,
> I think she means to tangle my eyes too!
> No, faith, proud mistress, hope not after it.
> 'Tis not your inky brows, your black silk hair,
> Your bugle eyeballs, nor your cheek of cream
> That can entame my spirits to your worship.
> You foolish shepherd, wherefore do you follow her,
> Like foggy south, puffing with wind and rain?
> You are a thousand times a properer man
> Than she a woman. 'Tis such fools as you
> That makes the world full of ill-favor'd children.
>
> (3.5.41–53)

Rosalind's vehemence and impatience reveal something other than an impartial supervising intelligence.[62] Her mockery responds dramatically to Phebe's scorn of Silvius, in the most prominent speech in their pageant of love:

> 'Tis pretty, sure, and very probable
> That eyes, that are the frail'st and softest things,
> Who shut their coward gates on atomies,
> Should be called tyrants, butchers, murtherers!
> Now I do frown on thee with all my heart,
> And if mine eyes can wound, now let them kill thee.
> Now counterfeit to swound; why, now fall down,
> Or if thou canst not, O, for shame, for shame,
> Lie not, to say mine eyes are murtherers!
> (3.5.11–19)

Phebe mocks the lover's extravagance by pretending to take his claims literally. This makes her rather less dignified and attractive than her prototype in Lodge, but it also makes her a good deal more like Rosalind herself, who will deal with Orlando in a similar vein in the next scene. Phebe's refusal to credit hyperboles is exactly the weapon that Rosalind will turn on her. Phebe thus appears to be a pastoral simplification of one side of Rosalind, just as Silvius is of another. If he represents her capacity for romantic extravagance, she represents her capacity for mocking her lover and the need she seems to feel, at this point in the play, for controlling him and protecting herself from fully acknowledging her feelings.[63] Once smitten, Phebe fills out another aspect of Rosalind's pastoralism, her sense of love's imperatives. Phebe's first utterance, after Ganymede/Rosalind leaves, is:

> Dead shepherd, now I find thy saw of might,
> "Who ever loved that loved not at first sight?"
> (3.5.81–82)

This is pure pastoral convention. The words of the departed shepherd "accord to the passions of the hearer," and they are true of all the lovers in Arden—Rosalind and Orlando, Silvius and Phebe, Celia and Oliver, and, for all we know, Touchstone and Audrey.

Rosalind's association with Silvius and Phebe is only the most explicit sign that she plays a pastoral role in the middle acts of *As You Like It*. Her vitality, wit, and sense of freedom are such that critics understandably treat her as the controlling intelligence in the play. But her freedom and control are bound up with her disguise and its constraints. She discovers the depths of her own love and Orlando's open-eyed persistence in his, because she can mock, tease, and openly show her hand to everyone except the person to whom she will eventually have to. The question, for her and for the play, is how the revelation of herself will come about. The problem is neatly presented by an implication Helen Gardner draws from her fine observation that "the center of *As You Like It*" is the "discovery of truth by feigning and of what is wisdom and what folly by debate." Thinking along these lines, Gardner says, "By playing with [Orlando] in the disguise of a boy, [Rosalind] discovers when she can play no more."[64] This represents Rosalind as the play's controlling intelligence, able to act on what the scenes in the Forest of Arden make known.[65] But Rosalind's playing with Orlando does not lead her to discover the limits of play. On the contrary, at the end of the mock-wooing scene (4.1), it is not at all clear that she is not ready to play through several more such scenes; this is presumably what she has in mind when she sends Orlando off with a fine display of teasing and fooling and makes him promise to return in two hours. Rosalind recognizes that she can play no more only because of events that are beyond her control.

The resolution of the play is precipitated by Oliver's arrival in the forest and Orlando's being wounded by the lioness from whom he rescues his brother. Rosalind—who has once more been impatient with her lover and who has been working off some of her energy by teasing Silvius about Phebe's love poem to her—swoons when she sees the bloody handkerchief that explains why Orlando failed to come (4.3.156). At the level of plot, there is really nothing in this episode that should force Rosalind to remove her disguise, but there is a great change in her strength relative to world. However she is costumed, she has revealed herself by swooning, and the first indication of this turning point is a motif that associates her with Silvius and Phebe. "Now counterfeit to swound," Phebe had challenged Silvius, and Rosalind attempts to disguise her fainting by claiming, again and again, that it was "counterfeit" (4.3.167–82). In the scenes with Orlando, Rosalind had been able to express her own love by seeming to mock his: the play's truest poetry was indeed the most feigning. But when she swoons, she can no longer pretend that she and her prose are in control: she cannot successfully feign that her body's expression of faining was mere feigning.

It looks as if the poise of pastoral masking is to be disrupted and caught up in the larger forces of romance and dramatic comedy. But from this point on, the workings of the play, whatever their sources in literary tradition, can be described as making good the claims of pastoral convention. The consequences of Rosalind's swoon are revealed when she next meets Orlando, and they play with another of Silvius and Phebe's motifs:

Ros.	O my dear Orlando, how it grieves me to see thee wear thy heart in a scarf!
Orl.	It is my arm.
Ros.	I thought thy heart had been wounded with the claws of a lion.
Orl.	Wounded it is, but with the eyes of a lady.

(5.2.19–24)

It is as if Rosalind intended him to produce this sentiment. Certainly she is no longer in a position to mock such an expression of devotion but can only return to her feeble pretence: "Did your brother tell you how I counterfeited to sound when he show'd me your handkercher?" (5.2.25–26). "Ay, and greater wonders than that," says Orlando, whereupon Rosalind, taking his meaning and at last having something on which to exercise her wit and energy, gives a playfully rhetorical account of the sudden love of Oliver and Celia. This little performance prompts a decisive action. Orlando is moved by the impending wedding to express impatience for his ("I can live no longer by thinking"), and Rosalind, as if to acknowledge that her hand is forced, concocts her story of the magician uncle as the guise under which she can reveal herself. This conjuncture of feigning and faining is one way in which the play works the magic it thematizes here. All it really takes to bring everything round is for Rosalind to reveal herself, but the various modes of "holiday humor"—wit, fancy, imaginative staging—make us half believe that their charm is an exercise of charms.

So far as plot goes, the scene could end with Ganymede's promise to bring Rosalind to Orlando, but its poetry is still to be played out. Silvius and Phebe enter, and when Rosalind tries to turn away the importunate shepherdess by telling her to love her "faithful shepherd," the two native lovers set in motion a little eclogue:

Phebe.	Good shepherd, tell this youth what 'tis to love.
Silvius.	It is to be all made of sighs and tears, And so am I for Phebe.
Phebe.	And I for Ganymed.
Orl.	And I for Rosalind.
Ros.	And I for no woman.

(5.2.83–88)

The claims of pastoral convention are not to be resisted. Rosalind's "And I for no woman" may protect her "cover"—it ostensibly denies that she is caught up in this round of love, while leaving open the meaning that she loves a man—but she cannot avoid the effect given here, that she too is chiming in. Her prose wit has one more gesture left to it. Phebe initiates the fourth and last round of the quartet:

> *Phebe.* If this be so, why blame you me to love you?
> *Silvius.* If this be so, why blame you me to love you?
> *Orl.* If this be so, why blame you me to love you?
> *Ros.* Why do you speak too, "Why blame you me to love you?"
> *Orl.* To her that is not here, nor doth not hear.
> (5.2.103–7)

This is a pretty enough answer by Orlando and could keep the music going, but it is too much for Rosalind, who cuts it all off with her "Pray you, no more of this, 'tis like the howling of Irish wolves against the moon." This is usually taken to be simply a healthy expression of good sense. But this comparison was proverbial for a vain desire,[66] so it suggests Rosalind's impatience not only with her fellow lovers but with her own disguise. As if feeling its force, she concludes the scene by prosing the conventionality of the quartet in which she has just participated:

> To-morrow meet me all together. I will marry you [Phebe], if ever I marry woman, and I'll be married to-morrow. I will satisfy you [Orlando], if ever I satisfied man, and you shall be married to-morrow. I will content you [Silvius], if what pleases you contents you, and you shall be married to-morrow. As you love Rosalind, meet. As you love Phebe, meet. And as I love no woman, I'll meet. (5.2.112–20)

The parallel phrases and the motif of meeting lay the ground for the final scene, in which Rosalind, promising "to make all this matter ever" (5.4.18), brings in Hymen, who unites the couples and leads them in a wedding dance.

Ending with marriages is hardly specific to pastoral and may have nothing to do with it. But in this play, as the characters come together in the guise of shepherds and foresters, pastoral conventions carry the comic dramaturgy and concerns. After the lovers' quartet there is a brief scene (5.3), a kind of prologue to the long finale, in which two pages—stock figures from Lyly's pastoral comedies but coming from nowhere in this play—sit down with Touchstone and Audrey to sing "it was a lover and his lass." The scene consists almost entirely of the song, whose dramaturgic effect is registered at its conclusion. Touchstone, predictably trying to trip up his companions, says: "Truly, young gentlemen, though there was no great matter in the ditty, yet the note was very untuneable." To which one page replies, truly and with perfect sufficiency: "You are deceiv'd, sir. We kept time, we lost not our time" (5.3.34–38). They did keep time in their singing, and it was not a waste of time. The song—the most innocent and idyllic in the play, the one springtime song in a play which usually sings of "winter and rough weather"—thus assimilates to its self-sufficient pleasures and to its pastoral moral ("And therefore take the present time") the various paces of Time about which Rosalind/Ganymede first displayed her witty wares to her charmed lover (3.2.302–33).

The final scene confirms the confluence of pastoral and comedy by remaining in the Forest of Arden to celebrate the coming together of its various inhabitants. Commentators, aware that most of the characters are courtiers, associate *As You Like It* with other plays in which a sojourn in a "green world" enables a return to court.[67] But where *Love's Labour's Lost*, *A Midsummer Night's Dream*, *The Winter's Tale*, and *The Tempest* bring the characters back to court or show them on the point of departure, *As You Like It* is content to finish its business in the woods. The Duke, no longer exiled, nevertheless says:

> First, in this forest let us do those ends
> That here were well begun and well begot;
> And after, every of this happy number,
> That have endur'd shrewd days and nights with us,
> Shall share the good of our returned fortune,
> According to the measure of their states.
> Mean time, forget this new-fall'n dignity,
> And fall into our rustic revelry.
> Play, music, and you brides and bridegrooms all,
> With measure heap'd in joy, to th' measures fall.
> (5.4.170–79)

"The measure of their states" indicates the differentiated and hierarchical social order that awaits them all. But for the moment society's measure is turned into the "dancing measures" in which only Duke Frederick and Jaques will not take part. The pastoral idea of space set apart for song meets and is adequate to what the comic theater provides.

As You Like It can end both conventionally and satisfactorily, because the play throughout is attentive to the motives and powers of pastoral convention. Just as *Lycidas* presses certain traditional usages to their limits, so *As You Like It* tests by dramatizing and validates in its dramaturgy two practices that are at the heart of pastoral—responsive rivalry in performance of set pieces and the translation of experience into song and other forms of verbal finish and display. Amiens's praise of the Duke—

> happy is your Grace,
> That can translate the stubbornness of fortune
> Into so quiet and so sweet a style—
>
> (2.1.18–20)

could be said of a hermit and perhaps of a stoic. One can also imagine the virtuous spirit controlling its fortunes in other styles than the sweet and quiet. The Duke's style is pastoral, because it is shared, held in common on the basis of a recognized strength relative to his world. This understanding of pastoral is made explicit at the end of Act 2, when Orlando breaks into the Duke's company and demands food. His wonder that "in this desert inaccessible" there is gentleness where he expected savagery makes him put up his sword and turn his demand into a plea—"If ever you have look'd on better days, / If ever been where bells have knoll'd to church," etc.—to which the Duke, enacting the idea of welcome and a common style, answers as responsively as if this were a formal eclogue (2.7.113–26). Then while Orlando goes to get Adam, the Duke says:

> Thou seest we are not all alone unhappy:
> This wide and universal theater
> Presents more woeful pageants than the scene
> Wherein we play in.
>
> (2.7.136–39)

This sense of a shared plight counts as pastoral because its speaker stands by his experience and awareness but does not presume on its centrality. He can imagine that his exile is a pageant merely played, like the scene between Silvius and Phebe. Hence he can display the quiet and sweet style of his life by having Amiens conclude this act with a musical version of the speech with which he himself began it—the song, "Blow, blow, thou winter wind."

But between the Duke's appeal to his fellows and Amiens's song comes Jaques's "All the world's a stage," which defiantly picks up the Duke's metaphor. The speech challenges and, so far as Jaques himself is concerned, denies the idea that rivaling performances bring foresters together. More broadly, it raises the question—played out by Touchstone and Rosalind, as well as by Jaques—of whether pastoral conventions can stand up to critical wit. In a sense, we have been arguing all along that they can, but we can conclude with a representative moment of pastoral convention and its testing. The first song we hear in Arden also engages an element of the Duke's speech, but attunes an experience less stubborn than the human ingratitude at the center of "Blow, blow thou winter wind":

> Under the greenwood tree
> Who loves to lie with me,
> And turn his merry note
> Unto the sweet bird's throat,
> Come hither, come hither, come hither!
> Here shall he see
> No enemy
> But winter and rough weather.
> (2.5.1–8)

The exclusive *huc ades* of the lover's pastoral appeal—"Come live with me and be my love"—here becomes a general invitation. The song beautifully plays out the idea of pastoral convention by making it impossible to tell whether the represented dweller in the greenwood is the singer or the companion invited to join him. But his present companion—and here again we see Shakespeare giving a more sharply dramatic form to something potential in pastoral practices—is Jaques, whose responsive song is a parody of this invitation:

> If it do come to pass
> That any man turn ass,
> Leaving his wealth and ease
> A stubborn will to please,
> Ducdame, ducdame, ducdame!
> Here shall he see
> Gross fools as he,
> And if he will come to me.
> (2.5.50–57)

This mockery ignores that what has brought the courtiers to Arden is not willfulness but a pastoral choice—free but within imposed limits or necessities. (This may be true of all "free" choices, hence the representativeness of pastoral; but pastoral choosers are aware of the constraints on them, hence the distinctness of the mode.) Jaques then acts out his defiance of pastoral convention by explaining "ducdame" as "a Greek invocation, to call fools into a circle."

So be it, as you like it. What is splendid about the play is that its lovers, its actors, its audience can accept this motto for themselves. *As You Like It* continually moves to attune what is discordant or dissonant, thus taking up a pastoral endeavor we have already observed in Sidney's double sestina and in *Lycidas*, with its hearing and absorbing of sterner pastoral voices. The attuning of discord is most direct in the woodland songs, in the last of which, the song of the deer, the foresters willingly "bear the burden," in the musical and physical sense both of the horns which they bring home as a trophy and of their symbolic import, about which Rosalind has just been teasing Orlando (4.1.160–76).[68] Dissonant utterance occurs throughout the play, and not only in the speeches of Touchstone and Jaques. It is at the heart of the pastoral kinship between Rosalind and Phebe. Phebe falls in love with Ganymede not, as in Lodge, because of his/her pretty face, but because of her mocking, irritated voice:

> Sweet youth, I pray you chide a year together,
> I had rather hear you chide than this man woo.
> (3.5.64–65)

The word Phebe settles on here is more frequent in this play than in any other of Shakespeare's. It engages a motif first sounded when the Duke praises "the churlish chiding of the winter's wind" and that later focuses his and Orlando's distancing themselves from Jaques. The Duke's sense that harsh sounds can be sweet is matched by the way various lovers, from Rosalind to Touchstone, mingle mockery and affection. But it is Phebe the chider who brings this word into the love plot, and it is Rosalind who puts it on full pastoral display. When Silvius brings Phebe's letter to her, Rosalind rags him by pretending that Phebe's conventional little love poem is "railing." Phebe's word sounds both within her poem—"Whiles you chid me, I did love"—and in Silvius's response when Rosalind has read it: "Call you this chiding?" "Alas, poor shepherd!" Celia says, as well she might (4.3.40–65). This playful juggling of harsh and sweet can be seen as fooling that liberates, as a salutary abrasiveness (best displayed here in Rosalind's wonderful remark, "She Phebes me" [4.3.39]), and as a working off of social and erotic energies: Rosalind's abuse has something to do with Silvius's arriving just when she was impatiently expecting Orlando. All these elements are again apparent in the pastoralism of the final scene. Touchstone's set piece on dueling and the virtues of "if"—Shakespeare's substitution for the love complaints with which Lodge's Montanus entertains King Gerismond—shows how verbal performance can disarm rivalry. As even Touchstone "press[es] in here ... amongst the country copulatives," Hymen draws the fools of love into a circle. Even Jaques, who mockingly hails "the couples coming to the ark" at the beginning of the scene, makes his exit by a ritual farewell that, with its final rhyme on "dancing measures," is as close as he can come to pastoral song.[69]

This account of the pastoralism of *As You Like It* should, like the play itself, have an epilogue. We have continually spoken of pastoral expression as due to and reflecting felt limitations, and we have spoken of pastoral conventions as practices that bring "shepherds" together after a separation or loss. What happens in the Forest of Arden is certainly initiated by the courtiers' loss of the world in which they belong, but the play is so assured and liberating that by its end we may simply take the world of Arden to be the world itself. *As You Like It* is usually thought to be one of the supreme achievements of Shakespearean comedy. On the other hand, even its most fervent admirers, its truest believers, have often felt the need to defend or explain away elements of the play, like the supposed unreality of the pastoral world, the "fairy-tale" nature of its plot devices, and the artificial character of its ending.[70] However strongly such reservations were felt in older criticism, they have been replaced by reservations grounded in sociohistorical observations. Recent studies emphasize that the world of the play is hierarchical and that it is in the final analysis dominated by men. The finest of these essays—which by no means intends to debunk the play, only to understand the conditions of its accomplishment—observes that "if *As You Like It* is a vehicle for Rosalind's exuberance, it is also a structure for her containment," and adds: "Several generations of critics—most of them men, and quite infatuated with Rosalind themselves—have stressed the exuberance and ignored the containment."[71] It is certainly the case that Celia says not a word once she is engaged to Oliver,[72] and that Rosalind's taking off her disguise, which we have treated as the "purpose" of the play, means that she is handed over to the Duke as a daughter and to Orlando as a wife. It is altogether an odd play—robust and liberating, and at the same time requiring a certain delicacy in treatment. Too great an insistence on social hierarchy or "patriarchal structures" seems to ignore the character of the play, while avoiding these matters would seem to miss some of the play's own lessons of critical self-awareness. What the title's wry permissiveness suggests is Shakespeare's own pastoral self-awareness, the sense of the play's limits he displayed by keeping his foresters in Arden and not following the ending of *Rosalynde*, in which there is a decisive return to the world of wars and kingdoms. Critics have often felt the connections of this play with *Hamlet*, through Jaques, and through various motifs and locutions, with *King Lear*. Presumably, the Duke and his company return to court better individually and as a society. But had Shakespeare actually brought them home, he might have set them on the road to the tragedies.

Notes

51. Harold Jenkins, "As You Lake It," in *Pastoral and Romance: Modern Essays in Criticism*, ed. Eleanor Terry Lincoln (Englewood Cliffs: Prentice-Hall, 1969), 103. This essay first appeared in *Shakespeare Survey VIII*, ed. Harold Jenkins (Cambridge: Cambridge University Press, 1955), 40–51.

52. Leo Salingar, *Shakespeare and the Traditions of Comedy* (Cambridge: Cambridge University Press, 1974), 293.

53. Jenkins, 117.

54. Rosalie L. Colie, *Shakespeare's Living Art* (Princeton: Princeton University Press, 1974), 261.

55. Ibid., 249, 250, 261.

56. Cf. the stage direction of 2.1: "Enter Duke Senior, Amiens, and two or three Lords, like "foresters."

57. Edwin Greenlaw long ago argued that Jaques derives from the melancholy solitaries of pastoral romance, like Sannazaro's Sincero, Sidney's Philisides, and Spenser's Colin Clout. "Shakespeare's Pastorals," *Studies in Philology* 13 (1916): 122–54; reprinted in *Pastoral and Romance*, ed. Lincoln; see esp. 88–92.

58. Renato Poggioli, *The Oaten Flute* (Cambridge, MA: Harvard University Press, 1975), 39.

59. Colie, 256.

60. Anne Barton, Introduction to *As You Like It*, in *The Riverside Shakespeare*, 366.

61. C. L. Barber, *Shakespeare's Festive Comedy* (Princeton: Princeton University Press, 1959), 233.

62. 3.2.295–7. The role Rosalind proposes to play is a standard one in Lyly's pastoral comedies.

63. Barber, 236.

64. G. K. Hunter, *William Shakespeare: The Love Comedies* (London: Longmans Green, 1962), 39.

Notes for Pastoral Convention

60. *Shakespeare's Festive Comedy* (Princeton: Princeton University Press, 1959), 233–34.

61. Ibid., 230.

62. Cf. Barber's remark that "she reminds them that they are nature's creatures, and that love's poses are contradicted by too absolute a cultivation of romantic liking or loathing" (230). Similarly, Thomas McFarland views her scoffing wit as proper medicine for the unhealthy emotions of not only Silvius and Phebe but Orlando. Shakespeare's Pastoral Comedy (Chapel Hill: University of North Carolina Press, 1972), 114–17.

63. Cf. Rosalie L. Colie, *Shakespeare's Living Art* (Princeton: Princeton University Press, 1974), 255: "Ganymede assumes with his disguise ... one proper pastoral love-attitude, that conventionally assigned the shepherdess, of coolness to the lover."

64. Helen Gardner, "*As You Like It*," in *As You Like It*, ed. Albert Gilman (New York: Signet, 1963), 225; originally in *More Talking of Shakespeare*, ed. John Garrett (London: Longmans, 1959).

65. For a more up-to-date account of Rosalind as in control of herself and the play, see Barbara J. Bono, "Mixed Gender, Mixed Genre in Shakespeare's *As You Like It*," in Barbara Kiefer Lewalski, ed., *Renaissance Genres* (Harvard English Studies 14) (Cambridge: Harvard University Press, 1986), 203–4.

66. In *Rosalynde*, Rosalind/Ganymede uses the comparison to dissuade Montanus from

loving Phebe. See *Narrative and Dramatic Sources of Shakespeare*, ed. Geoffrey Bullough, vol. 2 (New York: Columbia University Press, 1963): 242. In her Arden edition of *As You Like It* (London: Methuen, 1975), Agnes Latham notes that "dogs or wolves howling at full moon were a proverbial image of collective clamour." In addition to her references, cf. Robert Greene's pastoral romance *Menaphon*, ed. G. B. Harrison (Oxford, 1927), 61, and Michael Drayton, *The Shepheards Garland* 7.29–30.

67. See the comments of Mary Lascelles and John Wain quoted in The New Variorum edition of *As You Like It*, ed. Richard Knowles (New York: The Modern Language Association, 1977), 524, 526.

68. Cf. J. C. Scaliger, *Poetices* 1.4: "The contestants [in the original pastoral singing contests] were also crowned, and we even read of their wearing the horns of deer" (Padelford [chap. 1, n. 15], 26).

69. Anne Barton comments on Jaques's new character in the ending, in the context of a discussion of the way *As You Like It* attunes its discords. "*As You Like It* and *Twelfth Night*: Shakespeare's Sense of an Ending," in *Shakespearian Comedy* (Stratford-Upon-Avon Studies 14), ed. Malcolm Bradbury and David Palmer (London: Edward Arnold, 1972), 166.

70. Barton (171) gives a full account, along traditional lines, of the reservations that attend and are dealt with by the ending.

71. Louis Adrian Montrose, "The Place of a Brother in *As You Like It*: Social Process and Comic Form," *Shakespeare Quarterly* 32 (1981): 52.

72. As pointed out by Peter Erickson, *Patriarchal Structures in Shakespeare's Drama* (Berkeley & Los Angeles: University of California Press, 1985), 36.

HAROLD BLOOM

As You Like It: *The Invention of the Human*

> The popularity of Rosalind is due to three main causes. First, she only speaks blank verse for a few minutes. Second, she only wears a skirt for a few minutes (and the dismal effect of the change at the end to the wedding dress ought to convert the stupidest champion of petticoats to rational dress). Third, she makes love to the man instead of waiting for the man to make love to her—a piece of natural history which has kept Shakespeare's heroines alive, whilst generations of properly governessed young ladies, taught to say "No" three times at least, have miserably perished.

That is George Bernard Shaw (hardly a Bardolator!) in 1896, when the reign of Rosalind was at one of its heights. When I saw Katharine Hepburn triumphing as Rosalind on Broadway in 1950, the role still maintained its long ascendancy, though now, nearly a half century later, Rosalind has been appropriated by our current specialists in gender politics, who sometimes even give us a lesbian Rosalind, more occupied with Celia (or with Phebe) than with poor Orlando. As the millennium goes by, and recedes into the past, we may return to the actual Shakespearean role, perhaps about the same time we wrest Caliban away from his "materialist" admirers and restore him to his bitter "family romance" (Freud's phrase) with the household of

From *Shakespeare: The Invention of the Human*. © 1998 by Harold Bloom.

Prospero. Back in 1932, when Rosalind was all the rage, G. K. Chesterton, very much her admirer, nevertheless protested her popular reductions:

> About three hundred years ago William Shakespeare, not knowing what to do with his characters, turned them out to play in the woods, let a girl masquerade as a boy and amused himself with speculating on the effect of feminine curiosity freed for an hour from feminine dignity. He did it very well, but he could do something else. And the popular romances of today cannot do anything else. Shakespeare took care to explain in the play itself that he did not think that life should be one prolonged picnic. Nor would he have thought that feminine life should be one prolonged piece of private theatricals. But Rosalind, who was then unconventional for an hour, is now the convention of an epoch. She was then on a holiday; she is now very hardworked indeed. She has to act in every play, novel or short story, and always in the same old pert pose. Perhaps she is even afraid to be herself: certainly Celia is now afraid to be herself.

Whether Shakespeare was as content as Chesterton would have him be to end the picnic in the forest of Arden (named, in part, for his mother, Mary Arden), I somewhat doubt. I think that Shakespeare must have been very fond of this play. We know that Shakespeare himself played the role of old Adam, Orlando's faithful retainer, an old Adam free of all sin and invested with original virtue. Of all Shakespeare's plays, the accurately titled *As You Like It* is as much set in an earthly realm of possible good as *King Lear* and *Macbeth* are set in earthly hells. And of all Shakespeare's comic heroines, Rosalind is the most gifted, as remarkable in her mode as Falstaff and Hamlet are in theirs. Shakespeare has been so subtle and so careful in writing Rosalind's role that we never quite awaken to her uniqueness among his (or all literature's) heroic wits. A normative consciousness, harmoniously balanced and beautifully sane, she is the indubitable ancestress of Elizabeth Bennet in *Pride and Prejudice*, though she has a social freedom beyond Jane Austen's careful limitations.

Daughter of Duke Senior, the rightful if usurped Duke, Rosalind is too far beyond Orlando (a poor gentleman) to accept him as husband, but the forest of Arden dissolves hierarchies, at least for a blessed time. The bad Duke, the younger brother of Duke Senior, absurdly yields up the usurped dukedom to the rightful Duke, Rosalind's father, while the wicked Oliver as surprisingly gives up their father's house to Orlando, his younger brother and Rosalind's lover. It is not possible to historicize so mixed a pattern, and social commentaries to *As You Like It* do not take us very far into this play's curious and charming ethos. We do not even know precisely where we are geographically in this comedy. Ostensibly, the usurped duchy is in France, and Arden is the Ardennes, but Robin Hood is invoked, and the forest seems very English. French and English names are haphazardly distributed among the characters, in a happy anarchy that works splendidly. Though critics can and do find many shadows in the forest of Arden, such discoveries obscure what matters most about this exquisite play. It is much Shakespeare's happiest: death has been in Arcadia, but not so that we can be oppressed by it, since nearly everything else is as we like it.

Shakespeare has some two dozen masterpieces among his thirty-nine plays, and no one would deny *As You Like It* eminence, though a few (wrongly) consider it the slightest of the masterpieces. If Rosalind cannot please us, then no one in Shakespeare or elsewhere in literature ever will. I love Falstaff and Hamlet and Cleopatra as dramatic and literary characters, but would not want suddenly to encounter them in actuality; yet falling in love with Rosalind always makes me wish that she existed in our subliterary realm. Edith Evans performed Rosalind before I was old enough to attend; according to one critic, she spoke to the audience as though everyone in it was Orlando, and so captured them all. A great role, like Rosalind's, is a kind of miracle: a universal perspective seems to open out upon us. Shakespeare makes even Falstaff and Hamlet victims, to some degree, of dramatic irony; we are afforded a few perspectives that are not available either to the greatest of comic protagonists or to the most troubling of tragic heroes. Rosalind is unique in Shakespeare, perhaps indeed in Western drama, because it is so difficult to achieve a perspective upon her that she herself does not anticipate and share. A stage play is virtually impossible without some degree of dramatic irony; that is the audiences privilege. We enjoy such an irony in regard to Touchstone, Jaques, and every other character in *As You Like It*, except for Rosalind. We forgive her for knowing what matters more than we do, because she has no will to power over us, except to exercise our most humane faculties in appreciating her performance.

2

I have remarked already that Shakespeare himself played the role of old Adam, the faithful servant who goes off with Orlando to the forest of Arden. The virtuous Adam is "not for the fashion of these times," as Orlando says, but represents rather "the constant service of the antique world." *As You Like It* is Shakespeare's sweetest-tempered play; there is *Twelfth Night*, but in that play everyone except the superb clown Feste is a zany. Orlando, a youthful

Hercules, is certainly not Rosalind's human equal, but he is considerably saner than *Twelfth Night*'s loony Orsino, while Rosalind and Celia would be exemplary in any company, and in wisdom and wit are goddesses compared with those charming screwballs Viola and Olivia. I would grant to scholars that there are dark traces in the forest of Arden, for Shakespeare's overwhelming sense of reality does not allow him to depict an absolutely unmixed realm. Having made this point, I am delighted to observe that the forest of Arden is simply the best place to live, anywhere in Shakespeare. You cannot have an earthly paradise and still have a stage comedy that works, yet *As You Like It* comes closest. Old Adam (Shakespeare) is nearly eighty, and nothing is said of his (or any other) Eve. We are in a lapsed world, silver at best, but it has a woman beyond Eve, the sublime Rosalind. Eve, the mother of all living, is celebrated for her vitality and beauty, and not always for her intellect. The exuberant Rosalind is vital and beautiful, in spirit, in body, in mind. She has no equal, in or out of Arden, and deserves a better lover than the amiable Orlando, and better wits for her conversation than Touchstone and Jaques. Each time I read *As You Like It*, I indulge a favorite fantasy, that Shakespeare never had written *The Merry Wives of Windsor* (unworthy of Falstaff, who is represented there by an impostor), and did not kill Sir John off in *Henry V*. No, if Sir John was to be seen in love, then he, and not Touchstone, should have fled to the forest of Arden with Rosalind and Celia, there to exchange Mrs. Quickly and Doll Tearsheet for Audrey and Phebe. What prose Shakespeare might have written for Falstaff and Rosalind in their contests of wit, or for Sir John to flatten Jaques! There is a critical point to my fantasy, since Touchstone and Jaques combined do not make me miss Falstaff less. Shakespeare sensibly would have rejected my suggestion: Falstaff, greatest of scene stealers, would have gotten in the way of our seeing Rosalind all round, as it were, and might have impeded Rosalind in her own educational venture, the instruction of Orlando, neither as brilliant nor as dangerous a student as Prince Hal.

Shakespeare's invention of the human, already triumphant through his creation of Falstaff, acquired a new dimension with Rosalind, his second great personality to date, beyond Juliet, Portia, and Beatrice. Rosalind's role was the best preparation for the revised Hamlet of 1600–1601, where wit achieves an apotheosis and becomes a kind of negative transcendence. Personality in Shakespeare always returns me to the difficult enterprise of surmising Shakespeare's own personality. Like Shylock, Shakespeare was a moneylender, and evidently became known as being rather sharp in his business dealings. Except for that, we do not encounter much that seems to find fault with Shakespeare, setting aside the early venom of the distraught Greene, failed rival dramatist. There are deep shadows on the speaker of the

Sonnets, and some speculate that these are related to the anguish of bearing a wounded name in the later "Elegy" for Will Peter, if indeed that is Shakespeare's poem. Honigmann sensibly advises us to live with two antithetical images of Shakespeare, one genial and open, the other darkened and reclusive, Falstaff and Hamlet fused in a single consciousness. What, besides intellect, do Falstaff and Hamlet share? Nietzsche said of Hamlet that he thought too well, and so died of the truth. Can one joke too well? Falstaff dies because the order of play abandons him with Hal's betrayal; that is a death not by wit, but by the loss of love, akin to the little deaths that Shakespeare (or his speaker) endures in the Sonnets. Genre is a fluid dissolve in Shakespeare, but Falstaff was allowed only the mock comedy of *The Merry Wives of Windsor*, not the authentic comedy of *As You Like It* and *Twelfth Night*.

Rosalind's high good fortune—which exalts her over Falstaff, Hamlet, and Cleopatra—is to stand at the center of a play in which no authentic harm can come to anyone. We are permitted to relax into our apprehension of Rosalind's genius. Shakespeare the man seems to have had a healthy fear of being hurt or abused: the speaker of the Sonnets never gives himself away as fully as Falstaff does to Hal, or Hamlet to his dead father's memory. Cleopatra, until Antony dies, protects herself from too much abandonment to her love, and even Rosalind is careful to pace her relationship to Orlando. Yet the glory of Rosalind, and of her play, is her confidence, and ours, that all things will go well.

3

Touchstone and Jaques, in their very different ways, do not go well with Rosalind, or with her ideal context in Arden. Touchstone's indeliberate travesties far exceed his intentional fooleries; he is the total antithesis of *Twelfth Night*'s Feste, Shakespeare's wisest (and most humanly amiable) clown. Jaques, a more complex botcher, has withdrawn from the passions of existence, but not in the name of any values that Rosalind (or we) can honor. Many critics rightly note that Rosalind and even her Orlando (to a lesser extent) have remarkably few illusions about the nature of the high Romantic passion that they share. They do not merely play at love, or at courtship, but they are careful to entertain play as a crucial element in keeping love realistic. Poise is Rosalind's particular endowment, and Orlando learns it from her. Of Rosalind's poise, it can be remarked that this quality emanates neither from manners nor from morals. Rather, such balance ensues from an intricate spiritual choreography, denied to Falstaff only by his passion for Hal, and abandoned by Hamlet because he internalizes the open wound that is

Elsinore. Cleopatra is always too much the actress, attempting the role of herself, to rival Rosalind in grace and in the control of perspective. Is it an accident that Rosalind is the most admirable personage in all of Shakespeare? The very name seems to have had a particular magic for him, though he named his actual daughters Susanna and Judith. *Love's Labour's Lost*'s Berowne fails in his campaign to win the formidable Rosaline, and Romeo, before he meets Juliet, is also infatuated with a Rosaline. But Rosalind is very different from both Rosalines, who resist their admirers. No one knows the name of the Dark Lady of the Sonnets, but we can be reasonably certain it was not Rosaline or Rosalind.

First in poise of all Shakespearean characters, the admirable Rosalind is also his most triumphant, both in her own fate and in what she brings about for others. *Twelfth Night* is *As You Like It*'s only rival among Shakespeare's Romantic comedies, but it lacks Rosalind. The difference may be that *As You Like It* directly precedes the *Hamlet* of 1600–1601, while *Twelfth Night* follows directly after it, and Hamlet made another Rosalind unlikely for Shakespeare. Nietzsche thought Hamlet to be the authentic Dionysiac hero. Though Camille Paglia boldly speculates that Rosalind is a Dionysiac heroine, I am not altogether persuaded. Paglia strongly emphasizes Rosalind's mercurial temperament, a somewhat different endowment than the one Nietzsche associates with Dionysus. Though anything but an academic feminist, Paglia shares in our current concern with the supposed androgyny of Shakespeare's heroines who adopt male disguises: Julia, Portia, Rosalind, Viola, Imogen. I cannot assert that I completely apprehend Shakespeare's vision of human sexuality, yet I distrust both G. Wilson Knight's and Paglia's notions as to a bisexual ideal in Shakespeare, though these critics are superb readers. Rosalind in any case hardly seems such a figure, since her sexual desires entirely center upon Orlando, a Herculean wrestler and by no means a diffident young man. Universally attractive, to women as to men (in or out of the audience), she is shrewdly absolute in her choice of Orlando, and she undertakes his amatory education in the role of a preceptor who is determined that he shall graduate. It is extraordinary that a dramatic character could be at once so interesting and so normative as Rosalind is: free of malice; turning her aggressivity neither against herself nor against others; free of all resentments, while manifesting a vital curiosity and an exuberant desire.

Orlando is a dreadfully bad poet:

> Therefore Heaven Nature charg'd
> That one body should be fill'd
> With all graces wide-enlarg'd.

Nature presently distill'd
Helen's cheek, but not her
heart, Cleopatra's majesty,
Atalanta's better part
Sad Lucretia's modesty.
Thus Rosalind of many parts
By heavenly synod was devis'd,
Of many faces, eyes, and hearts,
To have the touches dearest priz'd.
[III.ii.138–49]

And yet Rosalind is as integrated a personality as Shakespeare created: she is not a picnic of selves, as Hamlet sometimes becomes. Her changes unfold persuasively and only deepen the selfsame continuity of her nature. One of the most hideous of our current critical fashions, both academic and journalistic, calls itself sexual politics, and the sexual politicians all urge us to believe that Shakespeare abandons Rosalind to "patriarchal male bonds." It is not clear to me how Shakespeare could have avoided this supposed desertion of his heroine. Are Rosalind and Celia to marry each other? They don't want to; Rosalind rushes to Orlando, and Celia (with startling speed) leaps toward the reformed Oliver. Was Shakespeare to kill off the superb Duke Senior, Rosalind's affectionate father? Or was Rosalind to reject Orlando for Phebe? Let it suffice to affirm that no one else in the plays, not even Falstaff or Hamlet, represents Shakespeare's own stance toward human nature so fully as Rosalind does. If we can point to his unshadowed ideal, then it must be to Rosalind. His ironies, which are Rosalind's, are subtler and more capacious than ours, and more humane also.

4

Most commercial stagings of *As You Like It* vulgarize the play, as though directors fear that audiences cannot be trusted to absorb the agon between the wholesome wit of Rosalind and the rancidity of Touchstone, the bitterness of Jaques. I fear that this is not exactly the cultural moment for Shakespeare's Rosalind, yet I expect that moment to come again, and yet again, when our various feminisms have become even maturer and yet more successful. Rosalind, least ideological of all dramatic characters, surpasses every other woman in literature in what we could call "intelligibility." You never get far by terming her a "pastoral heroine" or a "Romantic comedian": her mind is too large, her spirit too free, to so confine her. She is as immensely superior to everyone else in her play as are Falstaff and Hamlet in theirs. The best starting point truly to apprehend her is a single grand sentence she speaks, when Orlando protests that he will die if she does not have him. I have heard this great line thrown away too often, when actresses suffered bad direction, but clearly delivered it is unforgettable: "Men have died from time to time, and worms have eaten them, but not for love." For wit and wisdom, that can compete with Falstaff at his greatest, after the Lord Chief Justice has chided him for speaking of his own "youth": "My lord, I was born about three of the clock in the afternoon, with a white head and something of a round belly." That affirmation of agelessness is a personal triumph; Rosalind's triumph is impersonal and overwhelming, and remains the best medicine for all lovesick males. "Men *have* died from time to time, and worms *have* eaten them": death is authentic and material, "*but not for love.*" Falstaff takes the Lord Chief Justice's complaint, and explodes it with Falstaffian fantasia; Rosalind, an equal master of timing, deflates subtly and definitively the male refusal to grow up.

Chesterton said that "Rosalind did not go into the wood to look for her freedom; she went into the wood to look for her father." Though I worship Chesterton, that would have surprised Shakespeare; an undisguised Rosalind is not even in her father's presence until she reassumes female garments for her wedding. The search for the father has little importance in *As You Like It*, and Rosalind's freedom is central to her. Perhaps, as Marjorie Garber suggests, Rosalind goes into the forest in order to mature Orlando, to improve him both as person and as lover. Orlando actually is no more adolescent than most of Shakespeare's males: did Shakespeare or nature invent the emotional inferiority of men to women? Rosalind is too pragmatic to lament such inequality, and is content to educate Orlando. She shares with Falstaff the educator's role; Hamlet diagnoses everyone he encounters, and is too impatient to teach them. Rosalind and Falstaff both augment and enhance life, but Hamlet is the gateway through which supernal powers, many of them negative, enter as intimations of mortality. *As You Like It* is poised before the great tragedies; it is a vitalizing work, and Rosalind is a joyous representative of life's possible freedoms. The aesthetic representation of happiness demands a complex art; no drama of happiness ever has surpassed Rosalind's.

To be in love, and yet to see and feel the absurdity of it, one needs to go to school with Rosalind. She instructs us in the miracle of being a harmonious consciousness that is also able to accommodate the reality of another self. Shelley heroically thought that the secret of love was a complete going-out from our own nature into the nature of another; Rosalind sensibly regards that as madness. She is neither High Romantic nor a Platonist: love's illusions, for her, are quite distinct from the reality of maids knowing that "the sky changes when they are wives." One might venture that Rosalind as an analyst of "love," is akin to Falstaff as an analyst of "honor"—that is to say, of the whole baggage of state power, political intrigue, mock chivalry, and open warfare. The difference is that Rosalind herself is joyously in love and criticizes love from within its realm; Falstaff devastates the pretensions of power, but always from its periphery, and knowing throughout that he will lose Hal to the realities of power. Rosalind's wit is triumphant yet always measured to its object, while Falstaff's irreverent mockery is victorious but pragmatically unable to save him from rejection. Both are educational geniuses, and yet Rosalind is Jane Austen to Falstaff's Samuel Johnson; Rosalind is the apotheosis of persuasion, while Falstaff ultimately conveys the vanity of human wishes.

I have been urging us to see Rosalind in sequence, between Falstaff and Hamlet, just as witty and as wise but trapped neither in history with Falstaff nor in tragedy with Hamlet, and yet larger than her drama even as they cannot be confined to theirs. The invention of freedom must be measured against what encloses or threatens freedom: time and the state for Falstaff, the past and the enemy within for Hamlet. Rosalind's freedom may seem less consequential because *As You Like It* brushes aside time and the state, and Rosalind has no tragic sorrows, no Prince Hal, and no Gertrude or Ghost. Rosalind is her own context, unchallenged save for the melancholy Jaques and the rancid Touchstone.

5

Jaques, poseur as he is, gets some of the best speeches in Shakespeare, who must have had a certain fondness for this fake melancholic. Like Touchstone, Jaques is Shakespeare's own invention; neither of them figures in the play's source, Thomas Lodge's prose romance *Rosalynde* (1590). Whatever pleasure Shakespeare took in Jaques and in Touchstone, we are misled if we are persuaded by their negations (many scholars have been susceptible to Touchstone, in particular). Touchstone, authentically witty, is rancidly vicious, while Jaques is merely rancid (the Shakespearean pronunciation of his name plays upon a jakes, or privy). Both of them are in *As You Like It* to serve as touchstones for Rosalind's more congenial wit, and she triumphantly puts them in their places. Her amiable triumphalism prefigures Prospero's, as Marjorie Garber suggests, though Rosalind's mastery is a wholly natural magic, normative and humane, and shall we not call it Shakespeare's own? Jaques and Touchstone are different but related disasters that the speaker of the Sonnets avoids falling into, despite the provocations to despair amply provided by the fair young lord and the dark lady, the two loves of comfort and despair.

Reductionism, or the tendency to believe that only the worst truth about us is true, is a great irritation to Shakespeare, a grim joy to Jaques, and an obscene pleasure to Touchstone. Jaques is both a social satirist and a mocker of Arden; however, society is off stage, and we are in pastoral exile, so that the satirical stance of Ben Jonson is barely available to Jaques. That leaves only Arden, where Touchstone serves both as Jaques's rival and as his colleague, another malcontent. Touchstone, who is both funnier and cruder, sees country innocence as mere ignorance; Jaques is only a little kinder on this. The major target for both would-be satirists is erotic idealism, or romantic love. But their mutual critique is redundant; Rosalind is both an erotic realist and a superbly benign critic of romantic love, and she makes both malcontents seem inadequate to their chosen modes. She exposes Jaques's silliness and Touchstone's absurdity, and thus defends Arden and its affections from an unhealthy reductionism.

Yet Jaques has qualities that partly redeem his silliness, more for us than for Rosalind, since she does not need him. Shakespeare makes us need Jaques by assigning him two great speeches, the first celebrating his meeting with Touchstone:

> A fool, a fool! I met a fool i' th' forest,
> A motley fool: a miserable world!
> As I do live by food, I met a fool,
> Who laid him down and bask'd him in the sun,
> And rail'd on Lady Fortune in good terms,
> In good set terms, and yet a motley fool.
> 'Good morrow, fool', quoth I. 'No, sir', quoth he,
> 'Call me not fool, till heaven hath sent me fortune.'
> And then he drew a dial from his poke,
> And looking on it, with lack-lustre eye,
> Says, very wisely, 'It is ten o'clock.
> Thus we may see', quoth he, 'how the world wags:
> 'Tis but an hour ago since it was nine,
> And after one hour more 'twill be eleven;
> And so, from hour to hour, we ripe, and ripe,
> And then from hour to hour, we rot, and rot,
> And thereby hangs a tale.' When I did hear
> The motley fool thus moral on the time,
> My lungs began to crow like chanticleer,
> That fools should be so deep-contemplative;
> And I did laugh, sans intermission,
> An hour by his dial. O noble fool!
> A worthy fool! Motley's the only wear.
>
> [II.vii.12–34]

Touchstone, a truant court jester or "motley fool," refuses the title of fool until fortune has favored him, and puns rather pungently on "hour" and "whore." Whatever tale hangs upon this rancid hint of venereal infection, we cannot be certain, but Touchstone's effect upon Jaques is both profound and enigmatic, since it releases Jaques from his obsessive melancholy, for an hour anyway, and revises his sense of his role as satirist:

I must have liberty
Withal, as large a charter as the wind,
To blow on whom I please, for so fools have;
And they that are most galled with my folly,
They most must laugh. And why sir must they so?
The why is plain as way to parish church.
He that a fool doth very wisely hit
Doth very foolishly, although he smart,
Not to seem senseless of the bob. If not,
The wiseman's folly is anatomiz'd
Even by the squand'ring glances of the fool.
Invest me in my motley. Give me leave
To speak my mind, and I will through and through
Cleanse the foul body of th'infected world,
If they will patiently receive my medicine.

[II.vii.47–61]

Shakespeare seems to glance slyly here at his friend Ben Jonson, and perhaps also conveys something of his own insight into the court fool's dramatic possibilities, an insight that will be developed in the Feste of *Twelfth Night* and the great nameless Fool of *King Lear*. Duke Senior is quick to retort that the Jonsonian Jaques himself has manifested the flaws he now would censure:

Most mischievous foul sin, in chiding sin.
For thou thyself hast been a libertine,
As sensual as the brutish sting itself,
And all th'embossed sores and headed evils
That thou with license of free foot hast caught
Wouldst thou disgorge into the general world.

[II.vii.64–69]

Jaques defends himself with a Jonsonian apologia for the satirical playwright, who attacks types and not individuals. This defense is the transition to *As You Like It*'s most famous speech, where Jaques gives his own dramatic version of the Seven Ages of Man:

All the world's a stage,
And all the men and women merely players.
They have their exits and their entrances,
And one man in his time plays many parts,
His acts being seven ages. At first, the infant,
Mewling and puking in the nurse's arms.
Then, the whining schoolboy, with his satchel
And shining morning face, creeping like snail
Unwillingly to school. And then the lover,
Sighing like furnace, with a woeful ballad
Made to his mistress' eyebrow. Then a soldier,
Full of strange oaths, and bearded like the pard,
Jealous in honour, sudden, and quick in quarrel,
Seeking the bubble reputation
Even in the cannon's mouth. And then, the justice,
In fair round belly with good capon lin'd,
With eyes severe, and beard of formal cut,
Full of wise saws, and modern instances,
And so he plays his part. The sixth age shifts
Into the lean and slipper'd pantaloon,
With spectacles on nose, and pouch on side,
His youthful hose well sav'd, a world too wide
For his shrunk shank, and his big manly voice,
Turning again toward childish treble, pipes
And whistles in his sound. Last scene of all,
That ends this strange eventful history,
Is second childishness and mere oblivion,
Sans teeth, sans eyes, sans taste, sans everything.
[II.vii.139–66]

Powerful enough out of context, this speech has a very subtle reverberation within the play, since it enhances our sense of Jaques's reductionism. Jaques knows, as we do, that all infants do not incessantly bawl and puke, and that all schoolboys do not whine. The lover and the soldier are better served by Jaques's satirical eloquence, and we can imagine Falstaff laughing at those "seeking the bubble reputation / Even in the cannon's mouth." Shakespeare, an inveterate litigator, invests considerable gusto in the reference to the well-known practice of stuffing judges with capons.

Himself only in the middle of the journey, at thirty-five, Shakespeare (perhaps intuiting that two-thirds of his life was already over) envisions the silly old Pantalone of *commedia dell'arte* as a universal fate, preluding the second childhood of all humans who survive long enough "sans teeth, sans eyes, sans taste, sans everything." That last line is Jaques's triumph, it being a natural reductionism that even Sir John Falstaff could not dispute, and yet Shakespeare does, by entering as old Adam (a part as I've noted, he himself performed). Orlando staggers onto the stage, carrying his benign old retainer, who has sacrificed everything for him, and yet who is precisely not "sans everything." The rebuke to Jaques's reductionism scarcely could be more persuasive than Adam's quasi-paternal love for and loyalty to Orlando.

Jaques's fine complexity abides in the charm and energy of his negations. When he should be rhetorically crushed by Rosalind's unanswerable wit, he at first rebounds with a satiric gusto that wins our bemused affection:

Jaques. I prithee, pretty youth, let me be better acquainted with thee.
Ros. They say you are a melancholy fellow.
Jaques. I am so. I do love it better than laughing.
Ros. Those that are in extremity of either are abominable fellows, and betray themselves to every modern censure, worse than drunkards.
Jaques. Why, 'tis good to be sad and say nothing.
Ros. Why then, 'tis good to be a post.
Jaques. I have neither the scholar's melancholy, which is emulation; nor the musician's, which is fantastical; nor the courtier's, which is proud; nor the soldier's, which is ambitious; nor the lawyer's, which is politic; nor the lady's, which is nice; nor the lover's, which is all these: but it is a melancholy of mine own, compounded of many simples, extracted from many objects, and indeed the sundry contemplation of my travels, in which my often rumination wraps me in a most humorous sadness.

[IV.i.1–19]

"'Tis good to be a post" either goes right by Jaques, or else is evaded by his insistence that his melancholy is original and individual. But his self-affirmation is voided by Rosalind's next salvo:

Ros.	A traveler! By my faith, you have great reason to be sad. I fear you have sold your own lands to see other men's. Then to have seen much and to have nothing is to have rich eyes and poor hands.
Jaques.	Yes, I have gained my experience.
Ros.	And your experience makes you sad. I had rather have a fool to make me merry than experience to make me sad—and to travel for it too.

[IV.i.20–27]

The rather lame "Yes, I have gained my experience" is the mark of Jaques's defeat, but Shakespeare grants his melancholic a dignified end. With nearly everyone else in the play either getting married or returning from pastoral exile, Jaques nevertheless departs with a flair: "So, to your pleasures: / I am for other than dancing measures." He will go out with the judgment that marriage is a "pastime," and we wonder again whether he does not speak for a partial Shakespeare, perhaps for the man rather than the poet-playwright. Jaques may be only what Orlando calls him, "either a fool or a cipher," but his highly stylized linguistic gestures partly succeed in saving him from himself.

6

Touchstone, despite so many of the critics, and the performance tradition, is truly rancid, in contrast to Jaques, and this more intense rancidity works as a touchstone should, to prove the true gold of Rosalind's spirit. Little as I love Touchstone, it is impossible to resist wholly a character who can thus affirm his past (and future) career as courtier:

> I have trod a measure; I have flattered a lady; I have been politic with my friend, smooth with mine enemy; I have undone three tailors ... [V.iv. 44–48]

Touchstone fascinates (and repels) because of his knowingness; he is conscious of every duplicity, intended or not, his own or of others. He is what Falstaff proudly (and accurately) insists the fat knight is not: a double man. Though Rosalind now provokes oceans of transvestite commentary, she floats over it quite untouched, precisely because she is not a double woman. Endlessly volatile, she remains unitary, the perfect representation of what Yeats called Unity of Being. She may well be the least nihilistic protagonist in all of Shakespeare, though Bottom the weaver is her close rival, as are the great victims: Juliet, Ophelia, Desdemona, Cordelia, and the near-victim yet troubled survivor Edgar. We cannot imagine Rosalind (or Bottom!) in tragedy, because, as I have noted, she seems not to be subject to dramatic irony, her mastery of perspective being so absolute. Touchstone, an ironist even as Jaques is a satirist, is bested by Rosalind, not only through her superiority in wit but also because she sees so much more than he does. Jaques had quoted Touchstone, "a fool i' th' forest," at his most characteristic: "From hour to hour, we ripe, and ripe, / And then from hour to hour, we rot, and rot." After chanting a doggerel in response to Orlando's bad love verses, Touchstone addresses Rosalind:

Touch. This is the very false gallop of verses. Why do you infect yourself with them?
Ros. Peace, you dull fool! I found them on a tree.
Touch. Truly the tree yields bad fruit.
Ros. I'll graft it with you and then I shall graft it with a medlar. Then it will be the earliest fruit i' th' country; for you'll be rotten ere you be half ripe, and that's the right virtue of the medlar.
Touch. You have said; but whether wisely or no, let the forest judge.

[III.ii.113–22]

The forest, as Touchstone knows, will judge as we judge: Rosalind has impaled him. Rotten before he is half-ripe, Touchstone pursues his Audrey, whose good-natured idiocy is sublimely conveyed by her: "I am not a slut, though I thank the gods I am foul." Comparing himself to the exiled Ovid among the Goths, Touchstone delivers Shakespeare's ultimate exorcism of the spirit of Christopher Marlowe, who haunts a play wholly alien to his savage genius:

Touch. When a man's verses cannot be understood, nor a man's good wit seconded with the forward child, understanding, it strikes a man more dead than a great reckoning in a little room. Truly, I would the gods had made thee poetical.
Aud. I do not know what 'poetical' is. Is it honest in deed and word? Is it a true thing?
Touch. No truly; for the truest poetry is the most feigning, and lovers are given to poetry; and what they swear in poetry may be said as lovers they do feign.

[III.iii.9–18]

Many in the original audience must have appreciated Shakespeare's audacity in alluding to Marlowe having been struck dead, supposedly on account of "a great reckoning in a little room," the tavern in Deptford where the poet-playwright was stabbed (in the eye) by one Ingram Frizer, like Marlowe a member of Walsingham's royal Secret Service, the CIA of Elizabethan England. The great reckoning ostensibly was a costly bill for liquor and food, in dispute between Marlowe, Frizer, and Walsingham's other thugs. Shakespeare hints strongly that it was a state-ordered execution, with maximum prejudice, and that the government's subsequent campaign against Marlowe's "atheism" had resulted in misunderstanding of the verses and "good wit" of the poet of *The Jew of Malta*, whose great line "infinite riches in a little room" is ironically echoed by Touchstone. Elsewhere in *As You Like It*, the "dead shepherd," Marlowe, is quoted with the famous tag from his lyric "The Passionate Shepherd to His Love": "Whoever loved that loved not at first sight." Touchstone, entrusted as Shakespeare's implicit defender of Marlowe, also states Shakespeare's own aesthetic credo: "for the truest poetry is the most feigning." Marlowe, true poet, feigned and was misread. Shakespeare, at last free of Marlowe's shadow, gives us *As You Like It* as the truest poetry, because it is the most inventive. Touchstone's final words in the play praise the "If" of poetical feigning. Asked by Jaques to name in order "the degrees of the lie" or contradiction that leads to the challenge to a duel, Touchstone achieves his most brilliant moment:

> O sir, we quarrel in print, by the book; as you have books for good manners. I will name you the degrees. The first, the Retort Courteous; the second, the Quip Modest; the third, the Reply Churlish; the fourth, the Reproof Valiant; the fifth, the Countercheck Quarrelsome; the sixth, the Lie with Circumstance; the seventh, the Lie Direct. All these you may avoid but the Lie Direct; and you may avoid that too, with an If. I knew when seven justices could not take up a quarrel, but when the parties were met themselves, one of them thought but of an If, as, 'If you said so, then I said so'. And they shook hands and swore brothers. Your If is the only peacemaker: much virtue in If.
>
> [V.iv.89–102]

"Much virtue in If" is a fine farewell for Touchstone, and teaches us to bear his nastiness to the shepherds, and his sordid exploitation of the too-willing Audrey. Jaques, in the presence of Rosalind, loses satiric dignity; Touchstone, confronted by her, abandons the prestige of irony. The play belongs to Rosalind. To see the "how" and "why" of her greatness, the reason she must be the most remarkable and persuasive representation of a woman in all of Western literature, is also to apprehend how inadequate nearly every production of *As You Like It* has been to Rosalind.

7

As You Like It is a title addressed to Shakespeare's audience, yet the play also could be called *As Rosalind Likes It*, because she achieves all her purposes, which have little in common with the ambitions of the gender-and-power covens. Article after article deplores her "abandonment" of Celia for Orlando, or regrets the curbing of her "female vitality," or even insists that her appeal to males in the audience is "homoerotic" and not heterosexual. I have not yet seen an article chiding Rosalind for spurning the shepherdess Phebe, though I live in hope. Orlando, as all of us know, is not Rosalind's equal, but Shakespeare's heroines generally marry down, and Orlando is an amiable young Hercules, whom Rosalind is happy to educate, in her ostensible disguise as the forest-boy Ganymede. When Ganymede plays Rosalind in order to rehearse Orlando in life and love, are we to assume that her lover does not recognize her? Aside from straining credulity, it would be an aesthetic loss if Orlando were not fully aware of the charm of his situation. He is not brilliant, nor well educated, yet his natural wit is reasonably strong, and he is a livelier straight man for Rosalind than Horatio is for Hamlet:

Ros. Come, woo me, woo me; for now I am in a holiday humour and like enough to consent. What would you say to me now, an I were your very very Rosalind?

Orl. I would kiss before I spoke.

Ros. Nay, you were better speak first, and when you were gravelled for lack of matter, you might take occasion to kiss. Very good orators when they are out, they will spit, and for lovers lacking—God warr'nt us!—matter, the cleanliest shift is to kiss.

Orl. How if the kiss be denied?

Ros. Then she puts you to entreaty, and there begins new matter.

Orl. Who could be out, being before his beloved mistress?

Ros. Marry that should you, if I were your mistress, or I should think my honesty ranker than my wit.

Orl. What, of my suit?

Ros. Not out of your apparel, and yet out of your suit. Am I not your Rosalind?

Orl. I take some joy to say you are, because I would be talking of her.
Ros. Well, in her person, I say I will not have you.
Orl. Then in mine own person, I die.
Ros. No, faith, die by attorney. The poor world is almost six thousand years old, and in all this time there was not any man died in his own person, videlicet, in a love-cause. Troilus had his brains dashed out with a Grecian club, yet he did what he could to die before, and he is one of the patterns of love. Leander, he would have lived many a fair year though Hero had turned nun, if it had not been for a hot mid summer night; for, good youth, he went but forth to wash him in the Hellespont, and being taken with the cramp, was drowned, and the foolish chroniclers of that age found it was Hero of Sestos. But these are all lies: men have died from time to time and worms have eaten them, but not for love.

[IV.i.65–103]

I have quoted the last sentence of this before, and wish I could find occasion to use it again, for it is Rosalind's best, and therefore very good indeed. The allusion to the Marlowe/Chapman *Hero and Leander* reinforces the matrix of irony that celebrates Marlowe's influence as being absent from *As You Like It*, where the courtship proceeds from splendor to splendor as Rosalind almost uniquely (even in Shakespeare) fuses authentic love with the highest wit:

Ros. Now tell me how long you would have her, after you have possessed her?
Orl. For ever, and a day.
Ros. Say a day, without the ever. No, no, Orlando, men are April when they woo, December when they wed. Maids are May when they are maids, but the sky changes when they are wives. I will be more jealous of thee than a Barbary cock-pigeon over his hen, more clamorous than a parrot against rain, more new-fangled than an ape, more giddy in my desires than a monkey. I will weep for nothing, like Diana in the fountain, and I will do that when you are disposed to

be merry. I will laugh like a hyen, and that when thou art inclined to sleep.

Orl. But will my Rosalind do so?

Ros. By my life, she will do as I do.

Orl. O but she is wise.

Rosalind. Or else she could not have the wit to do this. The wiser, the waywarder. Make the doors upon a woman's wit, and it will out at the casement; shut that, and 'twill out at the keyhole; stop that, 'twill fly with the smoke out at the chimney.

Orl. A man that had a wife with such a wit, he might say, 'Wit, whither wilt?'

Ros. Nay, you might keep that check for it, till you met your wife's wit going to your neighbour's bed.

Orl. And what wit could wit have to excuse that?

Ros. Marry to say she came to seek you there. You shall never take her without her answer, unless you take her without her tongue. O that woman that cannot make her fault her husband's occasion, let her never nurse her child herself, for she will breed it like a fool.

[IV.i.135–67]

She is marvelous here, but he (*pace* many critics) is no bumpkin: "But will my Rosalind do so?" It is the wisest as well as the wittiest courtship in Shakespeare, far eclipsing the mock carnage of Beatrice and Benedick. Only Rosalind and Orlando could sustain their finest exchange, as their play-of-two concludes:

Ros. Why then tomorrow I cannot serve your turn for Rosalind?
Orl. I can live no longer by thinking.

[V.ii.48–50]

Again despite the critics, Orlando's tone is light rather than desperate, but sexual urgency is well conveyed, and signals that he is ready to graduate from Rosalind's school. Are we? Rosalie Colie noted that "the love at the center of the play is not a particularly pastoral love," which helps save *As You Like It* from the death of the pastoral convention. William Empson, in his classic *Some Versions of Pastoral,* returns us to the First Folio text of Touchstone's ironic address to Audrey:

> No trulie: for the truest poetrie is the most faining, and Lovers are given to Poetrie: and what they sweare in Poetrie, may be said as Lovers, they do feigne.

The pun on *faining* (desiring) and *feign* (simulate or pretend), highly appropriate for Touchstone and Audrey, would not work if we applied it to Rosalind and Orlando, since their desire and their playacting are one, even when Orlando cries out that he can live no longer by thinking. The subtlest moment in this masterpiece of all Shakespearean comedies comes in the Epilogue, where the boy actor playing Rosalind steps out before the curtain, still in costume, to give us her final triumph of affectionate wit, of faining and feigning in harmony:

> It is not the fashion to see the lady the epilogue; but it is no more unhandsome than to see the lord the prologue. If it be true that good wine needs no bush, 'tis true that a good play needs no epilogue. Yet to good wine they do use good bushes; and good plays prove the better with the help of good epilogues. What a case am I in then, that am neither a good epilogue, nor cannot insinuate with you in the behalf of a good play? I am not furnished like a beggar, therefore to beg will not become me. My way is to conjure you, and I'll begin with the women. I charge you, O women, for the love you bear to men, to like as much of this play as please you. And I charge you, O men, for the love you bear to women—as I perceive by your simpering none of you hates them—that between you and the women the play may please. If I were a woman, I would kiss as many of you as had beards that pleased me, complexions that liked me, and breaths that I defied not. And I am sure, as many as have good beards, or good faces, or sweet breaths, will for my kind offer, when I make curtsy, bid me farewell.

In these curious days for literary criticism, this Epilogue stirs up the expected transports of transvestism and transgression, but such raptures have little to do with Shakespeare's Rosalind and her final words. I prefer Edward I. Berry, who is splendidly on target:

> As the director and "busy actor" in her own "play," and the Epilogue in Shakespeare's, Rosalind becomes in a sense a figure for the playwright himself, a character whose consciousness extends in subtle ways beyond the boundaries of the drama.

Rosalind again makes a third with Falstaff and Hamlet, also figures for Shakespeare himself. "Play out the play!" Falstaff cries to Hal; "I have much to say in the behalf of that Falstaff." "Suit the action to the word, the word to the action," Hamlet admonishes the Player King. "I charge you, O men, for the love you bear to women," Rosalind adroitly pleads, "that between you and the women the play may please." The voice in all three, at just that moment, is as close as Shakespeare ever will come to letting us hear the voice of William Shakespeare himself.

MARTHA RONK

Locating the Visual in As You Like It

The Forest of Arden seems in one's memory to dominate *As You Like It.* Yet the first picture of Arden is given by Charles the wrestler only as distant hearsay. Although one might expect a pastoral play to be replete with visual staging and visual effects (as in the sheepshearing celebration in *The Winter's Tale*), in *As You Like It* whatever "pastoral" might be is hedged round and inadequate from the outset. The most vivid pictures come in words, words already set forth, both by another speaker and by convention. The forest, not visual, is emblem: "They say he is already in the Forest of Arden.... They say many young gentlemen flock to him every day, and fleet the time carelessly as they did in the golden world" (1.1.114, 116–19).[1]

In this essay I focus on the relation between the verbal and visual in *As You Like It* and how they vie for contested dominance, disrupting presentation of both character and scene. Specifically I focus on Rosalind and on the pastoral world, arguing that Shakespeare purposefully draws attention to the ways in which the one aspect of theater plays against the other such that what is presented is layered and qualified. Shakespeare thus underscores the artificial and unrepresentable nature of what is being represented, emphasizing the impossibility of that which seems theatrically most obvious (what one sees) and the vividness of that which one cannot see. As in the sonnets in which the couplets ask us to embrace the hyperbolic statement

From *Shakespeare Quarterly* 52, no. 2 (2001).

that the young man, having been described as ravaged by time, will live forever in these poems, so this play asks that we be both drawn into the reality of the stage's world and yet distanced from it, that we embrace both potency and failure. Now you see it, now you don't. *As You Like It* repeatedly destabilizes what we have seen and forces us to experience theater in the making. Any theatrical production offers a complex collage, many visual sign systems of text, space (off and onstage/above and below stage), costumes, gestures, and scenery. To some extent here I take for granted the materiality of stage production in order to focus on ways in which what is obviously set forth is simultaneously erased and refigured, and to ask, finally, to what end. What Shakespeare's theater enacts explicitly is how different sets of signs undercut one another and purposely problematize theatrical representation itself.[2] As such, *As You Like It* is more than an isolated play about lovers in the forest; it embodies a theory of theatrical production.

My intention here is to address various aspects of the visual in the play, including both literal seeing and *seeing as*,[3] in order to identify the differences and frictions between the verbal and visual; between ekphrasis (pictures in words) and actual staging; and between sight (falling in love at first sight, for example) and speech (falling in love through extensive dialogue). As we examine the plays, both as texts and visual productions, foreground and background shift and alter. This alteration does not merely reflect critical interests but is built into the plays' structure by means of various self-referential techniques that call attention to its construction and, more audaciously, as I hope to demonstrate, to failure.[4]

Although we cannot know Shakespeare's intentions and although the arena in which the visual appears cannot always be circumscribed, it is nonetheless crucial to try to grasp some of the ways in which visual insistence creates and addresses disjunction, the disjunction at the center of this play and at the center of Shakespeare's culture. That *As You Like It* participates in historically cultural questions concerning the visual/verbal matrix is both obvious and complex, and can be explored here only briefly but, I hope, suggestively by referring to the tradition of ekphrasis, a verbal representation of a visual representation, and to Reformation attitudes toward the visual itself.

Ekphrasis

First, the play participates, as I have argued elsewhere, in a tradition often associated with medieval drama, a tradition that includes the related modes of ekphrasis, tableaux, talking pictures, and allegory, as well as in the psychological aspects of early modern theater in which characters reveal themselves by means of monologue, dialogue, verbal play, and wit.[5] This tradition was maintained throughout the period by the popularity of emblems in books and on coins, on clothing, and in masques and processions. Renaissance writers were keenly interested in ekphrasis as a mode that embodied the antimimetic elsewhere. Sidney writes of "speaking pictures" that enable the poet to create a world other than the ordinary, a world more true because far-fetched and feigned, opening up a space for the imagined, the missing or unsaid or inconsistent.[6] As Murray Krieger argues, "This is why the apophatic visual image helps belie the notion of the natural sign and can move beyond its limitations: playing its fictional role within a complicated code, the apophatic visual image opens out onto the semiotic possibilities of the verbal image.... because it does not resemble its object, [it] is therefore free to appeal to the mind's eye rather than the body's eye."[7] Puttenham also manifests an interest in visual allegory—in both its potency (the "captaine of all other figures") and its role as a figure of duplicity, deferral, deceit (to say one thing and mean another or, more subtly, to say one thing and mean something off to the side).[8] Ekphrasis stops time and, in the case of Shakespeare, stops the forward movement of the plot in order to allow contemplation, spatial exploration of a specific character or moment. Thus in *Twelfth Night*, Viola stops in her argument with Orsino to reveal inarticulable aspects of herself (both her love and her mixed gender) by offering the picture of her fictional sister who "sate like Patience on a monument" (2.4.114), an emblem one can locate in emblem collections of the period. Gertrude's set piece, the picture of Ophelia drowning, reveals the confused motivations of a young woman who drowns because in her madness she chooses suicide *and* because the branch over the water happens to break. In *The Winter's Tale*, Hermione's appearance as a statue in a memory theater directed by Paulina insists that the past not be forgotten; her very impenetrability as stone suggests the character's interiority and, moreover, an interiority lasting over time, since, as Leontes remarks, the statue shows Hermione's age. These examples may make it seem as if we can clearly distinguish between a character's verbal or her visual aspects and between a picture in words and the visible character onstage.

Yet, to think of this in more general and speculative ways, where the visual is located may not always be clear. It may not appear in an arena that can always be separated off or circumscribed; we might ask, for example, where the picture or icon is located and what difference it makes whether the picture is drawn in words, usually offstage and enacted in "the mind's eye," or actually staged—the act of wrestling, for example. It might seem obvious which "image" is more potent, since the eye is deemed the site of seductive powers by both early modern and postmodern critics.[9] Pictures seem to bring before us a visual presence that a verbal representation cannot evoke and in theater the pictures walk and talk, appearing as actors in physical and embodied form. Theater forces an audience to stare at, gaze at, listen to, want to touch or fend off characters set forth in full view as like or unlike, desirable or repulsive.[10] Although I do not want to dismiss out of hand what seems patently obvious; I also do not want to accept the obvious without question. For what we actually see may depend more on what is noticed or attended to than on what passes before our eyes in a flux of myriad impressions.

In fact, it seems that what focuses attention and creates seeing in the plays is language of two sorts, both intensely figurative language (which often approaches the emblematic) and the overtly emblematic language of ekphrasis. As W.J.T. Mitchell suggests, ekphrasis provides an eerie hope/fear of overcoming the impossible by creating a sort of sight, even an especially potent sort: "This is the phase when the impossibility of ekphrasis is overcome in imagination or metaphor, when we discover a 'sense' in which language can do what so many writers have wanted it to do: 'to make us see.'"[11] The potency of the imagined visual seems to be everywhere underscored in the plays; as Theseus says in relation to the mechanicals' efforts in *Midsummer Night's Dream*: "The best in this kind are but shadows; and the worst are no worse, if imagination amend them" (5.1.211–12). Moreover, ekphrasis seems often to provide characters with a kind of etched-in depth, enabling us to "see" more fully and completely; it seems to import or project some form of otherness, even subjectivity, to character (if paradoxically) by shifting codes from dramatic to allegorical. In the gap between one representation and another, often in a highly emblematic moment of ekphrasis, an idea of the subject is created, largely because allegory demands contemplation and interpretation. It requires a speculative filling-in.[12] Ekphrasis is also central to the study of Shakespeare's theater because it parallels a theatrical act and provides a model for the interaction of the verbal and visual. That is, the tension between the verbal and visual enacts a semiotics of theater: the relation of emblem to word or page to stage. Again, if Shakespeare's theater directly addresses the situation of failure in the theater and in explicitly theatrical terms, ekphrasis performs both impossibility and its overcoming. The clarity of representation in an ekphrastic moment (Patience on a monument or Rosalind as the idealized Helen) often does not stand in the service of that which can be represented.[13]

Reformation

Second, the verbal and visual offer contested forms of representation which not only problematize the enterprise of play production but which specifically reproduce significant cultural anxieties concerning the value or danger of the visual.[14] Thus the questions I mean to address in connection with *As You Like It* are intensified by the Reformation concern with whether truth resides in image or in word. As Huston Diehl argues, Elizabethan and Jacobean tragedies articulate the anxieties created by the "reformers" systematic campaigns to rid the churches of all taint of idolatry and superstition."[15] John Foxe, for example, ridicules worshipers who see and adore the bread as body instead of attending to the invisible god.[16] The host was, as Jonas Barish comments, "too tangible, too readily turned into a fetish, as in Protestant eyes it had become in the ceremonies of reservation and adoration associated with it. It had been turned into a thing of spectacle, to be gazed upon and marvelled at."[17] Focusing on the handkerchief and on "ocular proof" in *Othello* (3.3.360), Diehl argues that Shakespeare "examines the truth claims of magic and empiricism, the limits of visual evidence, the basis of faith, and the function of memory and imagination in acts of knowing."[18]

At this historical period the eye was understood as a conduit between what one imagined as inside and outside, public and private, and thus between truth and falsehood. The eye was also a political tool for those in positions of authority, who used it to dazzle, to consolidate power, to urge a particular way of being seen; using the iconography of Fame from Cesare Ripa's *Iconologia*, for example, Queen Elizabeth had ears and eyes embroidered on the sleeves of her gown, illustrating her courtly vigilance. The argument between Ben Jonson and Inigo Jones over the precedence of verbal (soul) or visual (body) provides but one famous example of the early modern struggle between these two modes of representation and but one example of the way in which a competition of signs is embodied in the theatrical enterprise.[19] Calvin believed that an image could compel the mind to make a fetish of that image; as a result, his fear of imagery was directly related to his sense of its enormous potency: "'Men's folly cannot restrain itself from falling headlong into superstitious rites.'"[20] The general distrust of images—associated with Catholicism, luxury, idolatry, deception, the whore of Babylon—was coupled with a love of splendor and spectacle, a sense that the image could also transport the viewer to truth or reveal aspects of the divine. So divided an attitude impressed itself everywhere: on decisions Queen Elizabeth made about whether or not to hang a crucifix, on the destruction and reinstatement of church statues, and on the decrying of and simultaneous use of images in Reformation literature. Protestants wrestled with the image, at times using it and at times destroying religious paintings and woodcuts, often, determining, as did Calvin, that visual images can be too easily misused and lead to delusion and idolatry. "For what are the pictures or statues to which [the papists] append the names of their saints," Calvin rhetorically asks, "but exhibitions of the most shameless luxury or obscenity?"[21] In "A Warning Against The Idolatrie of the last times," William Perkins cautions his followers against the use of any images in worship and indeed against the use of the imagination to form any image at all: "A thing fained in the mind by imagination, is an idoll."[22] In the midst of such fear monarchs nonetheless employed all manner of visual devices to dazzle the populace. In 1570 Elizabeth appears with the allegorical figures of peace and plenty in a painting entitled "Allegory of the Tudor Protestant Succession." As John N. King writes, "By commissioning this allegory, Elizabeth involved herself in the fashioning of her own image as a peaceful Protestant ruler."[23] In response, illustrating the same potency of imagery, enemies of the queen tried to harm her by stabbing and poisoning her image. Because of the overdetermined cultural attitudes toward visual display and idolatry, the competition between the visual and verbal in Shakespeare takes on a pointedness that one might otherwise simply ascribe to the nature of the theater.

As You Like It: Rosalind

In the spirit of the Reformation, the antitheatrical writers of Shakespeare's day criticized everything popish, spectacular, showy, enticing to the eye. That which was seen was labeled seductive in a double sense, seducing one to lust and, in times of iconoclastic urgency, to break and destroy. Given this context, we might assume that certain visual scenes in Shakespeare's *As You Like It* might therefore be especially salient, that despite the lack of backdrops or elaborate props, they might be read (as the antitheatrical writers indeed must have done) as magical and powerful. Yet we must also consider that certain visual scenes might not be potent, might simply be taken for granted as part of the natural working out of the play, might pass by almost unremarked; whereas a verbal image, especially an odd or emblematic one, might jump out, as when Rosalind discusses her desires with Celia, referring to male and female genitalia and to vaginal depths and male ejaculation:

> CELIA You have simply misused our sex in your love-prate. We must have your doublet and hose plucked over your head, and show the world what the bird hath done to her own nest.
>
> ROSALIND O coz, coz, coz, my pretty little coz, that thou didst know how many fathom deep I am in love! But it

cannot be sounded. My affection hath an unknown bottom, like the Bay of Portugal.

CELIA Or rather bottomless, that as fast as you pour affection in, it runs out.

(4.1.191–200)

This dialogue avoids physical display to the physical eye but nonetheless provokes a strong mental image. That an audience doesn't literally *see* anything doesn't make this speech less visually shocking or revealing. One sees what cannot be staged and what cannot be said more explicitly.

When Rosalind speaks to Orlando, moreover, she asserts that as his wife she will be "more new-fangled than an ape" (l. 144), a speech that underscores both her verbal wit and, by means of the accumulation of animal imagery, a desire that is both male, as in "cock-pigeon," and female, as in "Diana":

> I will be more jealous of thee than a Barbary cock-pigeon over his hen, more clamorous than a parrot against rain, more new-fangled than an ape, more giddy in my desires than a monkey. I will weep for nothing, like Diana in the fountain, and I will do that when you are disposed to be merry. I will laugh like a hyen, and that when thou art inclined to sleep.
>
> (ll.141–48)

The vivid image of "more new-fangled than an ape," an image that suggests a range of meanings (newly made, made anew, created in strange fashion, ape-like, akimbo, insistent, superimposed) emphasizes the complexity of a Rosalind who is able to proliferate new images one after the other and who is differently gendered and differently erotic at different moments in the play. All of this takes place in an exclusively linguistic form, that is, in words that evoke not the costume of an ape but a mental image that might overwhelm or at least strongly compete with the figure of the shepherd Ganymede standing on the stage. The superimposition of the ape image draws attention to the layers of costuming already in place; indeed it focuses the eye on what might otherwise be taken for granted, neglected as "conventional": boy dressed as girl dressed as boy. The images also force an audience to attend to the superimposition of one sort of desire (human and social) on another (animal and asocial) and of one human form on another and its subsequent stripping away. The eroticized violation of her own privacy enacted by Rosalind creates a kind of seeing for all her audiences which is clearly beyond the literal. Our "seeing" here depends ironically on the "ape" and requires a kind of interpretation that displays and embarrasses.

Although this language is not, strictly speaking, emblematic, it does move a great distance in that direction by calling up the conventional amalgam of the human and bestial which attracts Shakespeare throughout his career: "mountaineers, / Dew-lapp'd like bulls" (*The Tempest*, 3.3.44–45), the "beast with two backs" (*Othello*, 1.1.116–17), the "poor, bare, fork'd animal" (*King Lear*, 3.4.107–8).

Thus, if we return to the question of visual potency, we might be tempted to reframe it: if, as is often the case in Shakespeare's plays, metaphor is made visual and the visual metaphoric, which is to be judged most arresting, possessing most *enargeia*, a liveliness so potent, as Christopher Braider describes it, as to convey presence: "the power of filling the beholder with an overwhelming sensation of dramatic physical presence"?[24] In addressing this question, it is important to notice that the "overwhelming sensation" to which Braider refers seems often to come in moments of ekphrasis in which verbal pictures vie for attention with the stage precisely because the allegorical is unfinished, enigmatic, layered, odd. Paradoxically, the stagy "elsewhere" competes with the stage. While Elizabethan writers such as Sidney frequently fall back on the platitude that painting is mute poetry, poetry a speaking picture, the issue is clearly more complex, unsettled, and unsettling.

The questions of where visual potency is located and how it is most significantly experienced are self-consciously raised also in *Midsummer Night's Dream*, a play that confronts the issue of representation head on, most obviously by means of the artifice of the play-within-the-play, in which the mechanical's play-business directly interrogates where "seeing" is located, exploring the tension between literal seeing and seeing in an interpretive way: *what is lion?* It appears as a fearful creature to fright the ladies, a mere emblem from a book, something that disfigures into its absence, "not a lion" (3.1.35), into name ("lion" [5.1.225], "Snug" [l. 223]), into split costume (3.1.36–37), into "no such thing" (3.1.43), into generalized "man as other men are" (l. 44), and into the specific ("Snug the joiner" [5.1.223]).[25] Such a vivid and disjunct representation occurs in *As You Like It* once Rosalind leaves the court for the forest, appearing both as the talkative Ganymede and as a portrait created by Orlando on paper and on the trees: "Hang there my verse, in witness of my love" and "Run, run Orlando, carve on every tree / The fair, the chaste, and unexpressive she" (3.2.1, 9–10). Already the question of how the verse is to capture Rosalind is raised by the word "unexpressive": unable to be captured in words, without words, lacking expression, a visual sign as female (only a picture, dumb), about to speak as male. It is not "she" but rather Orlando who cannot find the expressions he wants to present the object of his affections.

Rosalind enters reading the portrait on the paper. Rosalind reads herself off the page (as character must be read from script) and yet reads herself as warped into a picture and a poem, both of which are at odds in various ways with the speaker who is their purported source:

From the east to western Inde,
No jewel is like Rosalind.
Her worth being mounted on the wind,
Through all the world bears Rosalind.
All the pictures fairest lind
Are but black to Rosalind.
Let no face be kept in mind
But the fair of Rosalind.
(3.2.86–93)

The female portrait here, so codified and conventional as to be comic, is read aloud by the woman—played by a boy and disguised as a boy—who is being praised in the clichéd poetry of the yet-untutored Orlando. The gaps created among the various pictures, to which the poem itself draws attention, are vast: between what Orlando imagines he sees (having fallen in love at first sight) and what this conveys, between the portrait in verse and the figure of Ganymede onstage, between the various pictures words and eyes create, between this picture and "*all the pictures fairest lin'd.*"

Such confusion is extended in the second poem, in which Orlando compares Rosalind to ideal representations of women such as Cleopatra, Atalanta, and Lucretia. The problematics of representation are unavoidably thrust into view, especially as we are asked to keep the fair Rosalind's *face* in mind as the doubly cross-dressed boy reads the portrait that can match what an audience sees only by an effort of mind.

Nature presently distill'd
Helen's cheek, but not her heart,
Cleopatra's majesty,
Atalanta's better part,
Sad Lucretia's modesty.
Thus Rosalind of many parts
By heavenly synod was devis'd,
Of many faces, eyes, and hearts,
To have the touches dearest priz'd.
(ll. 141–49)

What interests me about this bad poem is that it is bad—a failure at representation because it relies on cliché, uses obvious rhymes, thumps along in regular rhythm. Yet it also highlights the more general problem of how representation fails, and it becomes interesting as Shakespeare's statement on such failure. More specifically, it draws attention to what the audience comes to recognize about Rosalind as the play progresses: that she is a "*Rosalind of many parts*," beyond description, "unexpressive"; and that what one *sees* is determined by potent images such as those of Cleopatra or Helen—that is, one sees according to preestablished patterns. The way we see is affected, most obviously, by what we believe we are seeing and what we name it, a point made over and over again by scholars interested in the homoerotic nature of Shakespeare's theater and critics curious about what members of the audience "saw" when they saw boys playing girls and boys with quite ordinary looks playing girls who were said to "look like" Helen.

One cannot but see by means of emblem and allegory, and, here as elsewhere in Shakespeare, emblem helps to define character. More frequently the emblem of a character provides some new depth. We learn of Viola's love-longing and even know her confused sexuality as she describes the "worm i' th' bud" (*Twelfth Night*, 2.4.111), that suggests genitals confusedly entangled and refers to the "little thing" (3.4.302) beneath damask skirts which the actor and Cesario possess but which Viola *lacks*. The actor playing Cleopatra looks like a boy dressed up onstage, but when this character is emblematized in the long ekphrastic monologue by Enobarbus, she is created as a mental image more visually realized, perhaps, than the costumed player could ever be. We see the actor onstage, in part at least, as Enobarbus has memorialized her, and certainly that is the Cleopatra we remember. Rosalind is Cleopatra here only fleetingly, yet the name itself, especially given the popularity of Cleopatra's image in the Renaissance, is more than imaginatively evocative. It is by means of negotiating the difference between literal and interpretive seeing that one is able to "see" Rosalind's complexity. Like the lion's face in *A Midsummer Night's Dream*, hers is disfigured, created by cosmetics and wigs. The play asks what it might mean to be a Rosalind: a character, a name ("There was no thought of pleasing you when she was christened" [3.2.262–63]), a metaphoric jewel, a face, the witty (cracked/uncracked) voice of a saucy lackey.[26] Later, of course, the deceived Phoebe further *un*-represents Rosalind in her see-saw description of a figure whose words and beauty vie for her praise and add up to make—she presumes—"a proper man" (3.5.115). The transition from still picture to saucy lackey also implies increasing physical gesture, as if text were to come alive before our eyes. As an interim move, gesture makes us attend to the shift in codes as Rosalind metamorphoses from the stilted, love-lorn, and adored lady to the verbally agile and nimble boy. In this way the play shows again its making and forces the audience to be aware of its artificiality.

Think not I love him, though I ask for him.
'Tis but a peevish boy—yet he talks well—
But what care I for words? Yet words do well
When he that speaks them pleases those that hear.
It is a pretty youth—not very pretty—
But sure he's proud, and yet his pride becomes him.
He'll make a proper man.
(ll. 109–15)

Many have discussed the play-within-the-play courtship scenes between Rosalind and Orlando as teaching them of one another, as preparing them for marriage. What interests me here is the simultaneous disjunction between the scenes of courtship and the ending, and between one representation of "Rosalind" and another, given the friction between verbal and visual insisted on by the play-within-the-play and the charged and erotic eeriness that such impossibility creates.[27] Rosalind is not only *not* the picture hanging from the trees and *not* the figure in the Epilogue, she is also *not* (or, again, not exactly) the picture she creates of herself within this framed inner world of the play. Although she signals her own complexity and wit when she describes herself as future wife, she will also *not*, one assumes, despite her claim to the contrary, cuckold Orlando (4.1.154–68). Thus she is and is not both picture and dialogue, is and is not either one or the other, is perhaps the unresolvable conflicts among them.[28] Thus one of the important ironies of Orlando's poetry is that it acknowledges these conflicts and failures so explicitly and so well:

But upon the fairest boughs,
Or at every sentence end,
Will I Rosalinda write,
Teaching all that read to know
The quintessence of every sprite
Heaven would in little show.
(3.2.132–37)

These artfully bad poems posit a Rosalind who is a heaven in show, a written text, and a sprite to be read—impossibly all of these. Critics are thus brought to argue over the status and coherence of character versus language—it is built into the play. As the poem says, Rosalind's essence is ***to be read***, to be, as she turns out to be, a textbook of language and stories and myths and rhetorical flourishes, and the one who gives language to Orlando, teaching him what to say to woo and have her. "Then you must say, 'I take thee Rosalind for wife'" (4.1.128). Although their conversations move them toward marriage as Orlando begins to learn wit and blank verse, the play nevertheless holds something back from perfect consonance by insisting on various disruptive images as well, by using the disruptive nature of collage.[29]

The move in the direction of closure and possible coherence in *As You Like It* is purportedly effected by means of extreme counterfeiting. Again, to use an analogy to another play, this seems similar to what happens when Hamlet uses counterfeit in order to move away from the "antic disposition" (one kind of counterfeit) to murder. His move to kill the king is effected by his acting, that is, by following the lead of the actors and by adopting an artificial pose in imitation of the overacting Laertes. He acts in order to act. Rosalind faints at the sight of the bloody napkin and calls it "Counterfeit" (4.3.172), but this counterfeit is, as Oliver says, "a passion of earnest" (ll. 170–71). In this moment of counterfeit, Rosalind faints at the sight of blood, an image that suggests menstrual blood, the blood of the virgin on the wedding sheets, the blood of violence, the violence of sex as the hymen is torn. It is a counterfeit that also leads to the final device ("I shall," Rosalind says, "devise something" [l. 181]) in which Rosalind returns as the duke's daughter and the god Hymen arrives to marry all the couples. Rosalind creates herself as capable of effecting magic. First she promises to "cure" Orlando (3.2.414), having learned tricks from her "religious uncle" (l. 336); at the end she promises concord and seems to call up the god Hymen to "bar confusion" and "make conclusion" (5.4.124, 125). Shakespeare is clearly drawing on moments of religious transformation in which one thing becomes another. Even if she looks the same, she will not be, moreover, girl and wife are not, as the play points out, the same either. Paradoxically, then, only by means of artifice—represented as artifice and named as such, especially inthe appearance of the walking emblem of marriage, Hymen—does the play wrap up and stop the endless play of poses, speeches, dresses, redresses, and meanings.

As You Like It: Pastoral

Artifice not only provides the transition out of the play and playing but is in many ways its very center. Especially in plays such as *Midsummer Night's Dream* and *As You Like It*, in which the world presented is so patently and conventionally artificial; one is acutely aware of discrepancies and fissures in representation. David Young discusses the contradictory presentation of love and nature, and, although his emphasis is on ultimate coherence, his essay notes the play's insistence on paradox and the ways in which it raises metaquestions about representation both by its artificial and mannered pastoral form and by what characters say about the form in which they are embedded.[30] Young refers especially to the characters' discussions of pastoral: "Truly shepherd, in respect of itself, it is a good life; but in respect that it is a shepherd's life, it is naught. In respect that it is solitary, I like it very well; but in respect that it is private, it is a very vile life" (3.2.13–17). Pastoral characters are already, one might argue, perfect examples of the tension between the visual and verbal since they appear in shepherd's garb, a defining mark of pastoral, and yet speak with the verbal sophistication of those at court. In the case of Rosalind the fissures and contradictions are multiplied by her cross-dressing and cross-talking—posing as a cynical teacher of rhetoric and its civilizing influences—which underscore her duplicitous and encoded nature. In many ways, then, her pose is itself an emblem of theatrical performance, of complex and contradictory representation.[31] As Robert Weimann points out:

> Theatrical disguise, like any playacting or deliberate counterfeiting, constitutes the rehearsal of what the actor's work is all about: the performer's assimilation of the alien text of otherness itself is turned into a play; it is playfully delivered as an almost self-contained dramatic action itself. In other words, the actor, in *performing* a character in disguise, *presents* a playful version of his own *metier*, a gamesome performance of his own competence in counterfeiting images of both identity and transformation.[32]

The genre of pastoral itself is designed to deceive and hence is also appropriate to a theater focused on deception, not only the visible deception of—as the Puritans were so fond of pointing out—commoners dressed as nobility or boys as girls but also the theme of deception, beginning in *As You Like It* with the deception between brothers. As Puttenham argues, pastoral is a literary form especially designed "to insinuate and glaunce at greater matters."[33] *As You Like It* not only acknowledges the deceptive nature of the pastoral but creates a larger deception by barely mounting the pastoral at all, by almost insisting on its failure to do so. Although it is true that the play suggests a pastoral world, it is also true that in Shakespeare's time the stage was but minimally dressed and outfitted, "the empty space."[34] As I remarked at the outset of this essay, the Forest of Arden is "seen" through the emblematic as given in words: Arden as golden world, as Eden, as the lost pastoral of a Merry England, and as outmoded literary form. This vision of the forest, initially presented by Charles, is picked up first by Duke Senior, who says he is glad for freedom from the court, and then by the First Lord, who provides a Hilliard-like portrait of Jaques and the weeping deer:[35]

> The melancholy Jaques grieves at that,
> And in that kind swears you do more usurp
> Than doth your brother that bath banish'd you.
> To-day my Lord of Amiens and myself
> Did steal behind him as he lay along
> Under an oak, whose antique root peeps out
> Upon the brook that brawls along this wood,
> To the which place a poor sequester'd stag,
> That from the hunter's aim had ta'en a hurt,
> Did come to languish....
>
> (2.1.26–35)

Again the scene seems set in some mythic past, by the antique root of an oak tree and a quarreling allegorical brook. As pastoral figure, Jaques is more emblematic and mannered than dramatic, more artificial than sad. This bookish pastoral is elsewhere, ungraspable, ridiculous, failed. Jaques becomes emblematically melancholic, self-consciously languid and isolated, at one with the injured stag suffering from an incurable wound (see Fig. 1). He is presented as obviously out of place, even if one could know what place it is. The pastoral deer are emblematic: Orlando describes himself as a doe that must find its fawn, Adam. The picture the First Lord paints of Jaques weeping over a deer is emblematic of all destroyed by hunting and/or social cruelty. In this remembered scene Jaques "moralizes the spectacle" and creates an ekphrastic moment that erases literal pastoral:

> ... 'Ay', quoth Jaques,
> 'Sweep on you fat and greasy citizens,
> 'Tis just the fashion. Wherefore do you look
> Upon that poor and broken bankrupt there?'
> Thus most invectively he pierceth through
> The body of the country, city, court,
> Yea, and of this our life, swearing that we
> Are mere usurpers, tyrants, and what's worse,
> To fright the animals and to kill them up
> In their assign'd and native dwelling-place.
>
> (2.1.54–63)

Further, the liberty and festive release that C. L. Barber refers to as an essential part of the pastoral play never quite materializes, although its allegorical possibilities are everywhere. Holiday is in the wrong season: "*winter and rough weather*" (2.4.8). There is no sheepshearing, as in *The Winter's Tale*; no fairies or flowers, as in *A Midsummer Night's Dream*; no nature goddesses, as in *The Tempest*. Moreover, throughout *As You Like It* the pastoral picture is represented and denied, especially in Act 2, in which the Forest of Arden is constantly interrupted and even obliterated by long set speeches that conjure up the court. In the context of the pastoral fiction, it is unsettling that so many such speeches usurp the stage and focus attention elsewhere. Especially given a sparsely furnished stage, the speeches about books in brooks or herds of deer ("fat and greasy citizens") or time ("And so from hour to hour, we rot, and rot" [2.7.27]) or "All the world's a stage" (l. 139) provide ekphrastic moments that create a different sort of seeing, erasing trees, as well as natural harmony:

> All the world's a stage,
> And all the men and women merely players.
> They have their exits and their entrances,
> And one man in his time plays many parts,
> His acts being seven ages.
>
> (ll. 139–43)

One might argue that in the pastoral plays of green worlds the vision is momentary in the mind and meant to evaporate. Not only do the courtiers return to the court but the world that has been visible onstage—a world of fairies in *A Midsummer Night's Dream* or of purported harmony among classes or of performative possibilities in terms of gender—evaporates as if it had never been. The underscoring of such evaporation, especially, of course, in Prospero's farewell-to-revels speech (4.1.146–58), but in all the plays as well, adds to the questions about representation in Shakespeare's theater. It is the design of the play to expose the artificial construction of what we have seen and to problematize its representation.

At this point, in order to draw some broad conclusions about the location of the visual and the differences between literal and interpretive seeing, I turn to one of the most extreme examples of artifice and ekphrasis in *As You Like It*, the scene in which Oliver produces the bloody napkin that causes Rosalind to "counterfeit": Oliver's speech describes how Orlando approaches him as he sleeps under an old oak (just as Jaques is described near the outset of the play: bookends). The speech relates a highly emblematic if ineffable scene, calling out for interpretation: something is hidden, something concealed. Oliver's portrait of himself also demands analysis, since he presents himself in the third person as an object and as an object quite other than he has been before: "wretched," "ragged," "sleeping on his back:" Orlando

> ... threw his eye aside,
> And mark what object did present itself.
> Under an old oak, whose boughs were moss'd with age
> And high top bald with dry antiquity,
> A wretched ragged man, o'ergrown with hair,
> Lay sleeping on his back. About his neck
> A green and gilded snake had wreath'd itself,
> Who with her head, nimble in threats, approach'd
> The opening of his mouth. But suddenly
> Seeing Orlando, it unlink'd itself,
> And with indented glides did slip away
> Into a bush, under which bush's shade
> A lioness, with udders all drawn dry,
> Lay couching head on ground, with catlike watch
> When that the sleeping man should stir; for 'tis
> The royal disposition of that beast
> To prey on nothing that doth seem as dead.
>
> (4.3.102–18)

This ekphrastic speech contains obvious imagery of a violent primal scene with snakes and mouths (although the phallic power here is associated with the female) which ultimately provides the transition to Oliver's conversion, the reconciliation of the brothers, and the marriages.[36] Thus it is an ekphrastic speech, conflating the unconsciously erotic and the spiritual as it gestures toward what cannot be represented except by a pictorial replacement—an especially potent vehicle given cultural suspicion, at least in some quarters, of any sort of picture. Like the play-within-the-play in *Hamlet*, this episode provides a way of contemplating the meaning of the play as a whole—the problematics of representing the relationships among the characters and especially the sexual anxiety attending both homoerotic and heterosexual couples. This scene provides the transition to marriage, which also includes fear of sexuality, violence, dismemberment, confinement to specific gender role. It does so by means of picture. The scene is also a somewhat perverse transition back to the page: a sign of the written, the emblematic, the still moment that can be contemplated, the dead with an uncanny ability to become alive, the allegorical—an embodiment and creation of anxiety. One knows one is "looking" at something horrific, even if one does not know exactly what to make of it.[37]

Why does this long speech drop into the play at this moment? Why does the play interrupt the witty dialogue with this static emblem that seems so at odds with what has gone before? Why does it seem both a moment of essential if mysterious truth and a digression?[38] Why is the charming and dramatic verbal courtship replaced by this wooden visual description of impending doom, which turns out also to be a screen for the courtship between Oliver and Celia, albeit, and perhaps importantly, hidden from view, played out in pictures without words? Why does this scene so move Rosalind that she dies onstage, imaging the little death to come?

The scene seems overly freighted with meaning but meaning that is also oddly unreadable, the blockage that, as Paul de Man suggests, allegory always provides: "Allegorical narratives tell the story of the failure to read.... Allegories are always allegories of metaphor and, as such, they are always allegories of the impossibility of reading—a sentence in which the genitive 'of' has itself to be 'read' as a metaphor."[39] Allegory thus offers both enormous satisfaction, since we seem to have encountered the root of all meaning, and enormous frustration, since that meaning is blocked.[40] This objectified picture, a recitation from memory, paradoxically supplies access to something deeply remembered, extremely detailed and extremely elusive, a sort of screen memory perhaps.[41] It represents what cannot be represented by giving it an artificial form seemingly at odds with the movement of dramatic plot yet mysteriously capable of moving it forward, not directly, as the scenes between Rosalind and Orlando do, but indirectly and allegorically, as if by magic.[42]

As You Like It carries a theory of theatrical production within it—as it insistently enacts disruption and the various ways in which any character, scene, or abstract idea might be represented. The impossibility embedded in ekphrasis and in a scene such as this awkward transitional scene suggests that it is impossibility of representation which is being dramatized: in the crossing-over and conflict between the visual and verbal; in the picturing and especially "unpicturing" of pastoral; in the fracturing of character into highly visual and highly verbal aspects. In other words, Shakespeare's plays repeatedly draw attention to failure, to the overcoming of failure, and to failure again—the failure to construct the very thing that the play sets out to construct. Thus each of the familiar techniques by which Shakespeare calls attention to the construction of the plays also reveals how each device, whether linguistic or visual, ultimately fails to represent fully or falls short: the play-within-the-play; the use of scripts within the script (Hamlet's letter to Horatio, Viola's memorized speeches of courtship, Rosalind's lessons taken directly out of rhetoric books); the endless references to roles and costumes; the insertion of ekphrasis, which interrupts the forward movement of plot; and the homology between acting and acting or play (playing around) and the play.[43] Moreover, Shakespeare's plays continually emphasize what cannot be said ("I cannot heave / My heart into my mouth" [*King Lear*, 1.1.91–92]) and what cannot be pictured: no matter how many efforts are made in *Hamlet*, for example (including but not limited to the dumb show and "The Mousetrap"), the primal scenes of penetration (of intercourse and of Hamlet Senior's murder) remain unseen—elsewhere, represented by other murders.[44] The fact that saying and seeing are often in opposition to one another, one undoing the other, contributes not only to the gap between them but to the instability of representation itself. One might turn to Bottom's assertion that although a "ballet" might be made of his dream in *A Midsummer Night's Dream*, nothing could truly capture it: "The eye of man hath not heard, the ear of man hath not seen, man's hand is not able to taste, his tongue to conceive, nor his heart to report what my dream was. I will get Peter Quince to write a ballet of this dream" (4.1.211–14).

To conclude: the allegorical content of ekphrasis argues that the act of acting is itself a type of allegory: that which *must* be interpreted and which remains nonetheless unreadable. Even as costume itself announces the contingency of character, so it underscores theater's reliance on deception and allegory. In fact, the entire mise-en-scène must be read as worldview, or, to put it another way, the play as a whole must be read even as one reads a single act such as the more obviously emblematic plays-within-the-play. Often it seems obvious that what occurs in small is emblematic—but not so obvious that the entire play might be read in similar fashion, not, as has been argued, as Christian or any other totalizing allegory but rather as decidedly feigned and strange. Puritans opposed to Shakespeare's theater had a clear sense of the dangerous and deceptive nature of the plays, and, indeed, the plays themselves ask for such interpretation.

Each of the plays-within-the-play focuses on a set of lovers, Orlando and Rosalind, Phebe and Silvius, Phebe and Rosalind, Touchstone and Audrey, Oliver and Celia, and each is "counterfeit," that is, in each, someone is fooled or disguised or misapprehended or rendered artificial in a way implying that all this coincidence adds up to something. Taken together, they seem to suggest that a world (not just the world of the court or of Arden) is being presented which must be interpreted, that something is behind what is seen. Things are not what they seem not only because Rosalind is dressed as Ganymede, but because throughout the play every character and scene is rendered purposefully artificial and "elsewhere": one sees what is onstage and also bears in mind what is offstage or only in the mind. Perhaps there is no way to mount a play without its evoking the idea of a veil, behind which must be something, something that is always hidden and screened from view. *As You Like It*, for all its comic ingenuity, also conveys a sense of something erased and missing, some deep aspect of character, some golden world: the Robin Hood days of "yore" (the old order that is represented and destroyed again and again in plays such as *Lear*), the incarnation of the sacred. Shakespeare's theater can be understood as compensatory in many ways for cultural loss, most obviously the loss of magic ritual as represented in the appearance in this play of the god Hymen, the female potency of Rosalind/Ganymede, the conversions of Oliver and Duke Senior.[45] Rosalind articulates her ability to perform magic at the end of the play and thus articulates not Shakespeare's creation of saints or idols (although it was idolatry that the antitheatrical writers opposed) but rather that which must stand in for such: "I can do strange things. I have since I was three year old conversed with a magician, most profound in his art and *yet not damnable*" (5.2.59–62, emphasis added)[46] Rosalind reminds an audience of what is missing. I concur with C. L. Barber's view that the play "reflects the tension involved in the Protestant world's denying itself miracle in a central area of experience. Things that had seemed supernatural events, and were still felt as such in Rheims, were superstition or magic from the standpoint of the new Protestant focus on individual experience."[47] Shakespeare's theater then becomes a variation on memory theater, structurally organized to keep before the eyes of the audience what is missing or about to disappear—hence the focus on and the erasure of the potently visual whether on stage or page. The audience is asked to see with the mind, to call up and remember that which is not literally present, and to accord it complex meaning and weight. Perhaps what we "see" is necessarily elsewhere. Visual moments are as weighty and disturbing as they are because they tend to evoke images missing from the culture, especially images fraught with allegorical and mysterious meaning.

Notes

1. Quotations of *As You Like It* follow Agnes Latham's edition for the Arden Shakespeare (London: Methuen, 1975); all other Shakespeare quotations follow *The Riverside Shakespeare*, ed. G. Blakemore Evans, 2d ed. (Boston: Houghton Mifflin, 1997).

2. See Patrice Pavis, *Languages of the Stage: Essays in the Semiology of the Theatre* (New York: Performing Arts Journal Publications, 1982): "Semiology is concerned with the *discourse of staging*, with the way in which the performance is marked out by the sequence of events, by the dialogue and the visual and musical elements. It investigates the organization of the 'performance text,' that is, the way in which it is structured and divided" (20).

3. See Ludwig Wittgenstein, *Philosophical Investigations*, trans. G.E.M. Anscombe (New York: Macmillan, 1958), 193–229. For example: "The concept of an aspect is akin to the concept of an image. In other words: the concept 'I am now seeing it as...' is akin to 'I am now having *this* image'" (213).

4. See Stephen J. Greenblatt, ed., *Allegory and Representation: Selected Papers from the English Institute, 1979–80* (Baltimore and London: Johns Hopkins UP, 1981), vii–viii.

5. See Martha C. Ronk, "Viola's [lack of] Patience: *Twelfth Night*," *The Centennial Review* 37 (1993): 384–99; and Martha C. Ronk, "Representations of *Ophelia*," *Criticism* 36 (1994): 21–43.

6. Sir Phillip Sidney, "The Defense of Poesy" in *The Renaissance in England*, Hyder E. Rollins and Hershel Baker, eds. (Boston: D. C. Heath, 1954), 610.

7. Murray Krieger, *Ekphrasis: The Illusion of the Natural Sign* (Baltimore and London: Johns Hopkins UP, 1992), 138–39.

8. George Puttenham, *The Arte of English Poesie ...* (Kent, OH: Kent State UP, 1970), 196–97.

9. See, for example, David Freedberg, *The Power of Images: Studies in the History and Theory of Response* (Chicago and London: U of Chicago P, 1989). According to W.J.T Mitchell, 'A verbal representation ... may refer to an object, describe it, invoke it, but it can never bring its visual presence before us in the way pictures do' (*Picture Theory: essays on verbal and visual representation* [Chicago and London: U of Chicago P, 1994], 152); but compare Krieger: "Once, like the Neo-Platonists, one pursues Plato's quest for ontological objects seen by the mind's eye rather than phenomenal objects seen by the body's eye, then the superiority of interpretable—and hence intelligible—symbols, visual or verbal, over the immediately representational arts, is assured" (21).

10. "The ambivalence about ekphrasis, then, is grounded in our ambivalence about other people, regarded as subjects and objects in the field of verbal and visual representation. Ekphrastic hope and fear express our anxieties about merging with others" (Mitchell, 163). "The 'differences' between images and language are not merely formal matters: they are, in practice, linked to things like the difference between the (speaking) self and the (seen) other; between telling and showing; between 'hearsay' and 'eyewitness' testimony; between words (heard, quoted, inscribed) and objects or actions (seen, depicted, described); between sensory channels, traditions of representation, and modes of experience" (5). Mitchell's work informs much of my thinking here.

11. Mitchell, 152.

12. See Angus Fletcher, *Allegory: The Theory of a Symbolic Mode* (Ithaca, NY: Cornell UP, 1964); and Craig Owens, "The Allegorical Impulse: Toward a Theory of Postmodernism," *October* 12 (1980): 67–86. On the rehistorizing of Renaissance ideas concerning interiority, see, for example, Katharine Eisaman Maus, *Inwardness and Theater in the English Renaissance* (Chicago and London: U of Chicago P, 1995).

13. See Paul de Man, "Pascal's Allegory of Persuasion" in *Allegory and Representation*, Stephen J. Greenblatt, ed. (Baltimore and London: Johns Hopkins UP, 1981), 1–25, esp. 1–2.

14. See Louis Adrian Montrose, "Of Gentlemen and Shepherds: The Politics of Elizabethan Pastoral Form," *ELH* 50 (1983): 415–59; and Louis Montrose, *The Purpose of Playing: Shakespeare and the Cultural Politics of the Elizabethan Theatre* (Chicago and London: U of Chicago P, 1996). See also Robert Weimann, "Textual Authority and Performative Agency: The Uses of Disguise in Shakespeare's Theater," *New Literary History* 25 (1994): 789–808; and John Dixon Hunt, "*Pictura*, *Scriptura*, and *Theatrum*: Shakespeare and the Emblem," *Poetics Today* 10 (1989): 155–71.

15. Huston Diehl, *Staging Reform, Reforming the Stage: Protestantism and Popular Theater in Early Modern England* (Ithaca, NY, and London: Cornell UP, 1997), 4.

16. In her discussion of John Foxe, Diehl also examines the reformers' profound concern over the devotional gaze: Foxe "ridicules 'our mass-men' for 'gazing, peeling, pixing, boxing, carrying, re-carrying, worshipping, stooping, kneeling, knocking.' ... Protestants object to the Mass because it deflects the worshipper's attention away from an invisible God, focusing instead on material objects and 'man-made' images. In an effort to break the habit of 'seeing and adoring the body in the form of bread,' John Foxe ridicules worshipers who 'imagine a body were they see no body'" (100).

17. Jonas Barish, *The Antitheatrical Prejudice* (Berkeley: U of California P, 1981), 164.

18. Diehl, 134.

19. See D. J. Gordon, "Poet and Architect: The Intellectual Setting of the Quarrel between Ben Jonson and Inigo Jones" in *The Renaissance Imagination: Essays and Lectures by D. J. Gordon*, Stephen Orgel, ed. (Berkeley: U of California P, 1975), 77–101. On the influence of reformation politics and iconoclasm on the period, see Ernest B. Gilman, *Iconoclasm and Poetry in the English Reformation: Down Went Dagon* (Chicago and London: U of Chicago P, 1986).

20. John Calvin, *Institutes of the Christian Religion*, quoted here from Ann Kibbey, *The interpretation of material shapes in Puritanism: A study of rhetoric, prejudice, and violence* (Cambridge: Cambridge UP, 1986), 47.

21. John Calvin, *Institutes of The Christian Religion*, trans. Henry Beveridge, 2 vols. (London: James Clarke, 1949), 1:96.

22. William Perkins, *The Workes of that Famovs and Worthy Minister of Christ in the Vniuersitie of Cambridge*, 3 vols. (London, 1612), 1:669–99, esp. 695.

23. John N. King, *Tudor Royal Iconography: Literature and Art in an Age of Religious Crisis* (Princeton, NJ: Princeton UP, 1989), 223 and 226 (Fig. 74).

24. Christopher Braider, *Refiguring the Real: Picture and Modernity in Word and Image, 1400–1700* (Princeton, NJ: Princeton UP 1993), 9. Cf. Stephen Orgel: "When Ben Jonson opened *The Masque of Beauty* with Boreas (the north wind) and January, he gave them the attributes he found in the standard Renaissance *Iconology* of Cesare Ripa.... Commentators since Burckhardt have assured us that the Renaissance spectator would have recognized these figures at once. Jonson apparently believed otherwise, for however standard the imagery, January begins the masque by explaining it.... One of our chief difficulties in producing Elizabethan plays on modern stages is the ubiquitousness of the dialogue; it does not only explain, it often parallels or duplicates the action. Even in the heat of combat, Renaissance characters regularly pause to describe in words the actions we see taking place" (*The Illusion of Power: Political Theater in the English Renaissance* [Berkeley: U of California P, 1975], 25–26).

25. As another pastoral comedy that ends with marriage, *Dream* also has many parallels to *As You Like It*. The mechanicals deconstruct (or, to use Peter Quince's language, "disfigure" [3.1.60]) "Pyramus and Thisbe" by their literalness and attention to visual props, to real lions, and to the breaking of illusion, as when Bottom addresses the onstage audience so directly as to stop the play. Thus the mechanicals' rehearsal and performance directly raise the question of where "seeing" is located, of the tension between literal seeing and seeing in an interpretive way. In the rehearsal the question each of the players asks about how to represent is not simply comic stage business; it is *the* central question concerning dramatic representation: is "moonshine" in language or verbal image; is it in the sky; can it be represented by a bush of thorns and a lantern carried by "the person of Moonshine" (3.1.61)? As Bottom cries: "A calendar, a calendar! Look in the almanac. Find out moonshine, find out moonshine" (ll. 53–54). If one could *find out*, Bottom seems to suggest, all problems of representation would be solved, but, of course, his very cry indicates the foolishness of the endeavor of grasping moonshine, of locating any authentic, unalterable source of meaning. Shakespeare's plays elude, often in such self-

conscious ways as this, *finding out*. At court, representation is further problematized by Philostrate's initial description of the play and players ("it is nothing, nothing in the world" [5.1.78]), by the mocking interruptions from the audience, and even by Theseus's defense of using the imagination to "amend" the play. Terence Hawkes points out that bad acting, such as we see in "Pyramus and Thisbe," has considerable value in that "it affords insight into the workings of drama itself" (27). On the notions of "self" presented by Bottom's description of moonshine, see Lloyd Davis, *Guise and Disguise: Rhetoric and Characterization in the English Renaissance* (Toronto: U of Toronto P, 1993), 13. See also Jean H. Hagstrum, *The Sister Arts: The Tradition of Literary Pictorialism and English Poetry from Dryden to Gray* (Chicago: U of Chicago P, 1958), 57–92.

26. "The metaphoric displacement of sexually threatening women into jewels, statues and corpses attests that these plays contain rather than affirm female erotic power" (Valerie Traub, "Jewels, Statues, and Corpses: Containment of Female Erotic Power in Shakespeare's Plays" in *Shakespeare and Gender: A History*, Deborah Barker and Ivo Kamps, eds. [London and New York: Verso, 1995], 120–41, esp. 137). For discussions of Rosalind as saucy boy, see Natalie Zemon Davis, "Women on Top: Symbolic Sexual Inversion and Political Disorder in Early Modern Europe" in *The Reversible World: Symbolic Inversion in Art and Society*, Barbara A. Babcock, ed. (Ithaca, NY, and London: Cornell UP, 1978), 147–90; and Juliet Dusinberre, *Shakespeare and the Nature of Women* (London: Macmillan, 1975).

27. For a discussion of the wrestling scene as a play-within-the-play and as accentuating the tension between performance and script, see Cynthia Marshall, "Wrestling as Play and Game in *As You Like It*," *Studies in English Literature* 33 (1993): 265–87.

28. Susanne L. Wofford discusses these threats of cuckoldry as functioning in an apotropaic manner in "'To You I Give Myself, For I Am Yours': Erotic Performance and Theatrical Performatives in *As You Like It*" in *Shakespeare Reread: The Texts in New Contexts*, Russ McDonald, ed. (Ithaca, NY, and London: Cornell UP, 1994), 145–69. Cf. Stanley Cavell, *The Claim of Reason: Wittgenstein, Skepticism, Morality, and Tragedy* (Oxford: Clarendon Press; New York: Oxford UP, 1979), 326–496.

29. In an earlier article on the play, I argue that Rosalind teaches Orlando to be worthy of her and of marriage by teaching him language by means of conventional rhetorical techniques (including lying and deceit); see Martha Ronk Lifson, "Learning by Talking: Conversation in *As You Like It*," *Shakespeare Survey* 40 (1988): 91–105. I am now less sanguine than I was about the coherence of character or play, more convinced that different techniques often work at cross-purposes.

30. See David Young, *The Heart's Forest: A Study of Shakespeare's Pastoral Plays* (New Haven, CT: Yale UP, 1972), 38–72.

31. See James M. Saslow, *Ganymede in the Renaissance: Homosexuality in Art and Society* (New Haven, CT and London: Yale UP, 1986), 83.

32. Weimann, 798–99.

33. Puttenham, 53.

34. See Peter Brook, *The Empty Space* (New York: Atheneum, 1968).

35. Patricia Fumerton describes Hilliard's *Young Man among Roses* (c. 1587–88) in a way reminiscent of Jaques: the painting "quintessentially expresses the problematics of representing sincerity through artifice, simplicity through ornament, and secret self through public display" (*Cultural Aesthetics: Renaissance Literature and the Practice of Social Ornament* [Chicago and London: U of Chicago P, 1991], 81).

36. Interestingly, the threatened death of Viola/Cesario under Duke Orsino's sword provides a similar transition in *Twelfth Night*, 5.1. See Joel Fineman, "Fratricide and Cuckoldry: Shakespeare's Doubles" in *Representing Shakespeare: New Psychoanalytic Essays*, Murray M. Schwartz and Coppelia Kahn, eds. (Baltimore and London: Johns Hopkins UP,

1980), 70–109, esp. 93; and Valerie Traub, "Desire and the Difference it Makes" in *The Matter of Difference: Materialist Feminist Criticism of Shakespeare*, Valerie Wayne, ed. (Ithaca, NY Cornell UP, 1991), 105.

37. Mitchell discusses Shelley's "On the Medusa of Leonardo Da Vinci in the Florentine Gallery" in relation to gender confusion with female snakes and vaginal mouths on men; one might also compare Viola's "worm i th' bud": "If ekphrasis, as a verbal representation of a visual representation, is an attempt to repress or 'take domain' over language's graphic Other, then Shelley's Medusa is the return of that repressed image, teasing us out of thought with a vengeance" (173). The passage in *As You Like It* seems an announcement of "that which we are not to look upon," although I am uncertain to what it refers. See also Bryan Wolf, "Confessions of a Closet Ekphrastic: Literature, Painting and Other Unnatural Relations," *Yale Journal of Criticism* 3 (1990): 181–203.

38. Both aspects of ekphrasis—digression and essence—are emphasized in Grant F. Scott, "The rhetoric of dilation: ekphrasis and ideology," *Word & Image* 7 (1991): 301–10.

39. Paul de Man, *Allegories of Reading: Figural Language in Rousseau, Nietzsche, Rilke, and Proust* (New Haven, CT, and London: Yale UP, 1979), 205.

40. As Joel Fineman suggests, there is a formal affinity of allegory with obsessional neurosis (both incompletable), "which, as Freud develops it in the case of the Wolfman, derives precisely from such a search for lost origins, epitomized in the consequences of the primal scene" ("The Structure of Allegorical Desire" in Greenblatt, ed., 26–60, esp. 45).

41. See Sigmund Freud, *The Complete Introductory Lectures on Psychoanalysis*, ed. and trans. James Strachey (New York: W. W. Norton, 1966), 200–201.

42. Fletcher argues that especially in the chance happenings in pastoral, accidents of fortune seem to be caused by something magical or occult: "Whenever fictional events come about arbitrarily through the workings of chance ('accidents') or are brought about by the supernatural intervention of a superior external force ('miracles'), this accident and this intervention have the same origin, in the eyes of religion and poetic tradition .... accidents always are the work of daemons" (187).

43. According to Keir Elam, "there is a further historical dimension to Shakespeare's verbal self-mirroring, a dimension that is not so much theoretical as cultural and artistic. Formal self-reflection is one of the dominant features of baroque art in all its forms, and there is no question that the poetics of Shakespearean comedy, in its pursuit of structural and rhetorical complexity, is governed by the spirit of the baroque. The pleasures of Shakespeare's eminently self-interrogating dramatic art are in this respect the same pleasures derived from the mirroring games of the visual and other art forms of the period" (*Shakespeare's Universe of Discourse: Language-Games in the Comedies* [Cambridge: Cambridge UP, 1984], 23).

44. Discussing "The Mousetrap" in *Hamlet* as Shakespeare's most profound examination of mimesis, Robert Weimann states: "*The Mousetrap* itself becomes ... a self-conscious vehicle of the drama's awareness of the functional and thematic heterogeneity of mimesis itself. Such mimeses ... provokes differing levels of contradiction, such as that between speaking and acting, or that between theory and practice, which, in their turn, link up with the thematic conflict, associated with the central figure of the play, between discourse and action, conscience and revenge" ("Mimesis in *Hamlet*" in *Shakespeare and the Question of Theory*, Patricia Parker and Geoffrey Hartman, eds. [New York and London: Methuen, 1985], 275–91, esp. 279–80).

45. See Phyllis Rackin, "Androgyny, Mimesis, and the Marriage of the Boy Heroine on the English Renaissance Stage," *PMLA* 102 (1987): 29–41.

46. See Michael O'Connell, "The Idolatrous Eye: Iconoclasm, Anti-Theatricalism, and the Image of the Elizabethan Theater," *ELH* 53 (1985): 279–310.

47. C. L. Barber, *Creating Elizabethan Tragedy: The Theater of Marlowe and Kyd*, ed. Richard P. Wheeler (Chicago and London: U of Chicago P, 1988), 101.

ROBERT LEACH

As You Like It—A 'Robin Hood' Play

Professor Stephen Knight has confidently asserted that 'Shakespeare's *As You Like It* is a consciously non-Robin Hood play',[1] and of course in a literal sense, this is true. Yet after Orlando's complaints and bitter exchange with Oliver, and after the negative remarks concerning the banishing of the old Duke, the very first positive statement in the play, tells of the Duke's retreat to

> the forest of Arden, and a many merry men with him; and there they live like the old Robin Hood of England. They say many young gentlemen flock to him every day, and fleet the time carelessly, as they did in the golden world.[2]

When I was preparing a professional production of *As You Like It* in 1995,[3] I found this an immediate pointer to something significant in the play which it shares with the Robin Hood tradition and especially the Robin Hood games of the late Middle Ages.

The Robin Hood May games and plays were widespread, especially in Britain's market towns, between about 1400 and 1600, and—despite the name—they were played almost throughout the summer, certainly between May and the end of July.[4] The May festival, often associated with Whitsun,

From *English Studies* 82, no. 5 (October 2001).

rather than May Day, was one of regeneration and renewal, a celebration of youth rather than of fertility as such. Its form comprised a constantly shifting and overlapping fusion of real life, fictions, playing and pretending. No doubt it varied enormously from place to place, but nevertheless usually it consisted of three basic elements.

First, the 'Robin Hood' and his band of young men, disguised in green costumes, entered the village. They represented, in at best a half-articulated way, the 'noble outlaw', some kind of 'natural' order as opposed perhaps to man-made legalities and structures which permitted, for instance, the gradual encroachment of enclosure upon common land. They may have been local lads who had been into the forest overnight, or they may have been a troupe from a nearby village, but their processional entry in their green costumes was obviously significant. They brought with them the bounty of summer in the shape of green leaves, branches of blossom, and so on, but also the means of enforcing their 'alternative values', bows and arrows, horns, and the like. On arrival, they set up a 'bower', a sort of combination of throne room and tiring-house. How elaborate this was might vary, but its significance is suggested by the fact that in 1566 the Churchwardens of St Helen's, Abingdon, paid as much as eighteen pence 'for setting up Robin Hood's bower'.[5] Even more splendid was the one Henry VIII and his queen were invited to in 1515:

> There was an arbor made of boughs, with a hall and a great chamber and an inner chamber very well made and covered with flowers and sweet herbs.[6]

The arbour, or bower, wherein Robin was enthroned as Lord of Summer with Maid Marian (played by a man, of course) as his Lady, was clearly important. It suggests the possibility of an alternative—local, or communal—power centre, and was often linked to the maypole itself.

> I have seen the Lady of the May
> Set in an arbour (on a holy-day)
> Built by the maypole ...[7]

The maypole, or tree, keeps the relationship with the unenclosed forest significantly alive.

The second 'movement' of the Robin Hood games was its core. It consisted of the entertainment which the young men provided, the centrepiece of which was a rudimentary drama. This was usually set in its outlines, but offered considerable scope for improvisation and for audience participation, especially in the various contests and combats at its heart. Three or four such plays survive, tantalisingly enigmatic, but sufficient to give us an idea of their dramatic form. The earliest is contained in a single sheet manuscript dating from about 1475, and is, according to David Wiles,[8] actually two plays. In the first, set by a linden tree (probably the maypole on the green), a knight and a sheriff plot to capture Robin Hood, who then enters to the knight. They compete at archery, at stone throwing, at tossing the heavy pole, and at wrestling, before they draw their swords and fight to the death. The knight is killed, Robin cuts off his head, and puts it in his green hood. Then Robin dresses in the knight's horse-hide garments and, with the head held high, processes triumphantly round. The second play in this scrap of manuscript includes an archery contest between Little John and Friar Tuck, a skirmish in which the sheriff captures these two outlaws, and then their rescue by Robin. Two other plays were published about 1560, and advertised as 'very proper to be played in May-games'. They are, first, *Robin Hood and the Friar*, which centres on a series of confrontations between Robin and a Friar: the Friar throws Robin into a stream, fights him with quarterstaffs, and after a general melee, is rewarded with membership of the band and also 'a lady free' which much delights him. The second play, *Robin Hood and the Potter*, which is perhaps incomplete, includes Robin breaking the pots of Jack, the potter's boy, and when the Potter himself arrives, a fight between him and Robin. Who is the victor remains unclear.

In these skeletal scraps of drama, there may be inherent social protest—Robin defeats authority in the shape of the knight, the sheriff's proxy; the Friar escapes his Order's vows for sexual adventure; the Potter, perhaps a representative of money-based trade, and hence embryonic capitalism, has his wares destroyed; and so on. Moreover, and perhaps equally significantly, it seems likely that the spectators for this loosely-controlled entertainment were at liberty to join in, and thus identify themselves with the young men who provided it. The boundaries between performer and spectator were significantly blurred. The system was perhaps similar to that in the Victorian fairground boxing booths, where anyone paying a small fee could go a round or two with the professional. This is of course the way (less the small fee) in which Orlando challenges Charles in *As You Like It*. In well over half the extant Robin Hood ballads, which have a clear relationship to the May game dramas, Robin (or occasionally Little John) meets and does some sort of battle with an opponent: usually, in a provocative echo of the St George mumming plays, Robin is defeated, after which his opponent is welcomed into the band, and often provided with the necessary green livery. Contests like these seem to have formed the core of the Robin Hood games. We hear of wrestling matches, quarterstaff combats, archery competitions, and—less expectedly—juggling contests, 'head-breaking' and so on.

Yet if there is a threat to authority in this, it seems to be implicit rather than overt. That the combats are sporting—even perhaps choreographed—rather than real is clear from the tone of the ballads. Thus, *Robin Hood and Little John*, even allowing for the ballad-makers' enthusiasm, offers a lively description of what is surely a rehearsed fight:

The stranger gave Robin a crack on the crown,
  Which caused the blood to appear;
Then Robin, enrag'd, more fiercely engag'd,
  And followed his blows more severe.

So thick and so fast did he lay it on him,
  With passionate fury and ire,
At every stroke, he made him to smoke,
  As if he had been all on fire.

O then into fury the stranger he grew,
  And gave him a damnable look,
And with it a blow that laid him full low,
  And tumbled him into the brook.

'I prithee, good fellow, O where art thou now?'
  The stranger, in laughter, he cried;
Quoth bold Robin Hood, 'Good faith, in the flood,
  And floating along with the tide'.[9]

The fight is performed rather than real, and other contests, too, such as leaping and vaulting, 'Drop Handkerchief' and 'Kiss in the Ring', were surely entered into in a similar spirit. There may have been occasionally jigs, interludes, clown's recitations and flytings,[10] and a description from 1589 enumerates 'pomps, pageants, motions, masks, scutcheons, emblems, impresses, strange tricks and devices, between the ape and the owl, the like was never yet seen in Paris Garden'.[11] Such games and contests seem to offer a way of releasing physically some forms of social tension, and provide a means of experiencing a loosening of shackles, without triggering genuine social consequences.

The third and final part of the Robin Hood game also has implicit social significance, especially concerning the solidarity of the Robin Hood players and the local spectators. The final 'movement' was the *quete*, the purpose of which was to make a communal celebration after the entertainments and competitive sports. Its first components were feasting, drinking, dancing and singing, and again many ballads give a flavour of this.

> A stately banquet they had full soon,
>   All in a shaded bower,
> Where venison sweet they had to eat
>   And were merry that present hour.
>
> Great flagons of wine were set on the board,
>   And merrily they drank round ...
>
> ... And every cup as they drank up,
>   They filled with speed again.[12]

Communal feasting is, of course, an important way of asserting togetherness, and contemporary records, like that of 1505, when the Robin Hood and his troupe from Finchhamstead were provided with 'supper' at Reading, are clear and adamant about this.[13] One of the features of King Henry VIII's Robin Hood adventure in 1515 was the venison and wine they were served. The second part of the *quete* was a collection of money, and the donation of badges or liveries to those who contributed, before the procession's final departure. The collection of money (which often seems to have been put to mundane purposes such as the repair of the church roof or mending the local roads), as well as the mutual identification through badges or costume, serve the same function as the feasting, that of bringing people together.

Such was the pattern apparently followed by Britain's most popular summer pastime during the two hundred years before *As You Like It* was created: a processional entry and the provision of the bower for an alternative ruler; a series of playful combats of various kinds, perhaps embedded in some sort of dramatic performance, which both cast down the proud and allow the participants to experience a sort of freedom; and a communal celebration, including not only feasting, dancing and singing, but also 'buying into' the alternative group. Knight lists well over a hundred references to Robin Hood games between 1426, the earliest reference to games played at Exeter, and 1590, when they were recorded at Cranston in Scotland.[14] Given this enormous, and widespread, popularity, it is little wonder that when the Elizabethan playhouses began demanding more and newer dramas from their hard-pressed playwrights, the writers should sometimes have turned to Robin Hood for matter. Yet, if we may judge by the 'consciously Robin Hood plays' surviving, few were able to use the material of the popular summer games in anything but a superficial manner.

Thus, it was partially appropriated for a small section of the anonymous *George-a-Greene* (1590), which uses a character from the Robin Hood saga as its protagonist, and introduces Robin himself, who enters across the fields with Marian and others. George fights and defeats Robin's sidesmen, Scarlet and Much, before engaging Robin himself inconclusively. Robin invites George to join his band and offers him a livery, and George provides Robin with cakes and beef. The pattern is clear, though the incident is comparatively minor in the play. In Peele's vigorous *Edward I* (1591), Lluellen and the Welsh, having been outlawed, decide to play at the game of Robin Hood, 'the Master of Misrule'. They dress in green, build a cabin, or bower, in the inner stage, and Mortimer, as the Potter, and Friar David, appropriately as Friar Tuck, compete for Maid Marian's favour, first, by singing a song, then in a fight with staves. Again, the debt to Robin Hood games is obvious, though as so often with Peele's drama, the resonances and implications he approaches are never wholly exploited. However, these two plays are the best that extant Elizabethan drama can achieve in its overt dealings with Robin Hood. The surviving later plays develop the character in ways which have little to do with the traditional Robin Hood. Thus, the two plays which comprise *The Downfall and Death of Robert, Earl of Huntington* (1598) by Munday and Chettle, for example, try to recast the old stories to make Robin a victimised nobleman, while the anonymous *Look About You* (1599), a high-spirited conglomeration of well-loved pantomime gags and dressings-up, has little beyond the character's name in common with the May games hero.

It was Shakespeare who understood what the Robin Hood games offered to the formal theatre. He saw that they provided a *structure for festivity*. If his comedies are indeed 'festive' in the sense that C.L. Barber has suggested, here is a pattern developed over two hundred years to express not only what is unique to the summer festival, or holiday, but also its social significance. Of course, this tradition was not all that Shakespeare drew on in *As You Like It*, but there is discernible both a structure and a layer of meaning in this play which is clearly akin to that of the May games. The play can be divided into three sections, or movements. In the first part, the central characters, who seem to represent natural truth against cruel and man-made circumstance, are banished to the greenwood. They become outlaws. To this end, they (or two of them) adopt disguise costumes, and Rosalind takes her equivalent of a bow and arrow, 'a gallant curtal-axe ... and a boar spear'. When they come to where people are living, they set up a bower ('fenced about with olive trees'). Once they are established thus, the play's second movement begins.

In this section, the characters engage in a varied series of not-too-serious contests and pageant-like activities, which yet suggest a forbidden but freer way of living. The games include the creation of love verses, in which Touchstone challenges Orlando; 'flytings' or contests of wit, such as those between Touchstone and Corin, and, later, Touchstone and William, as well as those of Jaques with Orlando, and then with Rosalind; and the pageant-like drama of Silvius and Phoebe, 'truly played', as Corin comments to Rosalind, who suggests that she may 'prove a busy actor in their play'. In this context, the wooing itself becomes a sort of sport, conducted in a tone reminiscent of that used by the ballads to keep Robin Hood's fights from being taken too seriously. This tone is demonstrated from the moment of Orlando's arrival in Arden. Celia declaims: 'There lay he, stretched along like a wounded knight'. When she adds that he was 'furnished like a hunter', Rosalind adds like a bad melodrama actor: 'O ominous—he comes to kill my heart'. Orlando approaches, and Rosalind immediately makes clear—in instructively light tones—the play-game idiom which the following action is to use. 'I will speak to him like a saucy lackey, and under that habit play the knave with him'. She makes clear that Orlando himself is also only playing: Rosalind's uncle taught her 'how to know a man in love ... you are no such man'. Obviously there is much more than a game going on here, but equally clearly the whole of the wooing is, on one level, an elaborate pageant, or game. Orlando is 'to imagine (Rosalind) his love, his mistress', just as an actor must imagine his partner to be other than what he really is. The game climaxes in the mock-marriage which Celia/Aliena conducts for them: 'I cannot say the words'. 'You must begin ... Then you must say ...' This playing is the second 'movement' of *As You Like It*, and its core.

The third movement, the *quete*, is found in the lead up to, and celebration of, the integrating multiple weddings before Hymen in the last scene. Here is a sort of magical solidarity when all the characters come together in song and dance, though with one exception, typically enough for Shakespeare-Jaques. For a moment, or a minute, they live an alternative, exalted way of ordering society. Yet it is only perhaps for the duration of a holiday—time, in the last scene, 'trots hard'. And at its end all the integrated group process together from the stage, except—again typically for Shakespeare—Rosalind, who remains to speak the Epilogue. The glimpsed alternative way is gently allowed to evaporate, and normal perceptions gradually return. The play has offered something that was 'not the fashion'; Rosalind is not 'furnished' appropriately; all must bid her 'farewell'.

Thus, structurally, the first movement of *As You Like It* brings the disguised outlaws to the forest where they set up their bower; the second sees a series of playful contests between the various characters which suggest the overthrow of normal hierarchies; and the third is a celebration of solidarity.

There is subversion, as well as energy, in the structure itself. Within the overarching architectonics of this structure, furthermore, there are a whole series of features which underline *As You Like It*'s likeness to a Robin Hood game. In the first act we see a fragmented miniature of the large pattern when Rosalind decides to 'devise sports' for herself and Celia, and they turn out to be the classically May-game sport of wrestling, and a witty 'flyting' with Touchstone. And later in the play, the venison feast is predicted in the scene of the slain deer, with its song and its triumphal procession. These displacements and 'prequels' not only hint at the overall structure, they also give it a particularly Shakespearean resonance.

Other facets of holiday embedded in the fabric of this play are many. There is for instance the place of the play's action. The Robin Hood guizers bring greenery from the forest to make the place of their games special: they recreate, perhaps only symbolically, Robin's greenwood. This is clearly echoed in Shakespeare's Forest of Arden, which provides a genuine counter to the tensions of Duke Frederick's court, even taking into account all the reservations about the idealisation of the greenwood in the Robin Hood ballads, and the double-edged approach to the forest in Shakespeare's play. In addition to this, holiday is opposed to the everyday routine of our normal working lives, it rebels against the clock's regimentation. It is not difficult to see that Robin Hood's world is quintessentially a timeless one, and works in opposition to the everyday. Thus, he fights repeatedly against representatives of the working world—the potter, the butcher, the jolly pinder of Wakefield, the tanner, the ranger, the pedlar, and many others. And after the combat the tradesman drops his money-earning in order ritually and symbolically to don Robin's livery. Effectively, he enters a world from which clocks have been banished. In the Forest of Arden, a similar timelessness pertains. Here, the fact that it is ten o'clock serves only to show us that

> 'Tis but an hour since it was nine,
> And after one more hour 'twill be eleven.
> And so from hour to hour we ripe and ripe,
> And then from hour to hour we rot and rot;
> And thereby hangs a tale.

Maybe the tale is Jaques's 'seven ages of man', which also reduces time to an absurdity.

Getting outside time like this is extremely subversive. It suggests youth has as much validity as age, holiday is as legitimate as working time, and 'old custom' is as sweet as 'painted pomp'. This is a world turned topsy-turvey, a state signified supremely through 'role reversal', a notable feature of the Robin Hood games. Wiles points to

> the woman who is a man (Maid Marian), the cleric who has no morality (Friar Tuck), large Little John, who is strongest yet subordinate, and Robin Hood, the youth who is the senior, the yeoman who is the lord.[15]

In *As You Like It*, there are similar role reversals: the inexperienced youth, Orlando, out-wrestles the seasoned professional, Charles; the lady, Rosalind, dictates the progress of the love affair; Touchstone, the satirical jester, gets married; and so on. The effect is implicitly to offer an alternative value system to that presented by the vicious and oppressive court of Duke Ferdinand, just as the Robin Hood games offered an alternative (if only a holiday alternative) to the conventions of Tudor England. An adviser to Henry VIII complained in 1536:

> In summer commonly upon the holy days in most places of your realm there be plays of Robin Hood, Maid Marian, Friar Tuck: wherein, besides the lewdness and ribaldry that there is opened to the people, disobedience to your officers is taught.[16]

Lewdness, ribaldry and disobedience to officers are the proper activities of holiday, but they contain within themselves the potential for revolt. There seems little or no evidence that the Robin Hood games ever sparked any meaningful political rebellion, though there are occasional instances when they may have inspired acts of social disruption. In Southaccre, Norfolk, in 1441, a group of labourers threatened the local landowner, calling themselves 'Robynhodesmen'; in 1497, Roger Marshall of Westbury, Staffordshire, was accused of fomenting a riotous assembly, and defended himself by claiming he had been playing a 'Robyn Hode' game; and in Edinburgh in 1561, the apprentices and craftsmen, rioted against the hanging of one of their own, having been 'stirred up to make a Robin-Hood'.[17] Three disturbances in almost two hundred years of countrywide popularity speaks loudly against the Robin Hood games as politically dangerous. Yet it seems to be the case that Elizabethan political officers were anxious to suppress the games. Partly this may have been on religious grounds, for Robin Hood boasted many features of paganism, and when a Christian zealot such as Hugh Latimer visited a parish to preach on a Sunday, only to discover 'the parish are gone abroad for Robyn Hode',[18] his ire was no doubt egregious. Partly also it may have been because the Elizabethan period saw a new wave of common land enclosures (participated in, ironically enough, by Shakespeare himself), with which Robin Hood games were obviously and overtly at odds. At any rate, Robin Hood games, immensely popular nationwide as late as 1570, were virtually extinct by 1590.

Yet the values of the games, and their way of structuring experience, found their supreme outlet in 1600. By adopting the structure of the Robin Hood games, *As You Like It* seems implicitly to endorse the values of holiday, and to propose, at least inferentially, an alternative to hierarchical, conventional, work-a-day society—inclusiveness. For a work which is 'a consciously non-Robin Hood play', *As You Like It* has therefore a remarkable resonance with the Robin Hood tradition, and especially with the traditional summer Robin Hood games.

NOTES

1. Stephen Knight, *Robin Hood: a Complete Study of the English Outlaw*, Oxford, 1994, p. 2.
2. *As You Like It*, World's Classics edition, used throughout.
3. Presented in the open air at Dudley Castle, May–June 1995.
4. The basic information on Robin Hood, and especially Robin Hood plays and games, is from: R.B. Dobson and J. Taylor, *Rymes of Robyn Hood*, London, 1976; J.C. Holt, *Robin Hood*, London, 1982; Stephen Knight, *op. cit.*; David Wiles, *The Early Plays of Robin Hood*, Cambridge, 1981.
5. John Brand, *Observations on Popular Antiquities*, new edition, London, 1900, p. 144.
6. Edward Hall, *Chronicle: Containing the History of England*, London, 1809, p. 582.
7. Sir Thomas Browne, quoted in William Hone, *The Every-Day Book*, vol. 1, London, 1826, p. 547.
8. See David Wiles, *op. cit.*, pp. 33–5.
9. 'Robin Hood and Little John', in Francis James Child (ed.), *The English and Scottish Popular Ballads*, vol. III, New York, 1965, p. 135.
10. See C.L. Barber, *Shakespeare's Festive Comedy*, Princeton, 1972, p. 51.
11. John Brand, *op. cit.*, p. 141.
12. 'Robin Hood and Maid Marian' in Francis James Child, (ed.), *op. cit.*, p. 219.
13. See David Wiles, *op. cit.*, p. 16.
14. Stephen Knight, *op. cit.*, pp. 264–184.
15. David Wiles, *op. cit.*, p. 58.
16. Quoted in David Wiles, *op. cit.*, p. 53.
17. See Stephen Knight, *op. cit.*, pp. 108–109.
18. Hugh Latimer, *Seven Sermons Before Edward VI*, London, 1869, pp. 173–4.

NATHANIEL STROUT

As You Like It, *Rosalynde*, and Mutuality

Over the years, critics have noted a variety of thematic oppositions in *As You Like It*: fortune versus nature, country versus court, a view of time "as the medium of decay" versus time "as the medium of fulfillment," "contrary notions of identity," "the conspicuous narrative artifice of the opening scenes" versus the "equally prominent theatrical artifice in the forest scenes," two different "manipulative modes," and, most recently, the concerns of a "generally privileged audience" versus "the concerns of wage laborers, servants, and clowns."[1] Even the play's title seems to refer to an opposition between audience and author, leading George Bernard Shaw, for one, to read it as a "snub" of the audience's taste: here is what you, the spectators, like (but I, the playwright, do not).[2] Are the oppositions placed in a kind of balance by the end of the play (at least in the character of Rosalind), dissolved by the play's skeptical treatment of seemingly clear-cut distinctions, or are they necessarily partial and constrained gestures toward recognizing the value of what might have seemed to Shakespeare and his audience to be culturally subversive attitudes?[3] It all appears to hinge on whether we think Shakespearean comedy creates harmony among discordant elements, acts like a solvent on social constructions of difference, or serves to contain (though not always completely) the threats to the dominant social and cultural order its characters might sometimes express or embody.

From SEL *Studies in English Literature 1500-1900* 41, no.2 (Spring 2001).

None of these formulations, however, addresses what I would argue is the most important aspect of drama: the dynamic nature of the relationship between audience and play, spectator and actor. A performance in a theater, after all, is a mutual experience—not necessarily an equal one on both sides, but one in which two different groups respond to each other as the play unfolds. A responsive audience will help actors perform better. Good acting will help an audience become better involved in what they are watching. Whether *As You Like It* received applause at the Globe depended on the skill of the actors to produce enjoyment for the audience, and the enjoyment of the audience rewarded the skill of the actors.

Applauding the actors also meant, of course, that the audience was participating in any number of theatrical conventions, not just the convention that applause expresses the pleasure one has received from a performance, but also such basic conventions as boys playing female roles, commoners playing dukes, and the same stage serving as court and as forest. It is currently fashionable to treat any awareness within a work of its foundational conventions as automatically reflecting deep skepticism about their status and value. But to note the conventional aspects of a human activity may merely be to record its very nature. Just as theatrical performances rely on conventions to be successful, so too do certain social performances—marriage, for instance. To the mutual relationship between actor and audience, I suggest, *As You Like It* parallels the mutual relationship between lovers, a relationship which, if it is to end with the couple getting married, similarly depends on conventions being accepted and experiences being shared, especially in Tudor and Stuart England, when "from contact to contract, from good liking to final agreement, most couples passed through a recognizable series of steps."[4] The play, in other words, and, as we shall see, in marked contrast to Thomas Lodge's *Rosalynde* (1590), its main source, establishes connections between past mutual interactions and future mutual outcomes: Rosalind and Orlando's liking for each other leads to their becoming man and wife; our liking for the play and its players leads to our applause at the conclusion of the performance.

One way to connect the past to the future is through the use of narratives, which bring the past into the present so that characters (and audiences) can respond to it. Shakespearean drama typically includes many reports of off-stage events and many accounts of what we are to imagine as having happened in the past lives of characters.[5] *As You Like It* was once criticized on the grounds that the beginning of the play relies too much on characters narrating background that their onstage listeners either already know (Orlando telling Adam about his past relations with Oliver) or do not at that moment need to know (Charles telling Oliver about recent events at court), but narratives occur throughout *As You Like It*, not just in the first scenes, suggesting that narration is not opposed to the play's theatrical core but central to it.[6] There are, for example, several accounts, like those in the first scene, that describe events or supposed events from a time before the play begins, including Celia's eight-line description of how Rosalind and she came to be such close friends that they are "like Juno's swans"; Touchstone's nine lines recalling his love for Jane Smile; Rosalind's fifteen-line fiction (as Ganymede) of her curing a youth in love; and Touchstone's seventeen-line tale of the duel he had "like to have fought."[7] There are also at least seven narratives of recent off-stage events, all but one delivered in the forest: in I.ii Le Beau narrates in ten lines the triple success of "Charles, the Duke's wrastler" (line 126); in II.i a lord takes thirty-four lines to describe how he and Amiens overheard Jaques "weeping and commenting / Upon the sobbing deer" (lines 65–6); in II.vii Jaques excitedly recounts for twenty-two lines his finding "a fool i' th' forest" (line 12); in III.ii Celia's narrative to Rosalind of how she came across Orlando "under a tree, like a dropp'd acorn" (line 235), never gets further than two short sentences, thanks to Rosalind's interruptions and the entrance of Orlando himself; in III.iv Rosalind tells Celia in four lines that she "met the Duke yesterday, and had much question with him" (lines 34–5) but did not reveal herself to her father; in IV.iii Oliver narrates his rescue from a lion by Orlando, a story of fifty lines; and in V.iv the second brother reports in a dozen lines the conversion of Duke Frederick and his companions "both from his enterprise and from the world" (line 162).

From beginning to end, then, in the court and in the forest, the characters of *As You Like It* keep telling stories to each other, enlarging the imaginative world of the play beyond the visible stage, both in space and in time. For Stephen B. Dobranski, the result is an increase in the illusion of realism: in his plays, Shakespeare "convinces us of the worlds that he creates by intimating suggestive details of his characters' past experience."[8] The details also help establish and reinforce the importance of mutuality. Lawrence Danson has argued that in Shakespearean comedy, and especially in *As You Like It*, "Shakespeare discovers the self in the matrix of the family."[9] To place a character in a family is to give him or her the illusion of a past life growing up in mutual relationships with parents, siblings, and relatives. Celia, for example, explains her present affection for Rosalind by stressing her prior mutual interactions with her cousin:

We still have slept together,
Rose at an instant, learn'd, play'd, eat together,

And wheresoe'er we went, like Juno's swans,
Still we went coupled and inseparable.
(I.iii.73–6)

Significantly, though, even Touchstone and Jaques, neither of whom is connected in the play to a family, are given past lives. Touchstone's, perhaps, is a joke: his love of Jane Smile and his avoiding a duel may merely be the court jester's comic fictions. Duke Senior's response to Jaques, on the other hand, when Jaques wishes for the satirical "liberty" (II.vii.47) of a professional fool, accuses him of forgetting his past, of forgetting what he used to be like himself (II.vii.64–9), an exchange that can otherwise seem "puzzling."[10] What we have done to and with others sometimes enables our subsequent actions, sometimes restricts them, and sometimes leads to completely opposite behavior on our part: Oliver can change for the better in the forest; Duke Frederick can change for the worse in the court when he suddenly banishes Rosalind.

That actions in the present are influenced by mutual interactions in the past may not seem a remarkable observation about a work by the author of *Hamlet*, but it is one of the important ways Shakespeare transformed aspects of Lodge's *Rosalynde* into *As You Like It*. Most studies of the relationship of the play to this source have focused on how the details of the prose romance are modified in the light of "the leaner efficiency which drama demands" or on showing "how little, in spite of the general similarity of the outlines, Shakespeare actually owed to Lodge."[11] The latter efforts, in turn, have led to locating the complexities of *As You Like It* in works and writers more sophisticated than *Rosalynde* and its author: in John Lyly's treatment of boy actors playing girls disguised as boys in *Gallathea*, for example, or in Sir Philip Sidney's artistically self-conscious treatment of pastoral conventions in the *Arcadia*, or in Rabelais's subversion of the conventional as mediated through the works of Sir John Harington.[12]

But a source can influence a work to be different along a common axis as well as to be similar. Looked at in this way, *As You Like It* is a reaction against two notable aspects of Lodge's narrative: its understanding of social relations and its presentation of how people explain the ways they act. In *Rosalynde*, male concerns are so much more important than female ones that the latter are effectively excluded from consideration by the time the work ends, and human behavior is repeatedly explained not as a reaction to what other people have done or how they feel about each other, but by reference to long lists of "infallible precepts" that are said to determine our actions.[13] To Shakespeare, on the other hand, love between men and women is grounded in mutual, not just masculine, behavior, and what has happened between people helps make possible what will happen.

In Lodge, a common explanation for a character's actions is some sort of variation on the claim that "nature must have her course" (p. 76), a claim asserted by the narrator, Adam, Alinda, Saladyne, and Rosalind, often in combination with equally deterministic proverbs, as in the narrator's "fire cannot be hid in the straw nor the nature of man so concealed, but at last it will have his course" (p. 8). The even more frequent euphuistic lists of explanatory analogies have a similar effect, as when Alinda teases Rosalind about her love for Rosader: "The wind cannot be tied within his quarter, the sun shadowed with a veil, oil hidden in water, nor love kept out of a woman's looks" (pp. 103–4). Also similar in effect is the recurring use of the myth of Ulysses and the sirens, which is applied by the narrator and six different characters to describe either the impossibility (the sirens being so alluring) or the effort (Ulysses having had to tie himself to the mast) of resisting the nearly irresistible, variously said to be men's desire to love women, Rosader's complaints about being mistreated by his brother Saladyne, Venus, Rosalind's voice, the idea of brotherly concord as urged by Rosader's and Saladyne's father, untrustworthy male lovers, and the pleasure women receive from men's wit. As this evidence suggests, Lodge's characters feel hemmed in by powerful forces, especially by the force of love, and, like Ulysses, they feel they must face these forces on their own. Love, declares Lodge's Phoebe to Rosalind's father, "whatsoever he sets down for justice, be it never so unjust, the sentence cannot be reversed; women's fancies lend favours not ever by desert, but as they are enforced by their desires; for fancy is tied to the wings of fate; and what the stars decree, stands for an infallible doom" (p. 155).

The trouble with such absolute claims, analogies, precepts, principles, and rules is that they impose an impossible rigidity on human behavior. *As You Like It*, as Helen Whall has shown, depicts the difference between mistakenly thinking one is "directly receiving infallible doctrines" and accurately recognizing that using analogies is inherently inconclusive.[14] To liken one thing to another does not make one thing into the other. And, as Maura Kuhn has shown, the word *if*, which occurs more frequently in *As You Like It* than in any other drama by Shakespeare, both promises a consequence (if that is true, then this will happen) and permits alternatives to be imagined.[15] On the one hand, that is, Rosalind (as Ganymede) can promise Orlando that "if you will be married to-morrow, you shall; and to Rosalind, if you will" (V.ii.72–4). On the other hand, Touchstone can use the word *if* to demonstrate how quarrels may be broken off thanks to the capacity of a conditional construction to raise new possibilities: "when the parties were met themselves, one of them thought but of an If, as, 'If you said so, then I said so'; and they shook hands and swore brothers. Your If is the only peacemaker; much virtue in If" (V.iv.99–103). In Lodge's *Rosalynde*, words such as *fortune* and *fate* outnumber instances of *if*; in *As You Like It*, the reverse is the case, and by a wide margin.[16]

A determinism such as Lodge's, it is true, is vividly expressed in *As You Like It* by Jaques when, after declaring that "All the world's a stage" (II.vii.139), he invokes another contemporary commonplace: the inevitable chronological succession of the seven ages of man.[17] To Jaques, the future always holds nothing more than "second childishness, and mere oblivion" (II.vii.165), a vision of human experience that, as Helen Gardner noted, leaves out any mention of "love and companionship, sweet society."[18] In fact, although the speech seems broadly inclusive at the outset—"all the men and women" (II.vii.140)—it narrows quickly to the life of a single male: "And one man in his time plays many parts" (II.vii.142). Even more telling, its list of roles—infant, schoolboy, lover, soldier, justice, old man, senile old man—is made narrower still by its exclusion of the two male roles in relation to women that are played, or that will be played, by the other main male characters in *As You Like It*—the roles of husband and of father. A passage from a 1605 letter by Harington suggests that pursuing the analogy between life and drama did not require the exclusion of such roles: "the world is a stage and we that lyve in yt are all stage players ... I playd my chyldes part happily, the schollar and students part to neglygently, the sowldyer and cowrtyer faythfully, the husband lovingly, the contryman not basely nor corruptly."[19] Because Harington was writing about himself in this letter, it is appropriate that he mentioned only male activities.

Jaques makes a universal assertion about "all the men and women," yet limits their mutual interactions to "the infant / Mewling and puking in the nurse's arms" (II.vii.143–4) and the lover writing poems "to his mistress' eyebrow" (II.vii.149).

Indeed, women are present in Jaques' list only as those two possessive adjectives. Another contemporary use of the theatrical analogy can once again help us see that Shakespeare has constructed the speech so that Jaques ignores any potential for mutuality. Thomas Heywood's prefatory poem to *An Apology for Actors* (1612) declares that "All man haue parts, and each man acts his owne," but then goes on to assign some roles to women that involve their interacting with men:

> She a chaste Lady acteth all her life,
> A wanton Curtezan another playes.
> This, couets marriage loue, that, nuptial strife.[20]

In *As You Like It*, after Hymen has blessed the four pairs of newlyweds near the end of the play, Jaques acknowledges marriage merely to the extent of predicting "nuptial strife" for Touchstone and Audrey—"And you to wrangling" (V.iv.191), he says to the former about the future of his new relationship. Whereas Hymen addresses the couples as couples (using the phrase "you and you" three times, at V.iv.131, 132, 135), Jaques talks only to the men—to Orlando, Oliver, and Silvius, as well as Touchstone—and starts out with Duke Senior, thereby placing the four new marriages in the context, not of Hymen's mutual love, but of "former honor," "land," and "great allies" (V.iv.186, 189). At the end of *As You Like It*, in other words, we can choose to think of marriage as merely a social convention in a patriarchal society, as a public expression of mutual feelings of love, or as an appropriate outlet for the mutual sexual desire that Touchstone earlier points to as an important motive for marrying: "As the ox hath his bow, sir, the horse his curb, and the falcon her bells, so man hath his desires; and as pigeons bill, so wedlock would be nibbling" (III.iii.79–82).

Rosalynde does not offer its readers these multiple possibilities. Like Jaques, it sees the world in masculine, not mutual, terms, despite the gender of the title character, despite Lodge's giving Rosalind (twice) and Alinda (once) the functional equivalents of soliloquies in which they debate with themselves the appropriateness of loving Rosader and Saladyne respectively, and despite Lodge's having Rosalind explain to Alinda (disguised as Aliena) that in criticizing women while disguised as Ganymede, "I keep decorum: I speak now as I am Aliena's page, not as I am Gerismond's daughter; for put me but into a petticoat, and I will stand in defiance to the uttermost, that women are courteous, constant, virtuous, and what not" (p. 37). The masculine bias of *Rosalynde* is immediately apparent from its preface "To the Gentlemen Readers." Although the similar prefaces to Lyly's *Euphues* (1578) and Robert Greene's *Pandosto* (1588) suggest that Lodge's is in part conventional, the first of Barnaby Riche's three prefaces to *Riche His Farewell to Militarie Profession* (1581)—"To the Right Courteous Gentlewomen, bothe of Englande and Irelande"—indicates that a different way of thinking about readers was available at the time.[21] Lodge, however, moves straight from his exclusionary preface to "The Schedule annexed to Euphues' testament, the tenor of his legacy, the token of his love" (p. xxx), in which he has Lyly's popular hero Euphues inform a friend (Philautus) that the ensuing story will greatly benefit the friend's sons. The narrative proper then opens with Sir John of Bordeaux's death bed bequests, advice, and "Schedule" (p. 7) to *his* sons. Prominent among Sir John's "infallible precepts" (p. 2) of paternal advice, moreover, is the claim that any woman, even "if she have all these qualities, to be chaste, obedient, and silent, yet for that she is a woman, shalt thou find in her sufficient vanities to countervail her virtues" (pp. 5–6).

Even Lodge's 1596 narrative *A Margarite of America: For Ladies Delight*, *and Ladies Honour*, which would appear by its title to be especially directed toward women (at least of a certain social class), and which is dedicated to Lady Russell, not a male aristocrat, has a preface addressed "To the Gentlemen Readers."[22] During the tale itself, the narrator acknowledges the audience mentioned in the work's subtitle on two occasions—once in regard to Margarite's feelings: "but what she dreamed I leaue that to you Ladies to decide, who hauing dallied with loue, haue likewise beene acquainted with his dreames"; and once in regard to the love poems of the villain: "which I offer to your iudgement (Ladies)."[23] The closest *Rosalynde* comes to directly addressing women is when the text's usual third person narrative voice suddenly, and uniquely, changes to the first person plural in order to describe how Rosalind and Alinda overhear two shepherds: "Drawing more nigh we might descry the countenance of the one to be full of sorrow, his face to be the very portraiture of discontent, and his eyes full of woes, that living he seemed to die: we, to hear what these were, stole privily behind the thicket, where we overheard this discourse" (p. 40). This momentary uniting of narrator, female characters, and "gentlemen readers" (who will soon "overhear" the shepherds' discourse by reading it on the page) contrasts with Shakespeare's constant blurring throughout *As You Like It* of a single, masculine point of view.

Not surprisingly, the final paragraph of *Rosalynde* reinscribes the values of Lodge's male-centered beginning as the work effectively excludes women not only from being readers, but also from being important to the story at all: "Here, gentlemen, may you see Euphues' Golden Legacy, that such as neglect their fathers' precepts, incur much prejudice; that division in nature, as it is a blemish in nurture, so 'tis a breach of good fortunes; that virtue is not measured by birth but by action; that younger brethren, though inferior in years, yet may be superior to honours; that concord is the sweetest conclusion, and amity betwixt brothers more forceable than fortune" (p. 165). Lodge, that is, conflates his "gentlemen readers" with the sons of Philautus, all of whom are to find lessons about male behavior from *Rosalynde*, not insights into how men and women interact.

As You Like It, of course, begins with a scene depicting a conflict between brothers, a conflict that revolves, in part, around Oliver's refusal to grant Orlando his inheritance from their father.[24] But this focus on males and their property shifts in the second scene, which has no exact parallel in Lodge, as we see Celia and Rosalind talking together. More important, the now well-known epilogue at the end of *As You Like It*, in contrast to the final paragraph of *Rosalynde*, addresses both men and women: "I charge you, O women, for the love you bear to men, to like as much of this play as please you; and I charge you, O men, for the love you bear to women (as I perceive by your simp'ring none of you hates them), that between you and the women the play may please. If I were a woman I would kiss as many of you as had beards that pleas'd me, complexions that lik'd me, and breaths that I defied not; and I am sure, as many as have good beards, or good faces, or sweet breaths, will for my kind offer, when I make curtsy, bid me farewell" (Ep. lines 12–23). "If I were a woman" has been the focus of much attention recently as a metatheatrical moment revealing that central convention of Shakespeare's theater: boys playing female roles.[25] It is also important to notice that the epilogue begins by referring to another theatrical convention: "It is not the fashion to see the lady the epilogue; but it is no more unhandsome than to see the lord the prologue" (Ep. lines 1–3). This final concern for convention is related to Rosalind's oft-noted engagement throughout the play with the problem of determining the extent of Orlando's love for her. As Ganymede, Rosalind, several times, tells Orlando that he has failed to follow the conventions for lovers: he looks too healthy and is dressed too neatly (III.ii.373–84); he is not sufficiently concerned with being on time to meet his beloved Rosalind, even if he thinks Ganymede is just pretending to be her (IV.i.38–41). How can Rosalind be certain Orlando is in love with her if he does not act like a lover? On the other hand, how can Rosalind trust conventional behavior to express true motives? Acting as a lover is expected to act can make a young man look as if he were in love when he is, instead, merely passing the time, merely engaging in what Rosalind jestingly calls early in the play the "sport" of "falling in love" (I.ii.24–5).

Whether of courtship or of the theater, conventions are meaningful only if the parties involved mutually accept them. Within the play, for example, Orlando's saying "I take thee, Rosalind, for wife" (IV.i.137) will not result in marriage if Rosalind says, "I do take thee, Orlando, for my husband" (IV.i.139), only in her disguise as Ganymede. Similarly, the boy actor's saying "If I were a woman" to the assembled onlookers in the theater has an impact only if we participate, for the main body of the play, in the convention that Rosalind is female. The boy actor's gender is, in a sense, up to our imaginations, and the success of his performance depends on our having been pleased enough by it to accept the invitation implicit in the play's title to like what we have seen. The epilogue underscores the importance of mutual enjoyment to an extraordinary degree. In its twenty-three lines, seventeen first person pronouns are linked to eleven second person pronouns through ten instances of the word *good* and several forms of to *like* and *to please*, all within the structure of a well-reasoned argument-assertion ("it is not" [line 1], "'tis true that" [line 4]), counterassertion ("but" [line 2], "yet" [line 5]), conditional statement ("if" [lines 3, 18]), and conclusion ("then" [line 7], "therefore" [line 10], "I am sure" [lines 20–1]).

We have seen that Jaques' seven ages speech clearly rejects the idea that mutual relationships are possible. It has not been sufficiently noticed that when Silvius describes being in love to Orlando, Phebe, and Rosalind (as Ganymede), he does nearly the same thing from the opposite direction:

> It is to be all made of fantasy,
> All made of passion, and all made of wishes,
> All adoration, duty, and observance,
> All humbleness, all patience, and impatience,
> All purity, all trial, all observance.
>
> (V.ii.94–8)

In a now classic study of the play, Harold Jenkins remarks that because "Touchstone is only once, and Jaques never, allowed a sight of Silvius before the final scene of the play," we should understand that "Silvius has not to be destroyed or the play will lack something near its center."[26] Certainly, Silvius's extravagant view of love would be quickly deflated by the cynical realism of the other two characters had they been present. Yet the absence in this scene of Celia and Oliver from those listening to Silvius's hyperbole is as important as the absence of Touchstone and Jaques: Silvius defines unreciprocated love, not a mutual relationship.

What Silvius says about love, in fact, differs significantly from what Rosalind says to Orlando earlier in the scene about the rapid progress of Celia and Oliver's feelings for each other. Rosalind describes a mutually experienced sequence of events: "your brother and my sister no sooner met but they look'd; no sooner look'd but they lov'd; no sooner lov'd but they sigh'd; no sooner sigh'd but they ask'd one another the reason; no sooner knew the reason but they sought the remedy: and in these degrees have they made a pair of stairs to marriage" (V.ii.32–8). No sooner do Rosalind and Orlando meet, look, and sigh in act 1, but Orlando gets tongue-tied and the two are separated from each other. In addition to its suddenness, then, Rosalind describes a mutuality in the relationship between Celia and Oliver that in V.ii is still missing from her relationship with Orlando (for she is still disguised as Ganymede) as well as missing from the relationship between Silvius (in love with Phebe) and Phebe (who at the moment thinks she is in love with Ganymede). "Neither call the giddiness of it in question, the poverty of her, the small acquaintance, my sudden wooing, nor her sudden consenting; but say with me, I love Aliena; say with her that she loves me; consent with both that we may enjoy each other" (V.ii.5–9). To Oliver, who speaks these lines to his brother, as to Rosalind, the rapidity with which Celia and he make "a pair of stairs to marriage" is not as important as their climbing those stairs together.

This mutual joy is not, however, shared by Orlando: "They shall be married tomorrow; and I will bid the Duke to the nuptial. But O, how bitter a thing it is to look into happiness through another man's eyes! By so much the more shall I to-morrow be at the height of heart-heaviness, by how much I shall think my brother happy in having what he wishes for" (V.ii.42–7). The phrasing suggests self-involvement—I can't be happy though my brother is. Surprisingly, Orlando is the character in the play whose lines have the highest frequency of the personal pronouns *I*, *me*, and *my*—not Jaques or Frederick or Oliver, all of whom might come to mind as speaking or acting selfishly. Orlando begins the play by asserting himself and his interests against his brother, and when he first meets Duke Senior, he sounds a similar note: "he dies that touches any of this fruit / Till I and my affairs are answered" (II.vii.98–9). The Duke, as has often been noted, though usually in contrast to Jaques, speaks throughout the play of community and of sharing—"Now, my co-mates and brothers in exile" (II.i.1); "Sit down and feed, and welcome to our table" (II.vii.105);

every of this happy number,
That have endur'd shrewd days and nights with us,
Shall share the good of our returned fortune.
(V.iv.172–4)

Orlando turns everything toward himself. "Fair youth, I would I could make thee believe I love" (III.ii.385–6); "then in mine own person, I die" (IV.i.93); "I can live no longer by thinking" (V.ii.50).

Rosalind has been said to be so self-aware that she can educate Orlando about the nature of love.[27] Orlando has been said to be self-aware enough to know that he is only "*playing* Orlando" in his exchanges with Ganymede: "I take some joy to say you are [Rosalind]," he says, "because I would be talking of her" (IV.i.89–90).[28] Yet in V.ii, it is the sudden love of Celia and Oliver, not anything Rosalind as Ganymede has said, nor anything Orlando has learned from her, that prompts him to end the game. "I can live no longer by thinking" is surely an extravagant, extreme statement. Orlando seems not to have heard (or not to have believed) what Rosalind has already told him, that "men have died from time to time, and worms have eaten them, but not for love" (IV.i.106–8). The actor John Bowe has explained that he performed the exchange with Ganymede in V.ii to show that Orlando there "realizes that the dream is no substitute for the reality."[29] But from Orlando's point of view, the dream is to marry Rosalind, the now unsatisfying reality is to pretend that Ganymede is the woman he loves. What Orlando wants are his wishes and dreams fulfilled, and the possessive pronoun in his very last line in *As You Like It* is the final indication of the importance, to him, of his feelings for Rosalind, no matter how conventionally extravagant his declarations of love sound to anyone else: "If there be truth in sight, you are *my* Rosalind" (V.iv.119; emphasis mine).

Because Rosalind displays "a wry awareness of her own extravagance while insisting on that extravagance as the only adequate expression of her feelings," because she seems to be so much in charge of her relationship with Orlando, it may bother us that she uses a string of conditional constructions near the end of the play to give him the final decision regarding their future together, despite his being so much less alert than she is to the tone of what he has been saying: "Believe then, if you please, that I can do strange things" (V.ii.58–9); "if it appear not inconvenient to you" (V.ii.65–6); "if you will be married to-morrow, you shall; and to Rosalind, if you will" (V.ii.72–4).[30] One way to understand this deference is that it reflects a natural hesitation to commit one's life to another. Rosalind, in Barbara Bono's words, has to "exorcise her own fears about love" during the course of the play.[31] Her deference also partly reflects the uncertainty of ever knowing the full truth about what is going on in the "unexpressed interior" within another person's "theatricalized exterior."[32] We have only outward appearances by which to judge others' inner feelings, as Rosalind knows when she says to Orlando: "if you do love Rosalind so near the heart as your gesture cries it out" (V.ii.61–3). Rosalind needs Orlando to commit himself to her, just as she is willing to commit herself to him, if the two are to enter into the mutual commitment of marriage.

The string of *if* clauses can also, I suggest, be seen as a gesture toward that mutuality, not in the modern sense, with its implication of a meeting of equals, but as the concept might be understood within the social context of a patriarchal hierarchy.[33] Although the marriage service in *The Book of Common Prayer* (1559) gives as one of "the causes for which matrimony was ordained" "the mutual society, help, and comfort that the one ought to have of the other, both in prosperity and adversity," mutuality in a hierarchical world must have always been to some degree unequal.[34] When "The Homily on Marriage" (1562) encourages "mutual love and fellowship" between husband and wife, for example, it does so through the unequal exchange of female submission for male forbearance.[35] No matter how strong their impulses "to controul or command, which yet they may do, to their children, and to their family," wives must "perform subjection" to husbands. A husband, in turn, should "yield some thing to the woman": by forbearing to assert authority all the time, "thou shalt not only nourish concord, but shalt have her heart in thy power and will." How these dynamics might work themselves out in an actual marriage is illustrated in a revealing story recorded by Harington: according to him, his wife once told Queen

Elizabeth that "she had confidence in her husbandes understandinge and courage, well founded on her own stedfastness not to offend or thwart, but to cherishe and obey; hereby did she persuade her husband of her own affectione and in so doinge did commande his."[36] In a hierarchical system, exchanges of mutual affection get imagined and phrased in terms of mutual deference to each other's authority: the wife's obedience commands the husband's love; by not always giving orders, the husband can put his wife's heart in his "power and will."[37] So, even though it is Orlando (and Silvius and Phebe) who is obedient to Rosalind's "commands" (V.ii.121) as she arranges matters so that their love can end in the mutual commitment of marriage, Rosalind must also acknowledge the authority of Orlando for the relationship to be mutual.

Orlando, of course, is too much in love not to marry. From his point of view, all that is necessary for his commitment is a reunion with Rosalind. But our sense of his certainty should not obscure the possibility of his refusing. The idea that the marriage could be broken off at the last minute is, I take it, an important implication of Touchstone's extended description of how an argument can move in a series of seven steps from "the Retort Courteous" to "the Lie Direct" and so to a duel (V.iv.92, 96). Like the progress toward Celia and Oliver's marriage, as described by Rosalind, the progress toward a duel, as described by Touchstone, follows from the mutual responses of the two parties, and, as we have seen, Touchstone concludes that a duel can be avoided even after the seventh step has been reached through a mutually agreed on *if* statement: "All these you may avoid but the Lie Direct; and you may avoid that too, with an If" (V.iv.97–8). Orlando and Rosalind, though, do not wish to avoid getting married; when they use "an If" it expresses their commitment to each other rather than serves as an escape clause from that commitment: "If there be truth in sight, you are my Rosalind" (V.iv.119); "I'll have no husband, if you be not he" (V.iv.123). Marriage is their mutual choice, what each of them would like to have happen.

As we have seen, Lodge ends *Rosalynde* by recalling its patriarchal beginning in which a dying father bequeaths his property to his sons and advises them about the inevitable dangers of women, an ending perfectly in keeping with the feelings of Lodge's characters throughout the narrative that they do not have much freedom to decide their own fates. In *As You Like It*, "we see persons in relation": to each other through their immediate actions on the stage, to their pasts, which are brought before the audience through the many instances of narration in the play, and also to their futures, which depend, in part, on the many choices they make—Celia choosing to accompany her banished cousin into the forest, Adam choosing to accompany his master as he seeks safety from his brother, Rosalind choosing not to reveal herself right away to either the man she loves or her father, Orlando choosing to save Oliver from the lioness, and Jaques choosing not to leave the forest with Duke Senior and the others, to list only a few.[38] Shakespeare, that is, ends *As You Like It* so that we understand how the title need not mean that the author is simply giving in to the opposing values of the audience. As depicted in the relationships between Orlando and Rosalind, Celia and Oliver, actor and audience, "as you like it" both expresses the freedom we have to choose whether we like or do not like a play or a person—it is up to Orlando and to Rosalind each to say yes to marriage; it is up to each of us whether to applaud after the epilogue or not—and also acknowledges that for lover and beloved, performer and spectator, sometimes the feeling is mutual.

Notes

1. There is a list of some basic oppositions in Geoffrey Bullough, ed., *Narrative and Dramatic Sources of Shakespeare*, 8 vols. (London: Routledge; New York: Columbia Univ. Press, 1958), 2:150–1. The quotations are from the more recent studies of Alexander Leggatt, *Shakespeare's Comedy of Love* (London: Methuen, 1973), p. 210; Mark Bracher, "Contrary Notions of Identity in *As You Like It*," *SEL* 24, 2 (Spring 1984): 225–40; Kent van den Berg, *Playhouse and Cosmos: Shakespearean Theater as Metaphor* (Newark: Univ. of Delaware Press, 1985), p. 88: Dale G. Priest, "*Oratio* and *Negotium*: Manipulative Modes in *As You Like It*," *SEL* 28, 2 (Spring 1988): 273–86; and Mary Thomas Crane, "Linguistic Change, Theatrical Practice, and the Ideologies of Status in *As You Like It*," *ELR* 27, 3 (Autumn 1997): 361–92, 389.

2. George Bernard Shaw, "Shakespeare and Mr. Barrie," rprt. in *Bernard Shaw: The Drama Observed*, ed. Bernard F. Dukore, 4 vols. (University Park: Pennsylvania State Univ. Press, 1993), 3:937–43, 937.

3. This list refers, respectively, to the views of C. L. Barber, who describes Rosalind with the phrase "inclusive poise" in his chapter on the play in *Shakespeare's Festive Comedy: A Study of Dramatic Form and Its Relation to Social Custom* (1959; rprt. Princeton: Princeton Univ. Press, 1972), pp. 222–39, 238; Cynthia Marshall, "Wrestling as Play and Game in *As You Like It*," *SEL* 33, 2 (Spring 1993): 265–87; and Crane, who elucidates a complex presentation of the relationship between the values of the socially dominant and those who lack cultural and political power, as reflected not only in the language of the play but also in the style of performance suggested by the change from William Kemp to Robert Armin as the company's regular comic actor. Marshall's illuminating discussion of the wrestling match between Orlando and Charles shares my interest in understanding how theatrical and social conventions function in the play, but where she sees an increase in our skepticism about conventional distinctions, I see a stress on the importance of mutual involvement in those conventions.

4. David Cressy, *Birth, Marriage, and Death: Ritual, Religion, and the Life-Cycle in Tudor and Stuart England* (Oxford: Oxford Univ. Press, 1997), p. 234. Courtship conventions are not included among the literary and dramatic conventions in the play listed in Kenneth Muir's *The Sources of Shakespeare's Plays* (New Haven: Yale Univ. Press, 1978), p. 131.

5. See Anthony Brennan, *Onstage and Offstage Worlds in Shakespeare's Plays* (London and New York: Routledge, 1989). His discussion of *As You Like It* does not include the intersection I describe between narratives and mutual interactions (pp. 237–88).

6. See, for example, Jay L. Halio, "'No Clock in the Forest': Time in *As You Like It*," *SEL* 2, 2 (Spring 1962): 197–207, rprt. in *Twentieth-Century Interpretations of "As You Like It*," ed. Halio (Englewood Cliffs NJ: Prentice Hall, 1968), pp. 88–97, 91: "as dramatic exposition this dialogue is at least ingenuous-if not downright clumsy."

7. William Shakespeare, *As You Like It*, in *The Riverside Shakespeare*, 2d edn., ed. G. Blakemore Evans (Boston: Houghton Mifflin, 1997), pp. 403–36. I.iii.75, II.iv.46–54, III.ii.407–21, V.iv.47. All subsequent citations of the play will be from this edition and will appear within the text by act, scene, and line number; please note that I have removed square brackets indicating emendations.

8. Stephen B. Dobranski, "Children of the Mind: Miscarried Narratives in *Much Ado about Nothing*," *SEL* 38, 2 (Spring 1998): 233–50, 234.

9. Lawrence Danson, "Jonsonian Comedy and the Discovery of the Social Self," *PMLA* 99, 2 (Spring 1984): 179–93, 187.

10. Robert Ornstein, *Shakespeare's Comedies: From Roman Farce to Romantic Mystery* (Newark: Univ. of Delaware Press, 1986), p. 146.

11. Brennan, p. 286; Marko Minkoff, "What Shakespeare Did to *Rosalynde*," *ShJb* 96 (1960): 78–89; rprt. in *Twentieth-Century Interpretations*, pp. 98–106, 106. See also Agnes Latham's introduction to the Arden Edition of *As You Like It* (London: Methuen, 1975), pp. ix–xcv, xxxvi: "Shakespeare owes his plot to Lodge but not a great deal else."

12. The argument for John Lyly is made by Leah Scragg in *The Metamorphosis of "Gallathea": A Study in Creative Adaptation* (Washington DC: Univ. Press of America, 1982), pp. 79–98; the one for Sir Philip Sidney by Brian Gibbons in "Amorous Fictions and *As You Like It*," in *"Fanned and Winnowed Opinions": Shakespearean Essays Presented to Harold Jenkins*, ed. John W. Mahon and Thomas A. Pendleton (London: Methuen, 1987), pp. 52–78; the one for Sir John Harington and Rabelais by Juliet Dusinberre in "As *Who* Liked It?," *ShS* 46 (1994): 9–21. I use Harington later in this essay for very different purposes.

13. Thomas Lodge, *Rosalynde*, ed. W. W. Greg (London: Chatto and Windus, 1907), p. 2. All subsequent citations of this work will appear within the text by page number.

14. Helen Whall, "*As You Like It*: The Play of Analogy," *HLQ* 47, 1 (Winter 1984): 33–46, 35.

15. Maura Kuhn, "Much Virtue in If," *SQ* 28, 1 (Winter 1977): 40–50, 44, 49; also see Priest, pp. 285–6.

16. By my count, *fate(s)* and *fortune(s)* occur over 200 times in the tale, compared to roughly 150 instances of *if*. In Shakespeare's play, the ratio is 25 instances of *fortune(s)* and none of *fate(s)* to 138 for *if*. Data here and later in this essay on the number and frequency of words in *As You Like It* are drawn from volume 1 of *A Complete and Systematic Concordance to the Works of Shakespeare*, comp. Marvin Spevack, 6 vols. (Hildesheim Ger.: Georg Olms, 1968–70).

17. The commonplaces are treated at length in Leo Salingar, *Shakespeare and the Traditions of Comedy* (London: Cambridge Univ. Press, 1974), pp. 256–98.

18. Helen Gardner, "*As You Like It*," in *More Talking of Shakespeare*, ed. John Garrett (London: Longmans, Green, 1959), pp. 17–32, rprt. in *Twentieth-Century Interpretations*, pp. 55–69, 65.

19. Sir John Harington, *The Letters and Epigrams of Sir John Harington together with "The Prayse of Private Life*," ed. Norman Egbert McClure (Philadelphia: Univ. of Pennsylvania Press. 1930), p. 31.

20. Thomas Heywood, "An Apology for Actors," in *The Seventeenth Century Stage*, ed. Gerald Eades Bentley (Chicago: Univ. of Chicago Press, 1968), pp. 10–22, 11.

21. Barnaby Riche, *Riche His Farewell*, rprt. in *Eight Novels Employed by English Dramatic Poets of the Reign of Queen Elizabeth* (London: Shakespeare Society, 1846), p. 3.

22. Lodge, *Margarite*, in *"Menaphon," by Robert Greene, and "A Margarite of America," by Thomas Lodge*, ed. G. B. Harrison (Oxford: Blackwell, 1927), p. 113.

23. Lodge, *Margarite*, pp. 170, 207.

24. For the patriarchal implications of this opening, see Louis Adrian Montrose, "The Place of a Brother' in *As You Like It*: Social Process and Comic Form," *SQ* 32, 1 (Spring 1982): 28–54.

25. The complex layering of actor, character, and character-in-disguise that can result from the use of the convention in plays by Shakespeare and his contemporaries has been treated in great detail by Michael Shapiro, *Gender in Play on the Shakespearean Stage: Boy Heroines and Female Pages* (1994; rprt. Ann Arbor: Univ. of Michigan Press, 1996), esp. pp. 119–42 for *As You Like It*; a useful summary of the varied recent critical positions on the epilogue is on pp. 132–3. The male homoerotic implications of the convention have been stressed most recently by Stephen Orgel in *Impersonations: The Performance of Gender in Shakespeare's England* (Cambridge and New York: Cambridge Univ. Press, 1996). For an interpretation stressing the importance of female homoeroticism in the play, see Jessica Tvordi, "Female Alliance and the Construction of Homoeroticism in *As You Like It* and *Twelfth Night*," in *Maids and Mistresses, Cousins and Queens: Women's Alliances in Early Modern England* (New York: Oxford Univ. Press, 1999), pp. 114–30.

26. Harold Jenkins, "*As You Like It*," *ShS* 8 (1955): 40–51, rprt. in *Twentieth-Century Interpretations*, pp. 28–43, 38.

27. See Marjorie Garber, "The Education of Orlando," in *Comedy from Shakespeare to Sheridan: Change and Continuity in the English and European Dramatic Tradition*, ed. A. R. Braunmuller and J. C. Bulman (Newark: Univ. of Delaware Press, 1986), pp. 102–12.

28. Bracher, p. 236 (emphasis his).

29. John Bowe, "Orlando in *As You Like It*," in *Players of Shakespeare: Essays in Shakespearean Performance by Twelve Players with the Royal Shakespeare Company*, ed. Philip Brockbank (Cambridge: Cambridge Univ. Press, 1985), pp. 67–76, 74.

30. Leggatt, p. 204.

31. Barbara J. Bono, "Mixed Gender, Mixed Genre in Shakespeare's *As You Like It*," in *Renaissance Genres: Essays on Theory, History, and Interpretation*, ed. Barbara Kiefer Lewalski (Cambridge MA: Harvard Univ. Press, 1986), pp. 189–212, 204. One possible fear that has not been fully recognized is the fear of childbirth, the natural consequence of marriage. Dobranski shows how "again and again, Beatrice conflates her feelings for Benedick with sex and pregnancy" (p. 238). After her first encounter with Orlando, Rosalind similarly associates her thoughts of him with children, telling Celia "some of it [her sadness] is for my child's father" (I.iii.11). Whatever the actual statistics on mothers dying in childbirth, on stillbirths and miscarriages, and on infant mortality, the perception of the time was that childbirth was fraught with risks, a view well expressed by Richard Hooker in *Of the Lawes of Ecclesiastical Polity* (V.74.1): "the fruit of marriage is birth, and the companion of birth travaile, the griefe whereof being so extreeme, and the daunger alwaies so great" (quoted from *The Folger Library Edition of the Works of Richard Hooker*, ed. W. Speed Hill, 3 vols. (Cambridge MA and London: Harvard Univ. Press, 1977–81), 2:406.

32. The terms are from Katharine Eisaman Maus, *Inwardness and Theater in the English Renaissance* (Chicago and London: Univ. of Chicago Press, 1995), p. 2.

33. For a different view of how the patriarchal context affects our understanding of Rosalind, see Kay Stanton, "Remembering Patriarchy in *As You Like It*," in *Shakespeare:*

Text, Subtext, and Context, ed. Ronald Dotterer (Selinsgrove PA: Susquehanna Univ. Press, 1989), pp. 139–49.

34. *The Book of Common Prayer, 1559: The Elizabethan Prayerbook*, Folger Library Edition, ed. John E. Booty (Charlottesville: Univ. Press of Virginia, 1976), pp. 290, 291.

35. "The Homily on Marriage," rprt. in *Certain Sermons or Homilies Appointed to Be Read in Churches in the Time of Queen Elizabeth of Famous Memory* (Liverpool, 1799), pp. 393–4.

36. Harington, *Nugae Antiquae: Being a Miscellaneous Collection of Original Papers, in Prose and Verse, Written during the Reigns of Henry VIII, Edward VI, Queen Mary, Elizabeth, and King James*, ed. Thomas Park, 3 vols. (London, 1804; rprt. New York: AMS Press, 1966), 1:177–8.

37. The classic instance in Shakespeare's works of this dynamic in a relationship between parent and child is Cordelia and Lear each kneeling to the other when they are reunited in *King Lear*, IV.vii.

38. Latham, p. xlvi.

Chronology

1564	William Shakespeare born at Stratford-on-Avon to John Shakespeare, a butcher, and Mary Arden. He is baptized on April 26.
1582	Marries Anne Hathaway in November.
1583	Daughter Susanna born, baptized on May 26.
1585	Twins Hamnet and Judith born, baptized on February 2.
1587–90	Sometime during these years, Shakespeare goes to London, without his family. First plays performed in London.
1589–91	Three parts of *Henry VI*.
1592–93	*Richard III*, *Two Gentlemen of Verona*, *The Comedy of Errors*.
1593–94	Publication of *Venus and Adonis* and *The Rape of Lucrece*, two narrative poems dedicated to Earl of Southampton. Shakespeare joins the Lord Chamberlain's Men, adding to its repertoire *The Taming of the Shrew*, *Titus Andronicus*, and perhaps the first version of *Hamlet*.
1595–96	*King John*, *Love's Labor's Lost*, *Richard II*, *Romeo and Juliet*, *A Midsummer Night's Dream*.
1596	Son Hamnet dies. Grant of arms to Shakespeare's father.
1597	*The Merchant of Venice*, *Henry IV, Part 1*, *The Merry Wives of Windsor*. Purchases New Place in Stratford.
1598–99	*Henry IV, Part 2*, *Much Ado About Nothing*, *Henry V*, *Julius Caesar*, *As You Like It*. Lord Chamberlain's Men moves to new Globe Theatre.

1601	*Hamlet*. The poem *The Phoenix and the Turtle*. Death of Shakespeare's father, buried on September 8.
1601–02	*Twelfth Night*, *Troilus and Cressida*.
1603	*All's Well That Ends Well*. Death of Queen Elizabeth; James VI of Scotland becomes James I of England; Shakespeare's company becomes the King's Men.
1604	*Measure for Measure*, *Othello*.
1605–06	*King Lear*, *Macbeth*, *Antony and Cleopatra*.
1607–08	*Coriolanus*, *Timon of Athens*, *Pericles*.
1609	*Cymbeline*. Publication of *Sonnets*.
1610–11	*The Winter's Tale*, *The Tempest*. Shakespeare retires to Stratford.
1612–13	*Henry VIII*, *The Noble Kinsmen* (with John Fletcher).
1616	Shakespeare dies at Stratford on April 23.
1623	Publication of the first Folio of Shakespeare's plays.

Contributors

HAROLD BLOOM is Sterling Professor of the Humanities at Yale University and Henry W. and Albert A. Berg Professor of English at the New York University Graduate School. He is the author of over 20 books, including *Shelley's Mythmaking* (1959), *The Visionary Company* (1961), *Blake's Apocalypse* (1963), *Yeats* (1970), *A Map of Misreading* (1975), *Kabbalah and Criticism* (1975), *Agon: Toward a Theory of Revisionism* (1982), *The American Religion* (1992), *The Western Canon* (1994), and *Omens of Millennium: The Gnosis of Angels, Dreams, and Resurrection* (1996). *The Anxiety of Influence* (1973) sets forth Professor Bloom's provocative theory of the literary relationships between the great writers and their predecessors. His most recent books include *Shakespeare: The Invention of the Human* (1998), a 1998 National Book Award finalist, *How to Read and Why* (2000), *Genius: A Mosaic of One Hundred Exemplary Creative Minds* (2002), and *Hamlet: Poem Unlimited* (2003). In 1999, Professor Bloom received the prestigious American Academy of Arts and Letters Gold Medal for Criticism, and in 2002 he received the Catalonia International Prize.

C.L. BARBER was Professor of literature at the University of California, Santa Cruz, and the author of *Shakespeare's Festive Comedy* (1959) and *Creating Elizabethan Tragedy: The Theater of Marlowe and Kyd* (1988). His death in 1980 was commemorated by the creation of "Shakespeare Santa Cruz," an ongoing drama festival.

RUTH NEVO was Professor of English at Hebrew University in Jerusalem until her retirement in 1990. In addition to *Comic Transformations in Shakespeare* (1980), she has also written *Shakespeare's Other Language* (1987) and translated the poetry of Chaim Nachman Bialik and Yehuda Amichai.

PETER ERICKSON teaches at the Sterling and Francine Clark Art Institute. He is the author of *Patriarchal Structures in Shakespeare's Drama* (1985) and *Rewriting Shakespeare, Rewriting Ourselves* (1991). He is also coeditor of *Shakespeare's "Rough Magic": Renaissance Essays in Honor of C. L. Barber* (1985).

MARJORIE GARBER is William R. Kenan, Jr. Professor of English and Director of The Humanities Center at Harvard University. Her books include *Coming of Age in Shakespeare* (1981), *Shakespeare's Ghost Writers* (1987), and, most recently, *Question Marks* (2002).

RENÉ GIRARD is Professor Emeritus in French Language, Literature, and Civilization at Stanford University. He has written literary studies of Stendhal, Shakespeare, and Dostoevsky, as well as *Violence and the Sacred* (1977), *The Scapegoat* (1986), and *I See Satan Fall Like Lightning* (2001).

TED HUGHES served as Poet Laureate of England from 1984 until his death in 1998. His poetry volumes include *The Hawk in the Rain* (1957), *Crow* (1972), and *The Birthday Letters* (1998), which detailed his controversial marriage to the poet Sylvia Plath. A translator of Seneca and Aeschylus, his *Tales from Ovid* (1997) was awarded the Whitbread Prize in 1998.

ANDREW BARNABY, Assistant Professor of English at University of Vermont, is the author (with Lisa Schnell) of *Literate Experience: The Work of Knowing in Seventeenth-Century England* (2002). He has also published articles on Milton, Bacon, and Marvell.

PAUL ALPERS is Professor Emeritus in English at the University of California, Berkeley. The author of many books, including studies of Virgil and Spenser, his *What Is Pastoral?* (1996) was awarded the Phi Beta Kappa Christian Gauss Award in 1996.

MARTHA RONK is the Irma and Jay Price Professor of English and Comparative Literature at Occidental College. She has written many articles on emblematic women in Shakespeare's plays, and her books of poetry include *State of Mind* and *Eyetrouble* (1998).

ROBERT LEACH teaches in the English Literature Department at the University of Edinburgh. A freelance theater director and acting teacher as well, he has published many volumes of poetry and theater history, most recently *Boy and Baggage* (2001).

NATHANIEL STROUT is an Associate Professor of English at Hamilton College. His essay on *Hamlet* appeared in a recent Modern Language Association volume, in its Approaches to Teaching series.

Bibliography

Alpers, Paul. *What Is Pastoral?* Chicago: University of Chicago Press, 1996.

Alulis, Joseph. "Fathers and Children: Matter, Mirth, and Melancholy in *As You Like It.*" *Shakespeare's Political Pageant*. Eds. Joseph Alulis and Vickie Sullivan. London: Rowman & Littlefield, 1996.

Barber, C.L. *Shakespeare's Festive Comedy*. Princeton: Princeton University Press, 1959.

Barnaby, Andrew. "The Political Consciousness of Shakespeare's *As You Like It.*" *Studies in English Literature 1500–1900* 36, no. 2 (1996): 373–95.

Barton, Anne. *The Names of Comedy*. Toronto: University of Toronto Press, 1990.

Belsey, Catherine. "Disrupting Sexual Difference: Meaning and Gender in the Comedies." *Alternative Shakespeares*. Ed. John Drakakis. New York: Methuen & Co., 1985.

Berry, Edward I. "Rosalynde and Rosalind." *Shakespeare Quarterly* 31 (1980): 42–52.

Bloom, Harold. *Shakespeare: The Invention of the Human*. New York: Riverhead Books, 1998.

Bono, Barbara J. "Mixed Gender, Mixed Genre in Shakespeare's *As You Like It.*" *Renaissance Genres: Essays on Theory, History, and Interpretation. Harvard English Studies* 14. Ed. Barbara Kiefer Lewalski. Cambridge, Mass.: Harvard University Press, 1986.

Brockbank, Philip, Russell Jackson, and Robert Smallwood, eds. *Players of Shakespeare*, vols. 1–3. Cambridge: Cambridge University Press, 1985, 1988, 1993.

Clarke, Kate. "Reading *As You Like It*." *Shakespeare, Aphra Behn, and the Canon*. Eds. W.R. Owens and Lizbeth Goodman. London: Routledge, 1996.

Cole, Rosalie. *Shakespeare's Living Art*. Princeton: Princeton University Press, 1974.

Daley, Stuart A. "Calling and Commonwealth in *As You Like It*: A Late Elizabethan Political Play." *The Upstart Crow* 14 (1994): 28–46.

Dusinberre, Juliet. "As Who Liked It?" *Shakespeare Survey* 46 (1993): 9–21.

Elam, Keir. "As They Did in the Golden World: Romantic Rapture and Semantic Rupture in *As You Like It*." *Reading the Renaissance: Culture, Poetics, and Drama*. Ed. Jonathan Hart. New York: Garland, 1997.

Erickson, Peter B. *Patriarchal Structures in Shakespeare's Drama*. Berkeley: University of California Press, 1985.

Fendt, Gene. "Resolution, Catharsis, Culture: *As You Like It*." *Philosophy and Literature* 19, no. 2 (1995): 248–60.

Ford, John R. "The Condition of My Estate: Conjuring Identity and Estrangement in *As You Like It*." *Upstart Crow* 18 (1998): 56–66.

Frye, Northrop. *A Natural Perspective: The Development of Shakespearean Comedy and Romance*. New York: Columbia University Press, 1965.

Garber, Majorie. "The Education of Orlando." *Comedy from Shakespeare to Sheridan*. Eds. A.R. Braunmuller and J.C. Bulman. Newark: University of Delaware Press, 1986.

Gardner, Helen. "*As You Like It*." *More Talking of Shakespeare*. Ed. John Garrett. New York: Theatre Arts Books, 1959.

Gay, Penny. *As She Likes It: Shakespeare's Unruly Women*. London: Routledge, 1994.

Girard, René. *A Theater of Envy: William Shakespeare*. Oxford: Oxford University Press, 1991.

Halio, Jay L., ed. *Twentieth Century Interpretations of* As You Like It. Englewood Cliffs, NJ: Prentice-Hall, 1968.

Halio, Jay L. et al. *"As You Like It": An Annotated Bibliography, 1940–1980*. New York: Garland, 1985.

Harner, James, ed. *The World Shakespeare Bibliography on CD-ROM: 1900–Present*. Cambridge: Cambridge University Press, 2000.

Howard, Jean E. *The Stage and Social Struggle in Early Modern England*. London: Routledge, 1994.

Hughes, Ted. *Shakespeare and the Goddess of Complete Being*. New York: Farrar, Straus & Giroux, 1992.

Hunt, Maurice. "Words and Deeds in *As You Like It*." *The Shakespeare Yearbook* 2 (1991): 23–48.

Jenkins, Harold. "*As You Like It*." *Pastoral and Romance: Modern Essays in Criticism*. Ed. Eleanor Terry Lincoln. Englewood Cliffs, NJ: Prentice-Hall, 1969.

Kerrigan, William. "Female Friends and Fraternal Enemies in *As You Like It*." *Desire in the Renaissance: Psychoanalysis and Literature*. Eds. Valeria Finucci and Regina Schwartz. Princeton: Princeton University Press, 1994.

Kinney, Clare R. "Feigning Female Faining: Spenser, Lodge, Shakespeare, and Rosalind." *Modern Philology* 95, no. 3 (1998): 291–315.

Knowles, Richard. *New Variorum Edition of Shakespeare: As You Like It*. New York: Modern Language Association of America, 1977.

Kott, Jan. "Shakespeare's Bitter Arcadia." *Shakespeare Our Contemporary*. New York: W.W. Norton, 1964.

Leach, Robert. "*As You Like It*: A 'Robin Hood' Play." *English Studies* 82, no. 5 (2001): 393–400.

Lewis, Cynthia. "Horns, the Dream-Work, and Female Potency in *As You Like It*." *The South Atlantic Review* 66, no. 4 (2001): 45–69.

Lynch, Stephen J. "Representing Gender in *Rosalynde* and *As You Like It*." *Shakespearean Intertextuality: Studies in Selected Sources and Plays*. Westport, CT: Greenwood Press, 1998.

Marshall, Cynthia. "The Doubled Jacques and Constructions of Negation in *As You Like It*." *Shakespeare Quarterly* 49, no. 4 (1998): 375–92.

———. "Wrestling as Play and Game in *As You Like It*." *Studies in English Literature, 1500–1900* 33, no. 2 (1993): 265–87.

McFarland, Thomas. *Shakespeare's Pastoral Comedy*. Chapel Hill: University of North Carolina Press, 1972.

Montrose, Louis. "'The Place of a Brother' in *As You Like It*: Social Process and Comic Form." *Shakespeare Quarterly* 32 (1981): 28–54.

Nevo, Ruth. *Comic Transformations in Shakespeare*. New York and London: Methuen, 1980.

Orgel, Stephen. *Impersonations*. Cambridge: Cambridge University Press, 1996.

Orkin, Martin. "Male Aristocracy and Chasity Always Meet: Proverbs and the Representation of Masculine Desire in *As You Like It*." *Journal of Theatre and Drama* 3 (1997): 59–81.

Parry, P.H. "Visible Art and Visible Artists: Reflexivity and Metatheatricality in *As You Like It*." *Forum for Modern Language Studies* 34, no. 1 (1998): 1–15.

Ronk, Martha. "Locating the Visual in *As You Like It*." *Shakespeare Quarterly* 52, no. 2 (2001): 255–76.

Slights, Camille Wells. *Shakespeare's Comic Commonwealths*. Toronto: University of Toronto Press, 1993.

Smith, Bruce R. "The Passionate Shepherd." *Homosexual Desire in Shakespeare's England: A Cultural Poetics*. Chicago: University of Chicago Press, 1991.

Stanton, Kay. "Shakespeare's Use of Marlowe in *As You Like It*." *'A Poet and a Filthy Play-Maker': New Essays on Christopher Marlowe*. Eds. Roma Gill and Constance B. Kuriyama. New York: AMS Press, 1988.

Strout, Nathaniel. "*As You Like It*, *Rosalynde*, and Mutuality." *Studies in English Literature, 1500–1900* 41, no. 2 (2001): 277–95.

Tiffany, Grace. "'That Reason Wonder May Diminish': *As You Like It*, Androgyny, and the Theater Wars." *Huntington Library Quarterly* 57, no. 3 (1994): 213–39.

Tomarken, Edward, ed. *"As You Like It" from 1600 to the Present: Critical Essays*. New York: Garland, 1997.

Traub, Valerie. "The Homoerotics of Shakespearean Comedy." *Desire and Anxiety: Circulations of Sexuality in Shakespearean Drama*. London: Routledge, 1992.

Willis, Paul J. "'Tongues in Trees': The Book of Nature in *As You Like It*." *Modern Language Studies* 18, no. 3 (1988): 65–74.

Wofford, Susanne L. "'To You I Give Myself, For I Am Yours': Erotic Performance and Theatrical Performatives in *As You Like It*." *Shakespeare Reread: The Texts in New Contexts*. Ed. Russ McDonald. Ithaca: Cornell University Press, 1994.

Young, David. *The Heart's Forest: A Study of Shakespeare's Pastoral Plays*. New Haven: Yale University Press, 1976.

Acknowledgments

Barber, C.L. "The Alliance of Seriousness and Levity in *As You Like It*" from *Shakespeare's Festive Comedy*: 222–239. © 1959 by Princeton University Press. Reprinted by permission of Princeton University Press.

"Existence in Arden" by Ruth Nevo. From *Comic Transformations in Shakespeare*: 180–199. © 1980 by Ruth Nevo. Reprinted by permission.

"Sexual Politics and Social Structure in *As You Like It*" by Peter Erickson. From *Patriarchal Structures in Shakespeare's Drama*: 15–38. © 1985 by Peter Erickson. Reprinted by permission.

"The Education of Orlando" by Majorie Garber. From *Comedy from Shakespeare to Sheridan*, eds. A.R. Braunmuller and J.C. Bulman: 102–112. © 1986 by Associated University Presses. Reprinted by permission.

From "Introduction," "Do you love him because I do!: The Pastoral Genre in *As You Like It*" and "'Tis not her glass, but that you flatter her: Self-love in *As You Like It*" by René Girard. From *A Theater of Envy: William Shakespeare* by René Girard: 3–5, 92–105. © 1991 by Oxford University Press, Inc. Used by permission of Oxford University Press, Inc.

"Active Ritual Drama and *As You Like It*' by Ted Hughes. From *Shakespeare and the Goddess of Complete Being*: 106–116. © 1992 by Ted Hughes. Reprinted by permission of Farrar, Straus and Giroux, LLC.

"The Political Consciousness of Shakespeare's *As You Like It*" by Andrew Barnaby from *SEL Studies in English Literature 1500–1900* 36:2 (Spring 1996). © 1996 by William Marsh Rice University. Reprinted with permission of *SEL Studies in English Literature 1500–1900*.

"What Is Pastoral? Mode, Genre, and Convention" by Paul Alpers. From *What Is Pastoral?*: 70–78, 123–134. © 1996 by The University of Chicago Press. Reprinted by permission.

"*As You Like It*: The Invention of the Human" by Harold Bloom. From *Shakespeare: The Invention of the Human*: 202–225. © 1998 by Harold Bloom. Reprinted by permission.

Ronk, Martha Clare. "Locating the Visual in *As You Like It*" from *Shakespeare Quarterly* 52:2 (2001): 255–276. © 2001 Folger Shakespeare Library. Reprinted with permission of The Johns Hopkins University Press.

"*As You Like It*—'A Robin Hood' Play" by Robert Leach. From *English Studies* 82, no. 5 (October 2001): 393–400. © 2001 by Robin Leach.

"*As You Like It*, *Rosalynde*, and Mutuality" by Nathaniel Strout. From *Studies in English Literature 1500–1900* 41:2 (Spring 2001): 277–295. © 2001 by William Marsh Rice University. Reprinted with permission of *SEL Studies in English Literature 1500–1900* 41, 2 (Spring 2001).

Index

VIVA Modern Critical Interpretations

Available Titles in the Series

Viva

Crime and Punishment
9788130906409 Rs. 175

The Chronicles of Narnia
9788130907468 Rs. 145

The Crucible
9788130906416 Rs. 125

Darkness at Noon
9788130906423 Rs. 145

David Copperfield
9788130918730 Rs. 145

The Death of Artemio Cruz
9788130907475 Rs. 145

Death of a Salesman
9788130906744 Rs. 125

The Divine Comedy
9788130918846 Rs. 175

Don Quixote
9788130904658 Rs. 125

VIVA Modern Critical Interpretations

Available Titles in the Series

Viva

Dracula

9788130906430 Rs. 195

Emerson's Essays

9788130906577 Rs. 175

Emma

9788130918839 Rs. 165

A Farewell to Arms

9788130918754 Rs. 175

Frankenstein

9788130907413 Rs. 145

The General Prologue to the Canterbury Tales

9788130918747 Rs. 175

The Glass Menagerie

788130907482 In Print

The Grapes of Wrath

9788130906751 Rs. 145

Great Expectations

9788130904597 Rs. 175

VIVA Modern Critical Interpretations

Available Titles in the Series

Viva

The Great Gatsby
9788130906454 Rs. 145

Gulliver's Travels
9788130906461 Rs. 195

Hamlet
9788130918877 Rs. 165

The Iliad
9788130907895 Rs. 145

Invisible Man
9788130906485 In Print

Heart of Darkness
9788130918815 Rs. 165

Jane Eyre
9788130918860 Rs. 195

Julius Caesar
9788130906492 Rs. 125

King Lear
9788130918853 Rs. 165

VIVA Modern Critical Interpretations

Available Titles in the Series

Viva

Long Day's Journey into Night

9788130904634 Rs. 99

Lord of the Flies

9788130904603 Rs. 145

The Lord of the Rings

9788130907956 Rs. 145

The Man without Qualities

9788130907499 Rs. 145

The Merchand of Venice

9788130906522 In Print

Macbeth

9788130906515 Rs. 125

Miss Lonelyhearts

9788130907437 Rs. 125

A Midsummer Night's Dream

9788130918914 Rs. 165

The Metamorphosis

9788130904573 Rs. 99

VIVA Modern Critical Interpretations

Available Titles in the Series

Viva

Moby-Dick

9788130906546 Rs. 165

Oedipus

9788130906768 Rs. 165

One Flew Over the Cuckoo's Nest

9788130907444 Rs. 125

One Hundred Years of Solitude

9788130907451 In Print

The Old Man and the Sea

9788130906553 Rs. 125

Othello

9788130918891 Rs. 165

Paradise Lost

9788130906560 In Print

The Pardoner's Tale

9788130904665 Rs. 125

A Passage to India

9788130906584 Rs. 145

VIVA Modern Critical Interpretations

Available Titles in the Series

Viva

Persuasion

9788130906591 Rs. 175

Pride and Prejudice

9788130906607 Rs. 195

The Red Badge of Courage

9788130906614 Rs. 145

Romeo and Juliet

9788130906621 In Print

The Rubaiyat of Omar Khayyam

9788130904641 Rs. 145

The Scarlet Letter

9788130907505 Rs. 175

Silas Marner

9788130906638 Rs. 125

Song of Solomon

9788130906645 Rs. 145

Sophie's Choice

9788130906652 Rs. 175